PRAISE FOR *MISS INDEPENDENT* AND NICOLE LAPIN

"The role of women in the workforce is changing, and today women are disrupting the workplace—for the better. Ladies, it's time to disrupt your own industry. Nicole will show you how."

—Sara Blakely,
founder and CEO of Spanx

"Nicole shows you that taking care of yourself and your finances is not just OK but the only way to succeed."

—Bobbi Brown,
founder of Bobbi Brown Cosmetics

"If you're a woman and you like money, you need to read this book. Immediately. You can't afford to miss this one, ladies!"

—Alli Webb,
cofounder of Drybar

"Nicole's books should be mandatory reading for all women looking to be independent, make money, and succeed in their careers."

—Tracy DiNunzio,
founder and CEO of Tradesy

"Nicole is the real deal. Her influence on women to get their finances and careers in order is unparalleled."

—Rebecca Minkoff,
founder of Rebecca Minkoff fashion brand

"Read Nicole's books to help master life and achieve more success than you ever thought possible."

—Rosie O'Neill,
cofounder and CEO of Sugarfina

"Taking care of yourself isn't just important for your health—it's crucial to your success in your career. Nicole understands this firsthand, and the steps she lays out will help you become your most heroic self."

—Julia Hartz,
cofounder and CEO of Eventbrite

"Nicole's advice is *on point*! Her material and delivery is current, real, and entertaining."

—Lavinia Errico,
founder of Equinox

"Nicole has done it again! Her honesty and realness will make you laugh and learn like you're hearing from your smart-ass best friend."

—Jason Feifer,
editor-in-chief of *Entrepreneur Magazine*

"At last! A book that's cool enough for my kickass daughters and smart enough for my CEO self!"

—Julie Clark,
founder of Baby Einstein

"Want it all? Who doesn't?! Nicole provides the secret sauce. She is a must-read for women looking to thrive in the workforce."

—Barbara Corcoran,
founder of The Corcoran Group
and investor on *Shark Tank*

"Nicole reminds us that we can only define success from within. We must first take care of ourselves, and we must set our own goals while setting aside unhelpful doubts."

—Payal Kadakia,
founder and CEO of ClassPass

"Nicole delivers expert financial advice straight up, no chaser, in a tone that's as lively as it is likable."

—Neil Blumenthal and Dave Gilboa,
co-CEOs and cofounders of Warby Parker

"Whether you want to branch out with your own startup or get ahead in your current job, Nicole knows just how to develop those skills to get you where you want to be. She's a perfect role model for young women."

—Brit Morin,
founder of Brit + Co.

"Essential reading for twenty-first-century women wanting to rise to the top of the economic ladder."

—Rebecca Taylor,
founder of Rebecca Taylor lifestyle brand

"Nicole does a fabulous job educating people about money while always keeping it fun and entertaining."

—Alexis Maybank,
founder of Gilt Groupe

"Nicole is truly inspiring and shares essential money tips for women who want to take control of their lives."

—Josie Natori,
CEO and founder of The Natori Company

"Like a confidence-boosting best friend, Nicole guides you through her own financial journey while showing you how to channel your inner badass."

—Paige Adams-Geller,
cofounder of PAIGE

"Nicole will help you not only build wealth but also the confidence to follow your own gut and create the strong powerful masterpiece that is your life. Every one of us needs a copy of her books."

—Julie Smolyansky,
CEO of Lifeway Foods

"Nicole enlightens and empowers in the smart signature voice of a truly super woman."

—Liz Dee,
CEO of Baleine & Bjorn Capital and
copresident of Smarties Candy Company

"Nicole is a wonderful role model for women today, one that so many of us can relate to. Take her guidance to heart, and it will change your life."

—Mariam Naficy,
founder and CEO of Minted

"Nicole has done it again! Equal parts vulnerable and smartass Boss Bitch—just our cup of (organic) tea. Now stop browsing the damn accolades and read the book!"

—Zoë Sakoutis and Erica Huss,
founders of BluePrint

"Nicole reminds us that if we try to be all things to all people, we are nothing to anyone. The only way to be of value to anyone else is to be of value to yourself first. Nicole's simple twelve steps get you a better version of your already fabulous self."

—Jodi Guber Brufsky,
founder of Beyond Yoga

"Nicole's advice is a swift kick in the pants to the young, ambitious, upstart women out there who want control over their lives, debts, and careers."
—Wendy Williams,
host of *The Wendy Williams Show*

"When someone calls you a 'Rich Bitch,' say 'thank you.'"
—Gloria Steinem,
women's rights icon

"*Rich Bitch* should be mandatory reading for every young professional woman who wants to take control of her financial destiny."
—Mindy Grossman,
CEO of WW

"A financial diet is like a regular diet: if you allow yourself small indulgences, you won't binge later on. Nicole offers you a plan you can stick to."
—Sanjay Gupta,
CNN chief medical correspondent

"Having the life you want isn't just about managing your career brilliantly. It's about getting control of your finances—starting *right now*. Nicole's sassy, smart, and super-easy-to-digest books will help you do exactly that."
—Kate White,
former editor-in-chief of *Cosmopolitan* magazine

"*Rich Bitch* gives a brash tutorial for women looking to take their share in today's bleak economic climate. Nicole leads the way brilliantly!"
—Karen Finerman,
CEO of Metropolitan Capital and panelist on CNBC's *Fast Money*

"Women are underrepresented among entrepreneurs. Nicole is a great guide to help us close that gap."
—Daniel Lubetzky,
CEO and founder of KIND Snacks

"Nicole brings to life in a highly readable way the real pitfalls and solutions of growing your wealth and career in a complex world."

—Nigel Travis,
CEO and chairman of Dunkin Brands

"Nicole's unfiltered, energetic advice speaks to anyone taking aim at their own financial destiny."

—Mike Perlis,
CEO of Forbes Media

"Financial expert Nicole Lapin zeroes in on the easy ways smart women dig themselves out of debt. Trust her: she's been there."

—*Glamour* magazine

"In a world where money is power, women need to take control of their finances. Nicole Lapin tells us how to do exactly that with her twelve-step plan."

—*InStyle* magazine

"Nicole Lapin is singularly qualified to demystify money for the millennial set . . . with a no-nonsense, chic style. She is on a mission to help women get wise with money in *Rich Bitch*, the no-fuss personal finance guide."

—*Elle* magazine

"Lapin translates complex financial concepts for Generation Yers."

—*U.S. News & World Report*

"Lapin is renowned for making finances approachable and using easy-to-understand language for budget tips."

—Mashable

"Financial smarty-pants."

—*Redbook* magazine

MISS
INDEPENDENT

A Simple 12-Step Plan to Start Investing
and Grow Your Own Wealth

NICOLE LAPIN

HarperCollins
Leadership

AN IMPRINT OF HarperCollins

Published by HarperCollins Leadership, an imprint of HarperCollins Focus LLC.

Any internet addresses, phone numbers, or company or product information printed in this book are offered as a resource and are not intended in any way to be or to imply an endorsement by HarperCollins Leadership, nor does HarperCollins Leadership vouch for the existence, content, or services of these sites, phone numbers, companies, or products beyond the life of this book.

This book is designed to provide readers with a general overview of how to start investing and growing wealth. It is not designed to be a definitive investment guide or to take the place of advice from a qualified financial planner or other professional. Given the risk involved in investing of almost any kind, there is no guarantee that the investment methods suggested in this book will be profitable. Thus, neither the publisher nor the author assume liability of any kind for any losses that may be sustained as a result of applying the methods suggested in this book, and any such liability is hereby expressly disclaimed.

ISBN 978-1-4002-2633-7 (eBook)
ISBN 978-1-4002-2632-0 (HC)

Library of Congress Control Number: 2021947249

Printed in the United States of America
22 23 24 25 26 LSC 10 9 8 7 6 5 4 3 2 1

To all the Rich Bitches
who never stop learning and growing—
themselves and their wealth.

Don't marry rich.
Be rich.

CONTENTS

INTRODUCTION

know, I know. The Kelly Clarkson song has probably been stuck in your head since you first picked up this book. (And maybe the Ne-Yo song too!) But if you're going to have a theme song you can't shake while you invest in yourself by learning how to, well, invest, then "Miss Independent" is a pretty good one.

The spirit of the song—and this book—is that our time is better spent embracing Miss Right in Front of You instead of searching for Mr. Right. Of course, the hours (and hours) we've already spent feeling less-than-independent are never coming back to us, as much as we wish, pray, or blame ourselves. In the finance world, we call that a "sunk cost," as in it's already happened—there's nothing we can do about it because it's in the past. But we do have full control of the time in front of us. We have the power to tell the mean girl inside our head who tells us all the excuses why we can't be Miss Independent to take a seat so that we can fully come into our own.

You'll never again be as young as you are today, and it's never too late to enhance your independence. So, if you're finally ready to spend your time growing and enjoying your own wealth, you're in the right place. If you want to increase your FQ (financial intelligence), you're in the right place. If you not only want to get your financial shit together but get it on point, you're in the right place. *Miss Independent* is the exact book to help you do and be just that.

Chances are you've realized that you can (and you should!) budget and save your ass off, but neither is going to get your net worth to look like your phone number. All of the budgeting and saving in the world won't comfortably cover that annual first-class trip to the south of France on your vision board, the Tesla you've had your eye on, or the trip to Walt Disney World with your family you've been hoping to take—not to mention an ample emergency fund and a well-heeled retirement on your terms and timeline. In fact, the reason I wrote this book is because, even though they are stellar personal financial tools that can provide basic financial stability, *you can't budget and save yourself to wealth.* But you can get there with everything you learn in *Miss Independent.*

Becoming Miss Independent is not just about having more money than you know what to do with so that you get all the fancy things and all the status (although that can be part of it—if that's your goal). It's about having the *freedom* that money affords you. Money is the means with which you support yourself and your family and the way you will reach many of your personal and professional goals—so it goes without saying that it can be a source of serious, potentially debilitating anxiety and stress. That stress can lead to poor decision-making and even cause major health problems, not to mention serious strife between relatives and significant others. Imagine the calm you will feel internally and interpersonally once those feelings are eliminated. Hallelujah! That freedom is priceless; and no matter where you come from, your age, or your income bracket, it's something that can be yours. Perhaps you've just never realized that it could be, until now.

You don't need to have read my other books (although, of course, I hope you will!) to be successful with this one. Maybe we are already friends, after you've worked hard to pay down your debt and stash a solid chunk of savings in the bank with *Rich Bitch*; taken control of your career with *Boss Bitch*; and gotten your mind and money right with *Becoming Super Woman.* Or maybe this is the first of my books that you've picked up, so we're just now getting acquainted. Either way, I'm here with open arms to help you each step of the way. And no matter how you got here, the next step (or twelve) is to make your money work for you with *Miss Independent.* I mean, you've worked hard for it—it's about time you let your money return the favor.

I'll let you in on a little secret: Millionaires don't make their money just from their salaries, no matter how big their paychecks get. They have an average of seven additional streams of income, many of which are passive, meaning their money is making money for them while they sleep. Literally. This income can be in the form of real estate investments, stocks and bonds, dividends, and many other methods of increasing your cash flow.[1] In fact, none of us can rely on a salary alone—even if it is six figures or more—to earn the financial independence that lets you walk away from any job or any relationship, and toward any opportunity, without thinking twice about being able to afford it.

The short explanation for how this happens is compound interest. You may have been introduced to the concept of compound interest by seeing how interest on your credit card snowballs out of control because of it. Basically, it sucks when it works against you, but it's truly amazing when it works in your favor. Compound interest has been called the eighth Wonder of the World: "(S)he who understands it, earns it; (s)he who doesn't, pays it."

Well, that's what we are going to do over the course of this book: Say hello to earning interest and goodbye to paying it. We are going to set up a system for you to be Miss Independent so that you can add zeros to your net worth without putting in a ton of work or risking the money you already have. Yes, both are not only possible but completely doable.

The reason it has probably felt impossible until now is because you've been told it is from people who don't actually know better. We've been brainwashed to think the world of investing is a fancy club and we're not on the list, and those who are on it are sworn to keep what happens hidden behind the red velvet ropes. Well, that's the first of many financial lies I'm going to debunk for you. Investing may be a club, but there's no bouncer and the people partying inside don't really know much more than those lined up on the curb.

The reality is that the old notion about the shoemaker walking barefoot or the dentist always having the worst teeth is often true in the financial world. Surveys have shown that about half of financial planners have not saved for their own retirement, even while they implore you endlessly to save for yours. The hypocrisy is as real as the knowledge is shallow. Investing in ways that minimize downside, or risk of losing your initial investment, isn't the stuff your accountant or financial advisor will tell you about. This might surprise you, but here's the truth: it's probably not even on their radars. Going to a financial advisor or broker is not like going to the doctor. In fact, it's closer to going to a real estate agent. Some are more helpful than others, but all are making money off your business, which means they may not be acting in your best interest. But I am. And I'll tell you who and what you can trust throughout your journey to becoming Miss Independent.

Consider this your bootcamp to get into tip-top financial fighting shape—and stay that way. When we are done, you'll have to do the maintenance, of course, but you'll have the right plan set up for your money to keep growing on its own, building you a lifetime of wealth. Real wealth. Your own wealth.

Just like I did in my other books, I will tell you all the ways I messed up along my journey so you don't have to repeat my mistakes. I'll share my signature "confessions," too, because money talk is so taboo, but someone has to go first. So, let it be me. Learn from me, laugh at me. As long as you're smiling and not scowling when you think about money, I'll take one for the team.

Whether your goal is to have rental properties, or an entire building bearing your name, or even just owning your house and fortifying your family nest, the lessons in the pages that follow will unlock opportunities you never thought possible. Fully enjoying experiences without obsessing about the cost. Living life without worrying if you have enough emergency cash should the proverbial shit hit the fan. Feeling totally empowered to take career risks knowing that you have a financial safety net. Leaving a crappy relationship with the full confidence that you can and will make it on your own. Upgrading your current home to your dream home, knowing the new mortgage won't hold you hostage. Flying first class instead of coach—always, not just as a special treat. You'll be living a super rich, full life in all aspects of the word *rich*, all on your own terms.

In *Miss Independent*, I will:

- Show you how to unlock additional income that will open doors of opportunity for you and your loved ones.

- Help you explore multiple pathways to grow your wealth.

- Steer you away from the many scams out there—because if it looks too good to be true, then it probably is.

- Set up (and automate) a rock-star portfolio so that your money can make more money.

- Put financial and legal plans in place to protect your wealth for your loved ones, even after you're gone.

Ultimately, I'm going to help you create—and afford—a life you're proud of. A life you can enjoy. A life where you're confident with money and in having your own back.

Just because the tricks and tactics to make your money grow aren't subjects you know now doesn't mean you can't become a Jedi master of them. You can. And after reading this book, you *will*.

Becoming wealthy isn't a full-time job. You don't have to sit in front of stock charts all day. You just need to devote about as much time to it as you would planning your next vacation. Picking up this book is a great place to start. From here, you can make your way through it, step by step or skipping around in a choose-your-own-adventure-style. Maybe you already have your personal balance sheet down; then head to Step 5: Automate Your World to learn how to automate your financial life. If you want to get super smart about stocks, then skip over to Step 10: Index Funds and Chill. If you have no idea what those things are, start at Step 1: Find Your Power and go in order as each step builds on the last.

Before we get started, I want to be super clear: I never worked at a bank and I don't have an MBA.[2] I wasn't born into wealth or privilege. There were days when I didn't have food to put in my mouth, much less a silver spoon. For much of my early career I either lived paycheck to paycheck, was in debt, and/or subsisted on a brown-rice-and-beans diet (it felt fancier than ramen). I tell you this because if *I* could become Miss Independent—totally financially set up and secure on my own—then *anyone* can, including you. I promise.

Everything I have learned when it comes to growing wealth is through my own trials, errors, and fuckups. I'm not your typical boring bean counter. I'm a woman, just like you, who wants a future that is independent of the depression that comes with being trapped in a terrible job with a terrible boss because I don't have the FU money to leave; independent of the fear that comes with leaving a bad relationship, simply because I need a place to live; and independent of the worry that comes with saving to raise my future child because I feel left out of the ways rich people do it. I don't talk in jargon like bankers and stock analysts because that crap is meant to keep people (especially women) out of the conversation and thus behind the wealth curve. P.S. I can tell you from being part of that world that the dudes (yeah, mostly dudes) who talk in it rarely know what the heck they are talking about. Money-speak is a language like any other. If you don't speak Japanese and you go to Japan, you'll be really confused. If you go to Wall Street and you don't speak the language of money, you'll be really confused. Until, of course, you learn it.

It's time for you to join—and master—the money conversation. It's time to leap over the wealth gap once and for all. *It's time to be Miss Independent.*

PART

I

FIND YOUR POWER

What's Your Money Problem?

I don't hate many things in life, but clichés are high on the list. Why? Because they are so commonly said that people don't stop to question them.

Well, I question *everything*. In fact, I question (and often refute) pretty much all conventional wisdom, especially when it comes to finances.[1] But, I will make one exception for this tried-and-true cliché: money is power. Because money *is* power—perhaps the most powerful power there is. And it's one that can easily be yours.

Think of the power of money as a tool. And just like you can use a hammer to build a house, you can use the same hammer to tear it down. Superpowers can be used for good or evil, and so can money; it can control you or you can control it. We, of course, are going to control it and use it for good. In this step, I will help you reframe your perceptions about money and show you how to take control of it so that the reverse never happens again.

UNMINDFUCK YOURSELF

There is very little else so emotionally charged as money. Not politics (unless it's about money). Not religion. Not much.

It's a mindfuck when people have money because they feel guilty about it. It's a mindfuck for people who don't have money because they feel ashamed about it. The full-force mindfuckery around money happens no matter what. And the only way it stops is if you reclaim its power for yourself.

Of course, everyone has free will and the power to make their own choices. But as we have already determined, money is what ignites that power. When you have it, your choices become more numerous and substantial. And when you don't, they become much more limited.

So, what kind of choices are important to you? What kind of power do you want wealth to give you? Maybe it's the choice to work because you want to and love it, not because you have to. Maybe it's the choice of where you want to live or travel, without limitations, or to help people you love or groups in need. Maybe it's the choice to leave a shitty relationship because you don't have to be stuck with someone who supports you financially. Or, as is the case with Beyoncé, maybe it's the choice to run the world. Hard stop.

The choices that money affords us are more valuable than the money itself. Those choices buy you freedom. And the lack of that has likely been the basis of many of your past moves and relationships, even if you haven't yet realized it, as mindfucks often go.

YOU'VE HAD THE POWER ALL ALONG

One of the main reasons I felt called to write this book is because too many women have told me that managing money is "a guy thing." Or worse, they've shared with me that they are staying in a horrible home situation because they don't have money of their own to leave with.[2] Girl, what?! Men are certainly not the only ones who can grow their wealth or use it to their advantage. In fact, data has shown that women have proven to be superior investors, which isn't surprising given that they make 85 percent of consumer purchases and thus have better insight into demand. Demand drives sales and sales drive stocks. Numbers don't lie—guys aren't better investors at all; they just talk about it more than we do. Whatever the hell you think they know that's so special or difficult is *all* within your reach. But only if you grab for it.

It's not a coincidence that we think differently about money than our male peers. This starts at a young age. Girls are typically told to be prudent and save their money, whereas boys are taught to go after good jobs and build their wealth. While it's not the rule, and there are always exceptions, studies say it's the most common theme of money conditioning among children. So, as adults, women are cutting back on the lattes and opting for at-home hair dye (just don't), whereas men are out there, looking for investment opportunities and constantly watching the job market. We've also seen that women, in particular, express a greater sense of negativity around their finances and managing money than men do. In a recent survey, nearly half of the women associated negative words—like fear, anxiety, inadequacy, and dread—with financial planning, compared to less than a third of the men.[3]

To make matters worse, every time a Disney princess finds her prince, or a Hallmark movie features a woman-unlucky-in-love who finds The One, part of the "happily ever after" is that he is going to take care of her. He'll pay for all the things and keep her safe. We eat it up like rocky road ice cream at the end of a stressful day. But here's the thing: What those movies don't tell you is that the prince sometimes turns out to be a frog and The One may not stick around forever. You truly only have yourself till death do you part. And the real princesses—make that *queens*—are the ones with palaces of their own.

The truth is, as smart as we are, as badass as we are, as truly "women's lib" as we are, some small part of us was raised to believe that we'd marry a rich man and *he* would take care of us.[4] If you've never had that thought, then you are either a stronger woman than I am or you're lying to yourself.

Think back to the people you've been with (or are currently with) and ask yourself: Would the dynamics of my relationships be different if I went into them with a fat inheritance or were otherwise financially set on my own? Or if I got a big promotion or came into money while I was in it? Would I have put myself first more often? Would I have put up with less shit? If money wasn't a factor, would I have chosen differently?

For a few lucky ladies, the answer is "no," but for the rest of us, I'll answer first: yes, 100 percent yes.

We *must* break this cycle. In Step 12: Keep It Together, I'll talk much more about some precautions you can take for yourself and your money, including prenups, insurance, and wills—but for now, just know that I will not stand by and let you go to your deathbed regretting that you stayed in a bad situation or didn't go after the love you wanted and deserved because you weren't brave enough to do something about it. Whether it's subtle or it screams, money changes the balance of power in all relationships—especially romantic ones. (Hello, I have a show called *Hush Money* that's based around that very premise.[5])

FYI In Sweden, the median income for women is close to parity with the median income of men. As a result, men have been found to share in the chores, child care, and cooking in more equal measure than anywhere else in the world. And women there spend less time doing housework now than they did twenty years ago, from five hours per day in 1990 to just four hours per day today.[6] That sixty minutes may not sound like a lot, but as I've discussed in all my books, time truly is your most valuable asset, in investing as in life. Here in the United States, women spend the equivalent of ninety-five more eight-hour work days per year on unpaid work than men, which adds up to almost $1.5 trillion (with a "T") in unpaid labor.[7]

As Cher once famously recalled: "My mom said to me, 'You know, sweetheart, one day you should settle down and marry a rich man,' and I said, 'Mom, I am a rich man.'"[8]

By the end of this book, you will be able to confidently call yourself "rich," not just by the numbers in your net worth (you'll have those, too, my dear), but also with everything that money comes with, including the power of choice. Choice with lots of options. And once that happens, the way you go into any new relationship will change for the better.

Of course, this is not a book about relationships.[9] It's a book about getting wealthy. But to understand *why* you need to be financially independent, we've got to have a real talk about what's really, truly been standing in your way for so long. I believe that the mental and emotional baggage we carry into our financial endeavors has slowed us down or stymied us the most. If your bags are like mine, they are heavy. It's time to put them down and realize, to paraphrase my favorite children's fantasy movie (whose plot doesn't revolve around getting the prince), *The Wizard of Oz*: you've always had the power, my dear; you just had to learn it for yourself.

CUT THE STRINGS

Significant others aren't the only ones who can hold power over you. Families and friends can come with similar complexities, footholds, and strings attached. If you feel like money is playing an unhealthy role in your relationships, whether it's parents who pay for stuff but violate boundaries because of it or a friend you work for who pays you less than he or she should because you grew up together, it's time to cut the strings.

You could very well take money from your parents or work with your bestie and have no hard feelings in any direction with no strings attached, just rainbows and butterflies. Well, awesome. But be really honest with yourself. *The true price of anything is how much you give up for it.*

So, if your parents give you a $1,000 allowance every month, but expect you never to leave your hometown because of it, it's not just $12,000 a year; it's the opportunity cost of passing up other options to stay there, not to mention the anxiety the whole setup has caused, which might just result in therapy costs. About 70 percent of millennials—the generation also most likely to live at home—who work full-time still receive money from their parents to help foot the bills, which only tethers them to their parents well into adulthood.[10]

Is it worth it? I can't answer that. Your therapist or your friends can't answer that, either. Only you can answer it. And only *you* have to wake up in your own life every day. So, ask yourself: Am I living the life I want for myself? A life I love and am proud of? A life in which I have the ultimate say and power in how it unfolds?

If you're living your life as a supporting character in someone else's story, I hope you have the strength to do a major rewrite. I'll say it again: time is your most valuable asset—and it's the one thing you're gonna need on your side the most in order to grow your wealth. You can always get more money if you lose it, but you can't get more time. The longer you wait, the more you lose. And the strings will only get thicker and harder to cut over time.

WHAT'S YOUR FINANCIAL TRAUMA?

If you read my last book, *Becoming Super Woman*, you know that I suffer from posttraumatic stress disorder because of my abusive childhood and my father's death from a drug overdose. (And if you didn't, now you know.) We tend to assume that trauma has to be an earth-shattering event that happened in our lives. But people who have grown up with food insecurity, with narcissistic parents, abuse, or neglect can suffer in ways similar to those who went through a traumatic event, like a car accident, attack, or sexual assault. Whether it is given a diagnosis or not, those events or chronic behaviors shape the way we conduct our adult lives. I believe and am living evidence that we *can* heal from trauma, but only if we recognize the traumatic event or events. It can even become a superpower, like it did for me, if you name and reframe it.

We all have traumas around money whether in the macro sense or in the micro sense. Macro money traumas could include: working during the dot-com bubble, living through the Great Recession, or dealing with the economic stress of the COVID-19 pandemic. Micro money traumas could include: being on food stamps as a kid, seeing your parents' home get foreclosed, having your money stolen, or being laid off.

Underlying any potential trauma is a layer of deeply ingrained financial mores you grew up with or ones you've been exposed to culturally. Family customs around finances could be: seeing your parents hoard, spend frivolously, or clip coupons. Societal influences around finance could be: watching your friends go into debt, impulse buy, or avoid conversations about money.

Whatever you were exposed to as a child, a teenager, or a grown-ass adult doesn't matter. You get to decide what impact finances have in your life from now on. You get to create the culture. Set the tone. Maybe you want to do everything the exact same way as when you grew up. Cool, just as long as you take a pause, question it, and then carry on independently and intentionally. But when you question it, if you decide it doesn't work for you now, then do something different. Just because it was always done a certain way, doesn't mean that's the way it needs to be done. You are capable of learning a better or different way.

I taught myself everything I know about money (and life) by rethinking (and, ultimately, rejecting) everything I saw my family do growing up. Essentially, I reparented myself in the way I chose to be raised. So, when I say you can break *any* cycle, I speak from some hefty experience (and therapy bills).

CONFESSIONS OF BEING
MISS INDEPENDENT

Locked Up

"Nicole, listen to me carefully."

"Mom? Where are . . ." I said back into the cordless phone.

"Listen to me!" my mother snapped with her thick Israeli accent that bounced off whatever echoey room she was in.

I had just walked into our apartment when the phone rang. After school, I would normally walk to the library with friends and then my mother would pick me up outside at 4:00 p.m. But that day she wasn't there (and back then, there were no cell phones). So, I walked home with my backpack and books, worried and confused. I was in seventh grade.

"Okay," I said, swallowing the crackly feeling in my throat like I was about to cry.

"Go to my room right now and look under the small gold light by my bed. That's where the combination for the safe is. Go! Do you see it?"

"Uh." I froze, and then beelined for her bedroom.

"Nicole, this is important. Do exactly as I say. Go fast. Do you see it?"

"Uh, yeah."

"Take off the paper on the bottom and go to my bathroom."

My hands were shaking as I removed the small piece of index card with a bunch of numbers written in red ink on it, trying not to rip it in my haste.

"Are you going? Open the cabinet under the sink. Move all the boxes of maxis out. That's where the safe is."

I grew up in an immigrant family. My parents both emigrated from Israel before meeting in Los Angeles. They went through a sordid, cinematic divorce when I was three. My father got full custody until a year before he died of a drug overdose, when I was in sixth grade. I had only been living with my mother for two years at this point, and while I always saw her use cash to pay for things, I didn't yet know that there was a safe under the sink behind the maxi pads.

"Read the paper with the numbers very carefully. You have to turn the dial on the safe one full time and then turn it to the left and to the right to the numbers as written."

My hands were not only shaking, they were sweaty, my chronic hyperhidrosis fully activated. I was equal parts scared and focused as I tried to figure out this lock during what seemed to be an emergency. I didn't know what had happened to my mother yet, but I did know this was not the time to ask.

"Nicole, are you doing it?" she barked.

"Well, yeah, I mean . . ." I couldn't figure out how to put a sentence together, but I did figure out that this lock was just like the one on my locker at school.

"Go slowly," she said with a calmer but equally desperate voice.

Bingo. It opened. Oh. My. God.

"I hear it opening. Did it open?"

"Yes," I whispered, looking at the neatly wrapped little bundles of hundred-dollar bills.

"Count out $25,000. The stacks should be in $5,000 packs, so that's . . ."

"Five packs. I know." It was similar (but so, so different) to the word problems I did in math class.

"Yes, five. Take the five and close the safe. Make sure it clicks. You must hear the click to know it's locked. Now, go to my closet and take out the big black purse with the gold straps. Put the cash in there. Then put a few sweaters on top of it so it doesn't fly away. Then put a sweater on yourself and go back to the library. On the other side of the parking lot is the police station. Go in the door there and give them my name and the money."

"Okay," I said as I put on one of my mother's sweaters, rolling up the sleeves that dangled past my little, pink, wet hands.

My childhood was chaotic, violent, and abusive. By this time, I was no stranger to police, social workers, or courts. So, bailing my mother out of jail wasn't a total shock to me, sadly. But I'll never forget those stacks of bills hiding out in the safe under the sink, behind the maxi pads. How orderly they appeared, all lined up like that, compared with the disorder all around me.

You may be thinking: "Damn, Lapin! Your past is heavy. I've got my own shit, but I've never had to bail my mother out of jail."

Well, I've taken the "I'll show you mine, if you show me yours" approach in all my books, and this one is no different. Money talks are the ones even the most badass women are squeamish to have. So, if someone has to go first to make it less so, I got you.

And you're right, my past was heavy. So I put it down. If yours is heavier, I feel for you, but you've got to let your arms rest too. If it's lighter, I'm not mad at you, but take it from me: anything extra you need to carry on top of your own adult baggage is too much.

EMOTIONAL REGULATION + MONEY = INDEPENDENCE

Did I hear you say, "Yeah, yeah, but, Lapin, I'm just not a numbers girl"? Well, I'll tell you straight up that any fifth grader can do the math that is required to set yourself up financially. So, no excuses. I started out as a poetry major in college. If *I* can figure this stuff out, so can you.

It's the humanities part of money, not the math part, that's pretty much always the hardest. And as bad as you think you are at crunching the numbers, you're probably worse with dealing with the emotions around them. We all are.

We have been conditioned for so long to assume this stuff is complicated. Don't get me wrong, I thought the same thing. It's like when I look at the cords and wires behind my TV. *Eek!* I just want to throw my hands up in the air and say: "I can't understand any of that. I don't know how to do it. Let's just call someone else to set it up."

Now, I'm a smart woman. I have figured out harder things in life than how to plug in an HDMI cord. It's a lie to myself that I "can't" do it. If there were a samurai sword at my throat ready to slice if I didn't plug in the HDMI cord, then I would absolutely figure out how to do it, and fast. But making sense of all the acronyms and gizmos seems like something only an "expert" can do. While I love my handyman more than is normal, I don't think he's actually *smarter* than I am. I just haven't put in the time to learn what he knows. (And I likely get overcharged for the work that he does as a result.)

The same thing happens in a lot of industries. For example, an *iatrogenic* disease is one that is caused inadvertently by the medical professionals themselves. Well, shit. No wonder the medical industry has an unnecessarily long word to explain *that*. The finance world has all sorts of similar jargon and fancy words for super simple concepts. Like a mutual fund "load" really just means "fees." Even the phrase "overdraft protection" gives you the feeling that it is a good thing for you when in reality it's charging you a crazy high fee when you don't have enough money in your account to buy something. Using cryptic or overcomplicated language (by the way, there's a word for that too: "sesquipedalian") is yet another way that bankers and financial services companies make us feel like outsiders, often for their own benefit, knowing most of us won't ask about or question it out of embarrassment.

By the end of this book, you'll know the language, and I promise that you'll think, *This was way easier than I thought*, in the same way I did after I watched a YouTube video telling me what a freaking HDMI cord looks like—and how to plug it in. These things are more complicated in your imagination than they are in reality. And tell the hater in your head who is about to say "but . . ." to shush. She no longer holds the power. You do.

ADMIT YOU HAVE A PROBLEM

I'm poking at your insecurities in this step because, just like in any twelve-step program, the first step is to *admit you have a problem*. Hey, we *all* have problems with money. The only problem that is unfixable is the one you don't admit you have.

So, let your problem speak. It's been nagging and distracting you for quite some time, I'm sure. Hear it out. You may want to invest but don't know where to start. You may have a mortgage you can't afford or student debt stalking you. You may have a big life event looming—buying a house, having a kid, going back to school to get a fancy degree—and constant stress about how the heck you're going to pay for it. You may have nothing saved for retirement and worry that you're going to be a nine-to-fiver until you literally drop dead.[11] Once you stop pretending like everything is all good and acknowledge your money problem, you'll likely see that it's not as insurmountable as you convinced yourself it was.

I know it's scary. I know it's uncomfortable to sit with your crap. But just like with any major growth opportunity, the thing you're most scared to do is the exact thing you probably should be doing. Chances are your problem is rooted in the belief that growing wealth is impossible based on what you've seen or been told at some point in your life. That totally makes sense, especially in light of these very grim statistics:

- 70 percent of people have less than $1,000 in savings.[12]

- 40 percent of US households where the head of the house is between ages thirty-five and sixty-four will run out of money before retirement.[13]

- 75 percent of Americans will run out of money before they die.

- One in five Americans don't save for retirement or emergencies.[14]

There are serious problems with growing wealth that are systemic, for sure. I will tell you how the financial system is definitely stacked against people who are outsiders throughout the course of this book.[15] I will rant about why the language and logistics are unnecessarily complicated. Trust me: I want to change the financial system for the better, and I will do everything I can to do that or die trying. But until real, systemic change happens, we have to figure out how to make the system work to our advantage. So, I will give you the solutions. Because there *are* solutions to every financial problem you can imagine . . . and, of course, admit you have.

By now you've guessed that, yes, the solution must start with *you*. Sure, I will teach you how to create the most incredible portfolio and system for making your money grow with very little risk and beautifully hedged tax exposure. I will give you the tricks and the tools—but I'm not going to change your life. I can't. I'll be rooting for you along the way like a total stage mom, for sure. I will give you the framework, but I'm no psychic about what macro- and microeconomic forces may come your way. So, you will have to do the blocking and tackling for yourself. You and only you are going to change your life. And you'll do it over and over again.

Markets go up and down. Careers go up and down. But you remain the constant. The terrain changes but the athlete is the athlete. Whether Tom Brady is playing in snowy Boston or sunny Tampa Bay, he is still Tom Brady. There will never be perfect conditions. There will never be stock charts or markets that go straight up, and I don't bet that there will be. Instead, I bet on myself to navigate it in a way that gets me across my goal line (in Step 2, we will find out where yours is). And you should also bet on yourself. Because *that's* the best investment of all. It's the only one guaranteed to pay the most interest in the long run.

INFORMATION IS POWERFUL . . .

. . . but it can also be painful. There's certainly not a lack of information about money out there. There are thousands of financial websites and millions of articles about money. And yet 75 percent of us are financially illiterate. What gives?

The answer is quite simple. It has to do with decision theory, which essentially shows us that when we are presented with too many options, we freeze. Inertia takes over. Let me give you an easy example of decision theory in action. I'm vegan. When I go to a regular restaurant and there's one or maybe two options on the menu that I can eat, I decide quickly what to order and enjoy my meal. But when I go to a vegan restaurant, I'm so excited by all of the choices (the apps! the sides! the desserts!) that it takes me forty-five minutes to order and then I'm still wondering if I made the right choice even while I'm eating, and sometimes even as I'm leaving the restaurant.

Do you find that you're overwhelmed by all of the financial information and resources out there? Only to get more confused and anxious the longer you surf the interwebs? (And don't get me started about social media.) That's another big reason I wanted to write this book. Unlike your money, more is not necessarily better when it comes to information.

MISS
INDEPENDENT
TIP

TRACK YOUR (TIME) SPENDING

How often do you complain about money? "In my life, Lapin? A lot," I hear you say. Now, how much time have you spent actually doing something about it? "Not much. I don't have time," you may answer. *Au contraire*, my future Miss Independent. Consider this:

ACTIVITY	HOURS SPENT
Vacation Planning	8 per vacation[16]
Researching New Boots	40 per year[17]
Throwing a Party	8 per party[18]
Scrolling on Social Media	2.5 per day[19]
Setting Up Investment Accounts	0.5 per day[20]
Financial Management	0.03 per day[21]
Reading About Finances	0.03 per day[22]

The next time you complain about not having money or the power that comes from it, really ask yourself how much time have you actually spent doing anything about it.

It's only once you admit you have a money problem and clearly define it that you can go after the power you've had all along. It's always been there within you. It's just soft spoken. It doesn't nag; it whispers. You can only really hear what it's telling you and start listening to it once you've let your problems say their piece.

Previously, you may have only been exposed to the power of money when it was used against you, by a man or by "the man." Or because you didn't have it, leaving you powerless to overcome a difficult financial situation. Or because you did have it, but had no idea how to manage it properly (let alone grow it) and so you lost it. That's okay. You just have to take it back. Get ready to be the one who holds it rather than the one it's being held over.

In our financial system, the delta (difference) between being a customer and being an owner is small. But for all the emotions and other mindfuck reasons, it appears huge just like objects appear closer than they are in your rearview mirror. That difficulty dysmorphia? We are leaving it behind and we aren't going back. We are only looking forward. And if you open your eyes wide, you'll see that there's so much wide-open road waiting for you ahead.

BOTTOM LINE

Conventional Wisdom: The language of money is impossible to understand without being an insider.

Not really. Any language you don't speak is going to be impossible to understand at first. If you went to any country and didn't know the language, you'd be pretty lost and confused. If you went to Wall Street and you didn't speak the language of money, you'd also be lost and confused until you learned to speak the language, proficiently and then fluently. And then you wouldn't waste any more time thinking about how it used to sound like gibberish; you would just use it to get around—and, ultimately, to get what you want.

Conventional Wisdom: The financial habits you are accustomed to are nearly impossible to break.

False. Habits are not easy to break, for sure, especially when they are learned at a young age from our friends and family. But the only way to live life on your terms is to start thinking and acting for yourself. And that may mean rethinking . . . *everything*.

Conventional Wisdom: Men are better at managing and growing money.

No.

PUT A PRICE TAG ON YOUR DREAMS

How to Reverse Engineer Your Goals

’ve lived in ten cities in twenty years, with four different apartments in New York City alone. I never set out to be a nomad. In fact, I set out to have a home and roots. But that’s not how life has happened for me.

I thought I was the queen of goals. But I am actually the queen of *rewriting* goals. I have written and rewritten a lot of them over the years, many of which I’ve shared with you in my books. Since my first book, if you’ve followed along, you’ve seen me change along with my goals as life (and shit) happened.

I like to break my goals down into categories, which go by my favorite F-words: family, finance, fun, and fitness (that last one is both mental and physical). But before now, I never really put price tags on each of those goals or looked ahead farther than ten years, and I didn’t have you do that, either. Well, it’s time. I’m not going to lie: the amount of money you are going to need to feel financially set for life is a lot. But it is likely less than you think or at least more manageable to come by than you imagine. In this step, I’m going to help you figure out what that concrete number is. Only then can you break it down into baby steps and make a plan to get there.

LET'S DREAM TOGETHER

How many times have you avoided stepping on the scale because seeing the number flash back at you would make it real? (And I'm being intentionally vague about "it," because body image issues can come in so many forms, whether it's weight gain or weight loss or no change whatsoever that you're struggling with.) I get it because I've done it . . . pretty much every week of my life. Avoidance or flat-out denial can feel like bliss. But we all know deep down, it's not. Just like in avoiding the scale, the anxiety of not knowing your numbers ultimately takes over whatever fleeting reprieve avoidance afforded you.

Like many women, I've had all sorts of body image and eating issues. Even at the doctor's office for my annual physical exam, I declined to step on the scale and just gave the nurse a rough estimate of my weight. I thought doing that would be less triggering and make for a less slippery slope toward the body image issues with which I've always struggled. But it actually called *more* attention to them. The nurse would sometimes have to ask a supervisor for clearance to skip my weigh-in, which made the whole uncomfortable subject that much more . . . uncomfortable. The longer you avoid hard issues in your life, the heavier the anxiety becomes.

And when it comes to your finances, the only remedy for that is to step on the scale—in other words, open your bills and financial statements—and get a true sense of your current net worth so that you can calculate the number you will need to live your dream life from there. Everyone is entitled to their own opinions and feelings; they are yours and they are valid. But facts are facts. And numbers are numbers. So, let's figure out what your practical number is so we can reverse engineer from there to get you the money to live the life you want. (Notice that I say "practical number," not "magical number." There is nothing magical or mystifying about this number; it's a cold hard numeral that you *must* know in order to grow your wealth.)

WHO NEEDS TO BE A MILLIONAIRE?

If I asked you to ballpark how much money you would need to live on for twenty years without working, what would you guess? A million bucks? Two million bucks? Five million bucks?

I am going to assume that anything you say right now is going to be a wild guess, and that's okay. But by the end of this book, you are going to know your numbers inside out. You're going to know them so well that if you're interrogated about them with a flashlight in your face, you won't flinch. Where were you last Friday night? Who were you with? What's your net worth? What's your asset allocation?

The only way to answer any question with ease is to know the answer (I know, thank you, Captain Obvious). And if you have more unanswered questions about your finances than answered ones, that's about to change. But there is only one person who can answer them: *you*.

The reason I started by asking how much money you think you'll need to live on for twenty years is because the average retirement age is around sixty-five, and the average life expectancy for women in the United States is around eighty-two. So, that gives you seventeen years or so, on average, to (it is hoped) live life to the fullest after you're done working (we'll get into these retirement calculations in way more detail in Step 8). Of course, you could pull an RBG (RIP queen Ruth Bader Ginsburg) and work until the very end, or you could peace out to some beach at forty and never wear anything but flip-flops and sarongs again. Adjust accordingly. This is not intended to be a calculation of *when* you will retire (although the number we come up with will be used in Step 8 for retirement planning); it's intended to be a calculation of how much money you'll need to have your own back when you do.

We are going to explore three distinct levels of wealth.

1. The first is affectionately called "Rich Enough," where your super basic expenses are covered (think brown-rice-and-beans diet) without any frills.
2. Then, we have the "Pretty Rich" level, which allows you to live comfortably with some indulgences but doesn't factor in a ton of future growth.

3. And, finally, we have the "Super Rich" level, which entails having more money than you can reasonably spend, a.k.a. baller status. Hey, if you have no interest in pricey handbags or boats or sizable donations to your alma mater, then that's totally fine. I would still encourage you to go through all of the exercises for each level, because the more concrete the numbers become to you, the less out-of-reach they feel.

RICH ENOUGH

I know that Rich Enough doesn't sound like, well, enough. But if you're like me, you're a survivor, a warrior. The phrase "strong woman" is redundant; I've never met a woman who wasn't strong.

The pandemic wasn't my first apocalypse, and I'm sure it wasn't yours, either. Long before the world was brought to a screeching halt by a spiky ball of super infectious virus, I lived in a world of apocalyptic whack-a-mole, starting with my rocky childhood. Coping with my parents' mental and financial instability instilled in me the fear of being broke and homeless. Yes, it's irrational, and, yes, I've done a ton of work on it but I'll never forget being told to flush the toilet only if it was number two to save money on water or to only turn the lights on when it was dark in order to save money on electricity. I've worked to harness those fears for positive growth and ambition rather than have them get the best of me. And what's empowered me to do that is knowing that I have my basic expenses covered for a few years into the future. I'll talk more about how the COVID-19 crisis changed the money game in the micro sense (how my advice has changed because of it) and the macro sense (how the world has changed because of it). But one important impact that the pandemic has already had is underscoring the need for our basic expenses to be covered . . . for a while.

According to Abraham Maslow's famous hierarchy of needs, there are five basic human needs: safety, esteem, love/belonging, self-actualization, and physiological needs (including air, water, and sleep). Each level of financial security satisfies different needs. Being "Rich Enough" satisfies that first basic need for safety because it accounts for the roof over your head, the food in your fridge, and other essential costs of living. To calculate your Rich Enough number, look at your regularly monthly expenses. These expenses are the core of what you need to survive[1] sans extras (like your gym member-ship, beauty regimen, entertainment, and what not):

MONTHLY EXPENDITURES	
Housing: mortgage or rent	
Bills: utilities, cell phone, and insurances	
Transportation	
Food	
Healthcare	
Child/pet costs (if applicable)	
Miss Independent Fund savings	
= Monthly burn	
x12 = Annual burn	

The median household income in the United States is about $63,000 before taxes.[2] The average annual burn rate, that is, how much you spend per month and per year, is about half of that, or about $30,000. On average, we spend only about $5,000 a year on entertainment, personal care, and clothes (with the rest going to taxes, ugh).[3]

Another positive outcome of the pandemic is that it showed many of us that we actually can do a lot more with a lot less. No fitness classes? No highlights? No problem. I mean, maybe it's not ideal, but these are "wants," not "needs." When thinking about your Rich Enough lifestyle, draw inspiration from your pandemic days with "natural" nails and dark roots (ombre, anyone?).

Now, multiply your annual needs by twenty to cover those twenty non-working retirement years that we estimated earlier. If we go off the average American needs, that's twenty years x $30,000/year = $600,000 needed to live Rich Enough in retirement. Sure, that's a lot of money, but it's not in the millions like you may have started out thinking. Of course, there are many ways you can make $600,000 in cash or broken up as interest payments from your investments—and we will go over all of them in the steps ahead. And if you want more tailored, specific calculations, use my wealth calculator at nicolelapin.com/tools. But for now, keep this $600,000 number in mind so your imagination and reality are at least in the same book, if not the same page.

Scan this code with your phone to access the Miss Independent Wealth Calculator:

WEALTH CALCULATOR QR CODE

THE 4 PERCENT RULE OF THUMB

This rule refers to how much of a nest egg a retiree takes out yearly so that she is living off her interest and not eating into her principal. For easy reference, a $1 million retirement portfolio would get you $40,000 per year for living expenses.[4] Then, $2 million would get you $80,000, $3 million would get you $120,000, and so on. Those returns mean you don't touch the lump sum that's earning you the interest that you use to live. Whether you are looking at a traditional retirement or hoping to live off your interest ASAP, this is a good overview of how much money you would need to earn different types of lifestyles with interest *only*.

PRETTY RICH

Whatever level of wealth you aspire to have is up to you. Don't forget that comparison is the thief of joy. If you decide for yourself what makes you happy, whether it's owning a Subaru or a submarine, make sure you don't start comparing yourself to what others' definitions of wealth are. Obviously, you can change your mind, but if you actually, deep down, in your quietest moments would be cool chilling on a lawn chair from Target in your backyard, then don't freak out when someone else posts a picture on Instagram from the fancy deck chair on their yacht. That's *their* goal, *their* truth, not yours. By the way, researchers have found that earning $75,000 to $100,000 a year is the sweet spot for optimal happiness.[5] Listen, if you want to make ten times that—I'll cheer you on every step of the way! But if that Target-lawn-chair life is your jam, then, girl, save me a seat. I'm gonna be your number-one fan on the way to financial happiness, as *you* define it.

If you feel best maintaining your current lifestyle, complete with occasional splurges like dining out or buying some designer duds, great. It's the Pretty Rich life for you. The first step in figuring out what you need to maintain that lifestyle is to calculate your current burn rate. We need an exact number so that you know what you're working toward on your own without feeling beholden to a job or another person to keep that flame alive.

The best way to win the wealth game is to make the rules. You are destined to win that way. But you'll be destined to misery, always feeling poor AF, if you keep changing those rules on yourself midplay. So, before we get to any investment strategies, we need to know where the goal we are working toward is—precisely. We've all seen referees in football games measure where a ball lands down to the inch. You will never see a ref say, "Oh, well, that was close enough to the yard line, let's just call it a goal!" And while football games are undoubtedly serious business, I want you to treat your life and the wealth you aim to create even more seriously. I used to have a vague sense of where my goal line was. But that doesn't work for the NFL and it no longer works for NML (that's me; my middle name is Miriam).

You might think that your Pretty Rich number is just your salary and you're done. Nope. A lot of people actually spend all the money they bring in each year. Some even spend more, while others manage to spend less. (We know which one you are!)

MONTHLY EXPENDITURES	
Your Rich Enough needs	
Dining	
Lifestyle (gym, beauty, memberships, and so on)	
Travel	
Clothing	
= Monthly burn	
x12 = Annual burn	

This might not feel like a groundbreaking development in your mission to become wealthy and make your money work for you (instead of the other way around, working for your money like most women do). But seeing these numbers clearly—maybe even for the first time—hopefully makes them less overwhelming. And clarity is a far better ally than confusion when it comes to working toward your Pretty Rich reality.

SUPER RICH

Now, this is where we start having some fun. (Although, like I said, a lawn chair from Target can be fun for you, and that's a-okay.) This is where we dream really big, with the biggest ticket items you think you could ever want: from a big boat to your name on a big building. Then, we calculate what those would actually cost you to have.

Here are some of the most common Super Rich dreams I hear from people:

- A sailboat

- A sizeable donation to my favorite charity or school

- A new Louis Vuitton (or whoever your favorite designer is) bag every year

Now, granted, there are a lot of different calibers and styles for all these items. But for the sake of this exercise, I'm going to pick what I think that item should reasonably cost but still satisfy that goal with two options, including one that gets you the spirit of what you may be looking for without actually owning it. So, here's what those items actually cost broken down by month:

DREAM ITEM	TOTAL COST	MONTHLY COST
A BOAT		
Option 1: 2001 Merritt Custom Sportfish	$2,895,000	$241,250[6]
Option 2: 1990 Douglas Sharp Design Yachtfisher	$588,000	$49,000[7]
A BIG DONATION TO MY ALMA MATER/FAVORITE CHARITY		
Option 1: $200,000	$200,000	$16,666
Option 2: $20,000	$20,000	$1,666

DREAM ITEM	TOTAL COST	MONTHLY COST
A NEW LOUIS VUITTON BAG EVERY YEAR		
Option 1: Dauphine MM Epi Leather Bag	$ 3,648	$304[8]
Option 2: Louis Vuitton on Tradesy: Duffel Brown Monogram Canvas Weekend bag	$648	$54[9]

I wanted to list out how much these seemingly unattainable things actually cost, because oftentimes we assume and convince ourselves that something is out of reach without even figuring out how high it actually is. I also wanted to show you an option that gets you the spirit of that big-ticket item without being the highest cost option. It's up to you to determine if you really want to own a fancy boat and if you will use it all the time, or you just want to float around in one over the weekends each summer. The price difference between the two is wide enough to figure out exactly what floats your boat (sorry, had to).

There is also science around the idea that we tend to conflate really big numbers—millions, billions, trillions. Same thing, right? Um, no. New research in psychology has found that we ignore mass suffering because the number of people lost is too big for our human brains to fathom.[10] Basically, the more people who die, the less we care about them, because we can't comprehend the difference between ten million people and fifteen million people. Get this: *million* wasn't even a word in the English language until the fourteenth century, and *billion* didn't come along until the seventeenth century. The delay in translating these orders of magnitude into our language shows that, for a long time, these numbers were not even discussed, because we had no frame of reference for them.[11]

Of the three levels of wealth we've defined in this step, Super Rich is the one that most satisfies Maslow's "esteem" need, which means the desire for approval and significance in the world. Sometimes people use money as a proxy for recognition and status. If that's you, own it. If fame is what you value, say that. Don't say you want to live a simple life when you don't. Set yourself up for success by clarifying *exactly* where you want to go.

If you were invited to a party at the home of a new friend, you would probably have a lot of questions before going, right? What's the address? What do I wear? Who will be there? What time should I go? Do I need to bring anything? Is there food? Booze? You need lots of specifics before heading out to a party at which you want to put your best (pedicured) foot forward. And you should have at least as many specifics for the celebration of this one wild ass life we have.

The reason I don't just have you come up with a number out of your ass that sounds nice, like "10 million bucks!", is because it's not the number that matters most or is even the hardest part to achieve. It's what you are going to *do* with that money that separates the financially secure from the truly independent. As I've always said, I advocate for a rich, full life in all aspects of the word, not just having money for the sake of having money. That's why when people say to me their goal is to have "a million dollars" or "a billion dollars," I always respond, "Oh, yeah? And what do you want to do with that million dollars or billion dollars?" Maybe you need more than a million or a billion, maybe you need less. First figure out your ideal life, which is meaningful to you and only you. Then reverse engineer it and figure out the price tag for *that*.

CONFESSIONS OF BEING
MISS INDEPENDENT

She Left a Little Sparkle Wherever She Went

There she was, my hero! I got up to where she was standing, surrounded by her team, and stood beside them, super awkwardly. I didn't want to interrupt, but I knew if I didn't just jump in there, I would psych myself out and miss my chance. After a few moments that felt like a sweaty century, they all turned to look at me. *She* (Kate Spade herself!) turned to look at me.

"Um, hi, um, Ms. Spade," I said as I held out my sweaty palm, then quickly wiped it on my skirt before extending it once more in her direction.

"Hi! I'm Katy and this is so-and-so and so-and-so from my team. What did you say your name is?" she said in a friendly voice, instantly calming my nerves.

"Oh, um, hi, everyone, and hi, um, Kate . . . Katy. I'm Nicole. I was . . ."

"We saw you up there on the panel. Really interesting points," Kate Spade said . . . to *me*!

Pretty in pink would be an understatement. She looked like the picture-perfect embodiment of the empire she built, wearing the most glorious silk fuchsia skirt and floral overcoat. Kate Spade, the brand and the woman, was feminine, colorful, and full of moxie.

"Oh, wow, thank you so much," I managed to stutter.

"You know, I got a degree in journalism and started at Condé Nast. It's a tough job, I know," she said with her warm, low, breathy voice. She was delightfully awkward. It was like she knew how to help a fellow introverted-extrovert sister. I felt a quick, unsaid understanding between us: the awkward in me sees the awkward in you.

I was moderating a panel about the business of fashion at an event for a big retail investor in New York City. All the major fashion powerhouses were in the room, including other eponymous designers like Kenneth Cole and Tommy Hilfiger. Of course, I wanted to meet and interview all of them for the business news show I was anchoring at the time. But after the stage portion commenced, I set out to find the one woman I needed to meet. I mean, I personally *needed* to meet her. I wanted to tell her about how I saved up to buy her iconic messenger bag, which I used as a work bag and which made me feel like a total badass. I was excited to tell her how much her brand meant to me, how much it spoke to me, and how the Kate Spade notebook on my desk, emblazoned in gold with the phrase "She Leaves a Little Sparkle Everywhere She Goes," motivated me to seize the day, every damn day. I was basically tickled, well, pink to put a face to my favorite brand, which touched pretty much every category in my home from my stapler to my dishware.

But I never got through all of my fangirling, because Kate asked more about *me* (me!), putting me in the spotlight and propping me up, almost in a maternal way. No bother; I assumed I would see her at another event and would then feel confident enough to properly praise her, and adequately thank her for the impact she had on my life and career.

Tragically, that never happened.

Kate's death hit me hard. I met her once; I certainly didn't know her well. But like many, I felt a sense of personal loss when the news of her suicide broke.

To the outside world, and to mere fashion novices and business mortals like myself, Kate was on top of the world. She sold her majority stake in her company to Neiman Marcus in 1999 for $34 million. Then in 2006, she sold the rest of her stake for $59 million. By the time I met her, she was laying the foundation for her second hurrah with American lifestyle brand Frances Valentine.

I would never speculate about the very personal details surrounding Kate's death. But I do know that Kate, or "Katy" as she was known to those closest to her, was not in need of money. She had all the money, admiration, and power in the world. But according to those who knew her best, it was the meaning and significance that she desired. It's a heartbreaking story that has played out with other seemingly "rich" celebrities across all industries, including actor Robin Williams, model Margaux Hemingway, and chef Anthony Bourdain. Money can be thought of as a proxy for meaning and can unlock many opportunities and possessions that bring us fulfillment, but at the end of the day, it can never take the place of its meaning.

Money without meaning is just paper (or these days just a number on your screen). How you use it makes all the difference—especially if you use it as a tool to unlock meaningful opportunities and experiences in your life and for those whom you love the most. Studies have shown that real happiness isn't derived from what you acquire but what it means to you. Now, if we can just put these two powerful forces together: money with meaning can be . . . *everything*.

THERE WILL BE TIME

Along with goal-setting (and resetting), I have another little addiction that might seem superficial but carries a lot of meaning for me: getting tattoos. My third (and likely not my last) tattoo is on the inside of my left forearm and reads, in tiny letters, "there will be time." It's a line from one of my favorite poems, T. S. Eliot's "The Love Song of J. Alfred Prufrock." The poem, and particularly this line from it, reminds me that even though everyone obsesses over how short life is, life is the longest thing we will ever know. So, there will be time for all the things we want to do. The YOLO (you only live once) hysteria of the last decade doesn't work for me. I'd rather work from a place of abundance with all my assets—with time being the most valuable—than from a place of scarcity.

I'm not giving you a pass to just chill on the couch and do nothing about growing your wealth because you've got all the time in the world tomorrow and the day after. No. But I do want you to take a beat (or several) to be thoughtful about *how* you use the long time horizons in front of you.

WHAT'S ON YOUR HORIZON?

Whether we like it or not, our longevity and sensitive biological clocks mean that women have to do more planning when it comes to managing and paying for big life events. It's real—just ask my thirty-year-old self, who essentially went through an existential fertility crisis when she realized that the biological window to have a kid of her own was closing. Whether you want ten kids or ten orchid plants, I don't care and would never judge. But if you *do* want a family of your own, then you *must* factor that in to your plans, because nothing is more time-, money-, and energy-intensive than having and raising bambinos.

Even when I was working on the earliest drafts for my second book, *Boss Bitch*, I knew that I wanted to talk in depth about my decision to freeze my eggs and other considerations around money, family, and relationships.

My editor at the time said, "But family planning isn't in business books." And I said, "Exactly."

Why? Because your money/work life and your personal/fun life are not separate and wrapped with their own little bows. It's just your one damn life, and it's impossible to separate the two. Yes, maternity leave is a legal right, and companies are much better than they were even ten years ago about accommodating mothers, but two months out of the office is a long time. A lot happens, and your job will likely be affected. That's just one of many reasons your career and your personal life cannot be planned separately.

In the past, I've prompted you to come up with your one-, three-, five-, seven-, and ten-year goals within the four Fs that I mentioned earlier (family, finance, fun, fitness). Now I want you to go beyond that. What does your fifteen-year plan look like? Twenty-year? Twenty-five-year? I know most days you can barely think about what you want to eat for dinner, much less what your life is going to look like in twenty-five years. But if you don't hold yourself to a goal, you are just shooting in the investment dark.

I calculated actual numbers for my three lifestyle tiers too. Here's how that breaks out:

RICH ENOUGH

MONTHLY EXPENDITURE	
Housing: mortgage or rent	$7,250
Bills: utilities, cell phone, insurance, and so on (excluding auto and health, see below)	$579
Transportation	$722
Food	$1100
Healthcare	$508
Child/pet costs (if applicable)	$0
Miss Independent Fund savings	$10,195
= Monthly burn	$20,390
x12 = Annual burn	$244,680

PRETTY RICH

MONTHLY EXPENDITURE	
Your "Rich Enough" needs	$20,390
Clothing	$1,250
Dining	$500
Lifestyle (gym, beauty, memberships, and so on)	$900
Travel	$3,500
= Monthly burn	$26,540
x12 = Annual burn	$318,480

SUPER RICH

DREAM ITEM	TOTAL COST	MONTHLY COST
A beachfront bungalow in Santa Monica	$1,000,000	$5,555
A big donation to my favorite women's advancement charity	$200,000	$16,666

Then I tried to fast-forward to see when I would want a certain level of income from my investments. Any salary I earned throughout this time would be extra, not needed. Here is how I planned out the lifestyle I want for the next twenty-five (gasp!) years:

5 years: Rich Enough

10 years: Pretty Rich

15 years: Pretty Rich

20 years: Pretty Rich

25 years: Super Rich

Now, you might want to be Super Rich in five years. Cool, get on with your bad self. My timeline is not yours and, honestly, I'll likely adjust mine as I go. But having a roadmap helps to navigate the decisions you're going to make in the steps to come.

Remember, the plan you "want" and the plan you "need" are two different things. Say you're thirty-five years old. Being Super Rich in five years is "nice to have" but perhaps not "need to have." Alternatively, if you're sixty years old and staring down retirement, then being Rich Enough in five years is likely "need to have."

The risk you take with your investments comes down to your time horizon. If you are dealing with a long-term investment horizon, you can plan your risk accordingly, likely taking a more aggressive route because, if the investment goes south, you'll have a longer time to recover financially. Alternatively, if you have a shorter-term investment horizon where you actually need the money (not just want it), I'm not going to let you piss it away in crazy-risky, exotic investments. If they go bust, then it's going to be hard to get that money back when you legitimately need it.

THE TIME VALUE OF MONEY

It's important to determine your time horizon because the glory of compound interest has to have time to work and bear fruit. The longer you give it to do its thing, the closer you will be to your goals. Basically, we need to figure out the length of time it will take for your investments to grow before you can reap the benefits. Of course, your five-, ten-, fifteen-, twenty-, twenty-five-year lifestyle goals can and likely will have some interruptions when you'll have to take a big chunk of money out of the growth cycle. Those times, often called a "major liquidity event," might include:

- Paying for a wedding

- Having and raising a baby

- Making a down payment for a home

- Paying for tuition for your kid(s) to go to school

- Buying a car, boat, or second home

Keep these potential biggie needs for liquidity in mind as we move forward with your plan to make your money work for you. Think of these five-, ten-, fifteen-, twenty-, twenty-five-year targets as your destinations, with the investment and savings strategy we're building as the vehicle that gets you there, and your regular income (a.k.a., your salary) as the fuel that powers the engine. Hey, I get it: A girl has got to pee or grab a snack along the way. Just remember: the more pit stops you make, the longer it will take to get you where you are going. Of course, if you get a more powerful engine (in other words, up your income game, which we will talk about in Step 3), you could make up for lost time. So, there are workarounds for every variable that might come up *as long as you plan for it*. Nothing—not a market crash or even a pandemic—should blindside you so much that you're left unprotected or unhedged.

FYI Lifestyle creep describes the phenomenon where you start making more money but don't become more wealthy. I've seen people go from making $60,000 to making $600,000 and yet not get any wealthier. Why? Because their spending increases along with their salary. Their former luxuries become necessities, and their standard of living comes to include must-have private schools, nice cars, and a nanny. You're likely earning more than you did five years ago, right? Are you actually saving more in relation to that? The creep is real and can push your time horizon out or, worse, eat into your Miss Independent Fund if you keep living above your means during times of decreased income like unemployment or retirement. For your goals and planning sake, it's wiser to keep your standard of living more consistent even after you get a raise so that your long-term wealth keeps growing—not just your short-term spending.

As you're calculating how much money you'll need to live a fulfilling life you love, it's always better to overestimate what that amount would be for you, Miss Independent, without anyone else's help. That means no co-parent, no inheritance, no alimony, nothing. I'm sure you'll get help along the way and I'm not saying don't take it. I *am* saying don't *expect* it—and then be pleasantly surprised when it's offered. If you think you can't do this on your own, walk over to the mirror right now. I'll wait. Look in it and remember who the fuck you are.

BOTTOM LINE

Conventional Wisdom: I just want to be a millionaire.

Cool. But what would you do with that million dollars? Maybe you want to be a monk, in which case you'll need far less than a million dollars. Or, maybe you want to travel to all seven continents with your children and bring a private tutor along, in which case you're going to need more than a million dollars. Being a millionaire might sound sweet. But what's sweeter is calculating—and then getting—the right amount of money to live the life you want.

Conventional Wisdom: Money can bring you power and significance.

When people say they want a lot of money, they normally mean they want a lot of power and significance. Because feeling esteemed is one of our basic needs, people often believe that money gives them that. Money can be seen as a proxy for power and significance, for sure. When you make and lose it, it can feel like a direct boost or blow to your sense of esteem. But, money will never deliver the true significance we crave. Remember: you've had that power all along, my dear; you just have to discover it for yourself.

Conventional Wisdom: The more money you want, the riskier you have to be.

Sure, an appetite for risk can yield some pretty sweet returns. But, what matters most is how long your time horizon is so that you can determine your own personal risk appetite. Generally speaking, the longer your horizon is, the riskier you can be with your investments. And the shorter your horizon is, the less risky you should be with your investments.

STEP

THE BIG THINGS MAKE
THE BIGGEST DIFFERENCE

Spend the Most Time on the Things that Matter Most

I'm sure you've heard other money experts out there spew this financial "wisdom": if you want to save more money, "Don't buy the latte." It's been said that you can save thousands of dollars per year by skipping your daily coffee shop order. While I understand the intention behind this financial advice, I call BS. In many areas of life, the little things matter: in relationships, in science, in cooking. But when it comes to growing your wealth, the big things matter *more*.

Think of it this way: What's going to matter more to your bottom line in the long run, the $3.50 you saved on that latte or the $3,500 you saved in interest by focusing on getting your credit score up and your interest rates down? That's why I've long said, buy the damn latte, get your ass caffeinated, and then get after the major ways to save and, even better, the major ways to earn.

Often I've seen women spend too much energy on and get overwhelmed by the insignificant areas of their finances and neglect the ones that will have the greatest impact. In this step, we are going to identify what those biggies are and master them for our present and future selves. That way, you can spend your time thinking about buying Starbucks stock or even your own coffee shop instead of stressing about the cost of a stupid latte.

STACKS ON STACKS

I've long said that it's much more productive (and fruitful) to focus on making more money rather than freaking out about pinching those pro-verbial pennies. Coming to your finances from a place of aspiration instead of deprivation will pay the most dividends later on. Think of the time you'll save buying your latte instead of grinding your own beans and fussing with coffee filters at home. If you harnessed that time for a money-making activity—like picking up freelance work, rebalancing your stock portfolio (more on that in Step 12), or even just arriving earlier at work to wow your boss and get that promotion—it would pay for that latte and then some.

One of the big reasons I wrote this book is because even with all the stacks on stacks you're making at work, you're never going to build real wealth unless you come up with a system to grow your money and then pro-tect it. The reality is that the salary increase you'll see over time at most jobs just isn't enough to keep pace with inflation and your growing lifestyle, and especially not a growing family should you decide to have one. Your salary is a great foundation to live on, but not an elevator to the penthouse. That's why, if you want to be Miss Independent, you need a steady flow of money from as many sources as possible. In the end, people who are truly financially independent know that it's not what you earn but what you *keep* that matters.

THOSE SEVEN FAMOUS STREAMS OF INCOME

As I mentioned in the intro to this book, millionaires have an average of seven streams of income. Here are some of the most common streams:

- Earned income is your salary.
- Profit income is what you earn from your side hustle.

- Interest income is the interest you earn on savings.

- Rental income comes from tenants and Airbnb guests who live or stay at properties you own.

- Royalty income comes from continued sales of your intellectual property, such as books, music, and acting.

- Dividend income is paid out from the stocks you purchase.

- Capital gains are the profit you make after selling an asset like stocks or real estate.

We talked about many of these revenue streams in my first three books, especially your salary and side hustle. In this book, I'll focus on helping you with those related to stocks and other investments. You can have any number and any variety of the streams listed or others you might come up with—just as long as you bring in more than one stream to protect yourself should another dry up. Other streams I've seen people use successfully to build wealth include:

- **Residual income** includes royalties and other commissions on work that you've completed, but for which you continue to earn a percentage of ongoing profits.

- **Affiliate income** is from companies that reward you for recommending their product (hello, my social media influencers!).

- **Resale income** is from selling the things you are no longer using.

- **Multilevel marketing income** comes from selling goods or services on behalf of a company in a system whereby participants receive commission on their sales as well as the sales of any participants they recruit.[1]

- **Blog income** comes from allowing advertising or sponsored posts on your personal blog.

There all different permutations of these streams based on your specific industry.

And if you're already experienced in yours and want to share your knowledge or inspire people, you could become an influencer or motivational speaker. That could lead to even more income streams including **media income** from appearances on TV, radio and podcasts, or contributing to print outlets; **speaking income** from events at which you have been hired to speak; or even **licensing income** from allowing your copyrighted or patented material to be used by another person or company.

The reason so many entrepreneurial experts (or, um, pontificators) online talk about these revenue streams ad nauseum is because earned income in and of itself won't get you from where you are to where you want to be, even if that earned income is in the six or seven figures. Think of the endless stories of celebrities and athletes and otherwise famous people who pissed away the millions they earned. The actress Kim Basinger famously bought a whole town in Georgia for $20 million and made $10 million on average per movie, but then went bankrupt. So did other Boss Bitches like Toni Braxton, Pamela Anderson, Janice Dickinson, T-Boz from TLC, Cyndi Lauper, Dionne Warwick, and La Toya Jackson. They all made millions—and then lost it all.

I'm not here to bash these babes. But I share these and other cautionary tales to remind you that your base earnings won't make you Miss Independent in the long run, especially without a solid (and automated, which we will get to in Step 5: Automate Your World) system in place. If for whatever reason you stop working, and therefore stop drawing a salary—whether it's to stay home with kids or travel the world or go back to school or, of course, to retire—our goal is to build you a money-making machine so that your money never stops working for you. But that machine needs money to start making money, so don't take the earned income you have for granted while you have it; after all, it fuels the other income streams I'm going to help you set up next. Sure, your salary could last forever. But I'd rather you be pleasantly surprised when it does than devastated in the unemployment line or in bankruptcy court after it runs out.

CONFESSIONS OF BEING
MISS INDEPENDENT

Where I Make My Money

When I started my company, Nothing But Gold Productions, in the aftermath of the Great Recession back in 2011, I didn't know if I could come up with the money to sustain myself or a company for the decade I have. I also quit a pretty sweet, six-figure news anchor salary to strike out on my own, and I was sure I'd never get back there again, but I justified the move knowing that I would be paid in additional happiness and freedom.

Fun fact: I started Recessionista.com—an online destination for real-talk financial advice targeting millennial women—out of the gate, as my first project. It was perfectly timed during the down economy, but when the economy finally turned around a year later, I was scared I wouldn't find a sustainable way to pivot. Little did I know it would be the first of many times I successfully pivoted my brand and business.

Over the years, I've made my money through many different income streams, and those streams change pretty much every year as I take on new projects or move away from others. You know that I'm an open book when it comes to my own finances, literally. I've shared my salaries and the nitty-gritty of my own balance sheets in all of my previous books, and this is no different. Here are the most consistent streams of income from my business (not including interest, dividends, and capital gains) with the approximate amount I make in a year from each:

Speaking income:	$100,000
Book royalty income:	$50,000
Online course income:	$75,000
Affiliate income:	$20,000
Brand deal income:	$400,000
Consulting income:	$50,000

TV and TV residual income:	$150,000
Licensing income:	$12,000
Producing income:	$45,000
Podcasting income:	$175,000
Resale income:	$20,000

Because the nature of running a full-service multimedia pro-duction company isn't consistent, there are some years when special project streams of income pop up and then drop off. There are also years when some of the above are pulling the weight for all the others. My company has brought in an average $1 million in revenue per year since it was founded—which is severalfold what I was making before from just my news anchor salary and more than I ever thought possible.

You didn't think I was going to muse about all of the different streams of income without telling you mine, did you? The more transparency we have about what other people are making in different ways, the better off we will all be. I've obviously signed up to go first by getting into the financial literacy business. I would be lying if I said it was always easy, but I never regret speaking my truth in hopes of getting others to feel comfortable doing the same. If you feel comfortable enough in your circle of friends to be the one to go first so that you can break the taboo of money and ultimately help your whole crew win, then I encourage you to pay that financial transparency forward by sharing about your own revenue streams.

BEHOLD THE POWER . . .

. . . of compound interest! Compound interest is what people are talking about when they tell you to "make your money work for you" (and also what they warn about in the case of ginormous mortgage payments or snowball-ing credit card debt). Focusing more on making money than coupon clip-ping is important, but making that money make you even more money is what separates the rich from the super rich. It's truly the secret to growing wealth overtime by doing pretty much nothing.

I'm sure some of you already know the difference between compound interest and simple interest, but I'm going to give you a quickie refresher. And if you know me, you know I try really hard with the sports analogies but don't always nail them, especially those involving golf. (As you might recall from a confession in *Rich Bitch*, I brought soccer cleats to my first golf lesson, thinking those were the "little spiky shoes" appropriate for the golf course.)

My athletic skill matches that of my sports analogies, so a really good bet against me would be $1.00 per hole (there are eighteen that I know of). It's almost guaranteed that I won't make the shot, much less know which of the clubs to pick. Now, a shark might say to me, "Let's make it interesting; let's double that dollar every hole." Well, it's only a buck. What's the worst that could happen? Let's see . . . a buck doubled would be two bucks for hole 2. Then, two bucks doubled would be a $4 bet for hole 3, then $8 for hole 4. This still seems doable, but wait. Let's see how much I'd be in the hole (har har) if I took this bet.

THE COMPOUND INTEREST GAME: EXPLAINED	
Hole 1:	$1.00
Hole 2:	$2.00
Hole 3:	$4.00
Hole 4:	$8.00
Hole 5:	$16.00
Hole 6:	$32.00
Hole 7:	$64.00
Hole 8:	$128.00
Hole 9:	$256.00
Hole 10:	$512.00
Hole 11:	$1,024.00
Hole 12:	$2,048.00
Hole 13:	$4,096.00
Hole 14:	$8,192.00
Hole 15:	$16,384.00

THE COMPOUND INTEREST GAME: EXPLAINED	
Hole 16:	$32,768.00
Hole 17:	$65,536.00
Hole 18:	$131,072.00

Guess you could say that situation escalated pretty quickly! I am thankful that I get how compound interest works, so I wouldn't fall for that shit. But it would be a pretty sweet deal for the shark. So, let's be the shark. And move the course to Wall Street.

Now, this exact doubling bet isn't one you're going to find in any particular stock or investment, but the concept is the basis of virtually every one you'll make, so it's important to make sure you really have it down. Compound interest is where your money grows on itself exponentially, making interest on interest—thereby "working for you." Simple interest, on the other hand, is where your money grows at a fixed rate without taking the growth it caused into consideration, so the interest is based only on the initial principal investment.

FYI

The Rule of Seventy-Two helps you quickly see how long it will take to double your money. You basically divide seventy-two by the interest rate you're getting. The answer is close to the number of years it will take for your money to double at that rate. So, it takes about seventy-two years to double your money at a 1 percent compound interest rate (72/1=72). It takes about thirty-six years to double your money at 2 percent (72/2=36). Your money doubles at 10 percent in 7.2 years (72/10=7.2). You get the idea.

Let's look at the difference between 10 percent growth with simple and compound interest using an initial $100,000 investment.[2]

	SIMPLE INTEREST	COMPOUND INTEREST
Year 1	$110,000	$110,000
Year 2	$120,000	$121,000
Year 3	$130,000	$133,100
Year 4	$140,000	$146,410
Year 5	$150,000	$161,051
Year 10	$200,000	$259,374
Year 15	$250,000	$417,725
Year 20	$300,000	$672,750
Year 25	$350,000	$1,083,471

Basically, in Year 1, you would get the same amount back, but from then on your money grows at very different speeds. The 10 percent of $100,000 is $10,000, so both examples make that in Year 1. In the simple interest example, you make an additional $10,000 fixed each year. But in the compound interest example, you make 10 percent of the greater amount—now, $110,000 the second year—which is $11,000. In each consecutive year, the 10 percent is calculated based on the new balance. At the end of twenty-five years, you end up with $350,000 if you were collecting simple interest (like with a bond, which we will talk about in Step 7), which isn't bad, but it isn't the million bucks you'd have if it was compound interest instead!

Compound interest can be calculated at different intervals, from daily to annually. (Some banks promise "instant" interest reports, but don't be fooled, that's basically the same as daily.) In the example above, I calculated it annually. But the frequency matters a lot. The basic rule is that the more cycles of compounding, the more compound interest you'll make. So, 10 percent interest once a year is less than 5 percent interest paid every six months, which is actually 10.25 percent a year. When it works in your favor, you want as frequent as possible, and when it works against you (like with a mortgage or credit card payment), you want the fewest possible cycles.

TYPICAL FREQUENCY OF COMPOUND INTEREST IN YOUR FAVOR:

Savings Accounts—daily

Certificates of Deposit—daily, monthly or semi-annually

Money Market Accounts—daily

TYPICAL FREQUENCY OF COMPOUND INTEREST THAT WORKS AGAINST YOU:

Credit Cards—monthly

Mortgages—monthly

Personal business loans—monthly

When compound interest works in your favor, it can truly be magical. It's an awesome hedge against factors like lifestyle creep (or inflation that we will dig into soon enough) that can cut into your wealth. But it can also be magical when it works against you because if you know the mechanics behind why it didn't work, you can then get it to work in your favor. For example, if you make your mortgage payment twice a month instead of once a month, you can save substantial interest in the long run (more on this in Step 9: Get Real About Real Estate).

KNOW YOUR NUMBERS

MISS
INDEPENDENT
TIP

The Truth in Lending Act requires that lenders disclose all the terms to borrowers, including whether the interest is simple or compound, and the full dollar amount to be repaid over the course of the loan (this can be scary). So, be sure to ask but also to understand the difference in jargon, because these rates are far from created equal:

APR (Annual Percentage Rate): This a simple interest calculation you'll usually see with credit cards and mortgages. It's pretty sneaky, because it doesn't account for the compounding nature of the debt. So if the APR is listed at 25 percent and you charge $1,000 on your card and don't pay it off, you'll owe $1,280 after a year, closer to a 28 percent Effective Annual Rate.

EAR (Effective Annual Rate): This is a compound interest rate calculation. You may wonder why the heck we don't just use this all the time. I tend to agree when it comes to credit cards, but there are some loans, like auto or personal loans, that use simple interest so APR is actually the most accurate calculation.

APY (Annual Percentage Yield): This is the other side of APR. APR is listed when you're paying (like with debt), APY is listed when you're getting paid. You usually see this listed on savings accounts.

Oftentimes you'll see the more favorable (for the lender!) rate advertised, which is why APR is bolded on credit-card flyers to look like you're not going to pay up the wazoo when you carry a balance. Whatever the advertised rate is, your new instinct should be to ask for the flip side of the interest coin or those not bolded. Caveat emptor.[3]

STACKS BEFORE TAX

The example about growing your money with compound interest to more than a million bucks over twenty-five years got your attention, right? Of course it did. But, of course, this is a fictitious example to illustrate the concept of compound interest. It's important to note that it won't happen exactly that way in reality because that example doesn't take into account other important factors, like taxes.

I don't need to tell you that taxes are a big fucking deal. They can make a huge difference in making or breaking your wealth, but tax rates are not well understood. Let's say you made a million bucks one year and had a 37 percent tax rate (the highest rate in 2020).[4] What would you be left with? Not a million bucks clean is right. To make matters worse, the calculation isn't straightforward, so you would be left guessing until April 15. Maybe $900,000? Nope. $750,000? Good guess, but wrong-o.

After going through the IRS math, you'd you would be left with about $670,000 and that doesn't even account for state taxes, local taxes, or property taxes.[5] If you live in a super-high-tax state like New York or California, that number could be way less, closer to $500,000.

You simply can't ignore the hit taxes can have on your finances. That's why the financial experts who talk more about skimping on the latte than the things that will make the largest difference in your wealth drive me crazy. I mean, how many lattes can you buy with that $500,000 you just paid in taxes in this example?! Exactly.

Before you roll your eyes at me, we've got to talk about some general tax strategies. Even though it probably sounds like as much fun as a colonoscopy, these tactics can save you from needlessly paying more in taxes the more money you make, and thus get you to your financial dreams sooner. I fully get that it's "high class" or "champagne" problems to pay more in taxes, because that means you're making more money. I'm not saying to do anything sketchy or illegal, but there are ways to maximize your money fully under the letter of the law. This obviously is not a book about taxes, but I want you thinking about two biggies in particular as we continue on our Miss Independent journey: capital gains taxes and real estate taxes.

WTF ARE CAPITAL GAINS?

When you make money on an investment (yay!), and you will, you have to pay capital gains taxes (boo!). There are two types of capital gains (or "cap gains") taxes: short-term and long-term. Both are taxes but are triggered after different periods of time and come atcha with different rates.

Short-term capital gains apply when you sell an investment before a year is up. Today, the rates are currently the same as ordinary income tax. If you're already a high-income earner (and if you're not, you will be soon) that's a shit ton. Remember from the little pop quiz I just gave you, the top federal tax rate is now at 37 percent, and if you combine that with state income taxes, the rate might be 50 percent or higher.

Long-term capital gains, on the other hand, are taxes you pay on investments you hang on to for a year or longer. The tax rate for those gains is much lower than short-term capital gains, as they are taxed at 20 percent for the highest earners and 0 percent for the lowest earners. Wherever possible, when you do sell investments, try to do so after a year, so you are taxed at a much lower rate.

If you happen to lose money on your investments, then the short-term losses can be used to offset the short-term gains. The long-term losses can also be used to offset the long-term gains. If you still have more losses beyond that, they can be used to offset the other kind (short-term) as well. So, if you lose $1,000 and earn $2,500 in the short term, you would be taxed on $1,500 because the $1,000 offsets the $2,500. But let's say you also had $1,500 of long-term losses; that can also be used against the $2,500, giving you a net taxable gain of 0.

THREE WAYS TO MASTER CAP GAINS

- Wherever possible, keep higher cost investments (like mutual funds) growing inside tax-deferred accounts like a 401(k), IRA, defined benefit plan, annuity, and the like, so that you're letting it compound in a tax-free environment (future tax-free environment in the case of Roths). Did I lose you? Peek ahead to Step 8: Retire in Style for a quick crash course.

- Try not to have mutual funds outside of vehicles like the ones I just mentioned, because even if you're not selling the fund, the folks managing it are selling the investments, a lot, and you're hit with the bill for all that movement without even selling it yourself. Lose you again? Pop over to Step 10: Index Funds and Chill.

- If you do have any investment, including a mutual fund, outside of retirement or annuity vehicles, hang on to them for more than a year.

Here's a quick example of how, if you're not careful, fees and taxes can be the enemy of all your good investment work. Let's say you're making 7 percent return on a mutual fund and paying 3 percent in fees. You now have a return that nets you 4 percent after said fees. But, if you're in the top tax bracket in a state like New Jersey, then you can kiss 50 percent of that gain goodbye if you sell it before a year's time. That leaves you with 2 percent of a return after fees and taxes. Remember the doubling-your-money equation? The more you lower your rate of return, the longer it will take for you to double your money.

What's the point of bringing this up before we've even dug into WTF those types of investment vehicles are? Because taxes and fees are not afterthoughts but rather things that must be top of mind from the jump. I want you to go into this with your eyes open, maybe even smizing (smiling with your eyes) a little.

THINK REALLY HARD ABOUT WHERE YOU WANT TO LIVE

As you continue to grow your wealth, preserving it through tax efficiency can be addicting. (And, hey, if you're going to have an addiction to something, that's a pretty good one to have!) In Step 9: Get Real About Real Estate, we will talk all about home buying, but before we get into the brass tacks, maybe start reconsidering where you live. Hear me out.

Do you know what your city and state tax rates are where you live now? Many people only care to check when it comes time to retire, but there's no reason you can't do it now to plan ahead or investigate what it would be like to live elsewhere. Maybe there is a legitimate reason that you can never leave Los Angeles or Manhattan, with no ifs, ands, or buts. In that case, skip ahead (chances are you'll come back to this question at some point). If you are flexible, however, or could be in the future, it's definitely worth thinking about saving 10 to 15 percent of *everything* you do by moving to a more tax-friendly place.

Getting your financial butt in shape will mean saving more, but what if you could do that just by living in a place with no state income tax, like Florida, Wyoming, Nevada, Texas, South Dakota, Washington, Alaska, or Tennessee? Or states like New Hampshire or Tennessee, where your interest and dividend income aren't taxed at the state level, which often yields more tax savings? Depending on your income and tax bracket, a move from San Francisco (where taxes on the highest earners are more than 13 percent) to Dallas (where the state income tax is zero) could increase your spending and saving power significantly. I've definitely done my fair share of lusting over homes in those places. Just seeing what the same amount of money will get you in different areas is enough to pack up the car. But then, seeing what that could do to your finances—in some cases, the savings in taxes alone can pay for your entire house—is when you make moves (after removing your face from your palm, of course).

It's not just a move in the United States that could make a huge difference. There are lots of younger expats in places where living expenses are super low, like Fiji, Bali, and Costa Rica. When your money goes further on living expenses, you have more to contribute to your wealth-making machine.

And if you're thinking, *"Um, Lapin, do you want me to just peace out and set up a smoothie stand on the beach?"* No, dear reader. Major companies and innovative startups have opened offices in exotic places, including Facebook, Procter & Gamble, Google, and so many more.

Many of us have proven to ourselves or our bosses that we can work at least part of the time remotely, allowing for greater flexibility when it comes to where we live.[6] I lived in Arizona for a while because a) I love it there, b) it's way cheaper than Manhattan, and c) I could. I broadcasted on CNN from my living room and recorded my podcast from my closet. I mean, Kelly Ripa did her show from the Bahamas and Tom Hanks hosted *SNL* from his kitchen. Not to mention, the ultimate Boss Bitch Sara Blakely ran her Spanx empire from home with her four kids under the age of eleven running around in the background. Millions of others found ways to work collaboratively over Zoom and GoToMeeting from their own dining-room tables. People just made it work. It shows that your space and quality of life are that much more important if you're going to be both living and working, at least part of the time, from there.

In relationships, in our day-to-day lives, the little things make all the difference, for sure. But when it comes to our finances, it's the *big* things that really do make all the difference. Be more efficient and effective with those first, and try not to get distracted by the little things. That way, you can buy all the lattes you want, whenever you want—and then sip them while sitting on the wraparound porch in front of your tax-haven of a home.

If you only take one step today, or for the next year or even five years on your journey to becoming Miss Independent, cool. It's your journey, not mine. But my suggestion is that if you're gonna take a step at all, channel your inner kid and make it a leap—and skip a few boxes of financial hopscotch with one smart move.

BOTTOM LINE

Conventional Wisdom: I've heard of millionaires having an average of seven streams of income, but I'm not a millionaire.

Exactly. And the only way to get there is to stop relying on your salary alone to grow your wealth. What you take home in the form of a paycheck will barely keep pace with inflation and your cost of living long-term, and certainly won't make you rich. There are lots of viable streams of income out there—most of which I'll cover in this book—so that you can keep the money fountain going even if another dries up.

Conventional Wisdom: Interest is interest is interest.

Wrong-o. Compound interest and simple interest are wildly different things, and the former can make or break you (and your wallet). Because compound interest earns interest *on itself*, it's one of the most surefire ways to make your money work for you and grow your wealth exponentially over time. But for that same reason, when it works against you—like with credit card debt or a mortgage—it can eat into your earnings faster than you can say "Super Rich." So, keep your eye out for compound interest, and play it to your advantage before it plays *you*.

Conventional Wisdom: I only need to think about taxes when it's time to file 'em.

On average, women think about sex eighteen times per day. I want you to be thinking about your taxes almost as often. No, they're not as sexy—but you know what *is* sexy? Making money. And if you're not thinking through opportunities to (legally) reduce your tax burden, then you're going to end up forking over a truly unsexy amount of cash to Uncle Sam and his state-level equivalent at the end of the year. Talk about financial buzzkill.

STFU, YOU'RE NOT TOO OLD

Set Yourself and Your Balance Sheet Up for Success Now

*D*o you know what it means when someone drops the "H-bomb" in conversation? It happens when someone went to Harvard, but is too embarrassed to say so, and avoids saying it altogether by mentioning instead attending "a small liberal arts school in Boston." Embarrassed? Are you kidding me? By going to arguably the best university in the world?! Yes. Some people are embarrassed by their own prestige.

As you know, I draw many parallels between taking care of your financial health and taking care of your physical health, but this is one way that they differ. When you take on a physical feat, like running a marathon or committing to a healthier lifestyle, you can—and probably do!—shout it from the rooftops. But our financial goals and successes are much more closeted. When was the last time you heard someone exclaim, "My portfolio just went up!" or post on Instagram that the last bit of credit card debt was paid off? Because regardless of whether we have a lot of money or we have none, we all have complexes about money and prestige. That doesn't mean we don't need the same support from family, friends, and society to validate our financial goals and ensure that we stay on the path to financial victory. In fact, we need *more* of it.

You don't have to be college-aged (or have gone to Harvard, although if you did then say it loud and proud, my friend) or even close to it to get yourself there. Sure, the sooner the better. You are never as young again as you are today. In this step, I'm going to teach you about the time-value of money, and why today is as good a day as any to get your finances organized on your way to being Miss Independent, baby.

SHOW ME THE MONEY

I'm sure you've heard the old adage: "A dollar today is worth more than a dollar tomorrow." That's the time-value of money, in a nutshell. Money in the present is worth more than an equal amount in the future, because it can be put to work. Let's say you win the lottery. First of all, lucky you! (I never win anything.) You are given two options for collecting your $1 million winnings: you can either take a lump sum payment of $1 million today, or get ten annual payments of $100,000 each (totaling $1 million over that span of time). Which option do you choose? The time-value of money says to take the lump sum payment *right now,* because it gives you the ability to put the money to work earning interest or growing via some other investment vehicle like stocks or real estate.

Let's get one thing straight: you can't put *any* of your money to work—not even your swanky lottery winnings—if you don't first take stock of what you have. This is your baseline. It's your personal balance sheet with your assets (what you own) and your liabilities (what you owe). Remember, all of your financial goals come back to your net worth and the money you'll need to live the life you want. Or, for the math nerds out there:

Net worth + money needed to achieve dreams = financial goals

My hope is that, while you might have some work to do, you will feel empowered by seeing that your financial picture is not as dire as the mean girl inside your head made it out to be. This is the most important selfie you'll take: a financial selfie. And this kind is done with no filter or retouching.

Here's a comprehensive template to calculate your net worth. It reflects the assets and liabilities that many people have, but not everything they could have. (The possibilities are truly endless!) There are some savings and investment vehicles on here that we haven't gone over yet; don't worry, we'll get to 'em in the steps to come. Just fill out what you can, and then as we move through more advanced concepts in Part II of this book you can refer back to this list and keep filling it out until it's complete. (You can also download this list from my website.[1]) However you complete it is up to you:

BALANCE WORKSHEET	
YOUR CURRENT ASSETS	
Cash and Savings	
Cash	
Checking Accounts	
Savings Accounts	
Money Market Accounts	
Certificates of Deposit (CDs)	
Other (alimony, child support, etc.)	
Investment Assets	
Stocks	
Bonds	
Mutual Funds (index funds)	
Stock Options	
Life Insurance (cash value only)	
Annuities (surrender value only)	
Real Estate (income-producing only)	
Other (REITs, commodities, cryptocurrency, etc.)	

BALANCE WORKSHEET	
Retirement Assets	
401(k), Roth 401(k), and/or Employee Savings Plan	
Profit-Sharing Plans and/or Pension	
Traditional and Roth IRA	
Other (SEP, Simple, qualified accounts, etc.)	
Non-Income-Earning Assets	
Home Equity (all non-income properties)	
Furniture and Electronics	
Jewelry	
Vehicles (car, boat, motorcycle)	
Other (alternative investments like memorabilia, collectibles, etc.)	
Total Assets	$
YOUR CURRENT LIABILITIES	
Mortgage	
Car Loan	
Credit Card Debt	
Student Loans	
Taxes (not withheld)	
Current Unpaid Bills	
Life Insurance (amount borrowed)	
Other Debt (friends and family, etc.)	
Total Liabilities	$
NET WORTH (ASSETS – LIABILITIES)	$

Calculating your net worth is found simply by subtracting your liabilities (everything you owe) from your assets (everything you own). You don't need to be a millionaire to have a net worth. Everyone has one but not everyone takes the time to calculate it. A recent study found that women control 32 percent of the world's wealth, and yet many women don't know their net worth.[2] Research has shown that 70 percent of households underestimate their net worth, and 40 percent of people underestimate their wealth.[3] In short: we're selling ourselves, well, short.

At the end of Part I, you will find a new, sparkly, aspirational balance sheet with everything we talk about throughout the rest of this book. Keep coming back to it. Add numbers, take numbers away, see how it all comes together.

Scan this code with your phone to access a balance worksheet you can print:

BALANCE WORKSHEET QR CODE

NEW RULES

We've all got bad habits, but biting your fingernails or staying up late binging Netflix aren't as damaging to your bottom line as leaving your financial future to the "professionals" to "figure it out." Don't give me that BS. We both know that you are fully capable of writing, reading, and revisiting your own personal balance sheet. If you can successfully track down your ex's new girlfriend on Instagram or get to the fourth page of an Amazon product review, then you can absolutely follow your own money trail.

For the rest of this book, we are basically going to be zooming in on the Endgame portion of the three Es in the Spending Plan you came up with in *Rich Bitch*. To briefly refresh your memory, a basic spending plan tailored for your lifestyle and spending choices should include:

- 70 percent goes to the **Essentials** (food, housing, transportation)

- 15 percent goes to the **Extras** (latte, mani-pedis, trip to Tulum)

- 15 percent goes to the **Endgame** (your future self and everything we are going to talk about next, including saving, investing, retirement)[4]

Now, I would be thrilled if you rejiggered these basic guidelines to give even more to your Endgame—18 percent or even 20 percent, if you could swing it—but at this point, if it's just 1 percent, let's start there. Regardless of how much you have or can put into retirement, if you don't know how to manage $1,000, you'll never know how to manage $1,000,000.

I talked about lots of different ways money is power in Step 1, but you may have noticed that I didn't say "knowledge is power." Why? Well, for starters, you know that I'm allergic to clichés. Also, it's just not true as it relates to your money. Financial knowledge *isn't* power, it's *potential* power. You can study your face off for the ten thousand hours Malcolm Gladwell says it takes to become an expert and highlight the shit out of this book, but you'll never be Miss Independent by doing that alone. Taking a few hours to actually, physically, run your own numbers and make a plan is where the real power comes from. Execution is power.

knowledge → execution → repetition → power

PUT IT TOGETHER

We have a tendency to over- or underestimate the money we have and the money we think we need to live the life we want. By now you know that I am the biggest advocate for knowing exactly what both of those numbers—what you have, and what you're gonna need—are. The two also work together as you create your financial destiny. Think about it: the more you have, the less you'll need, and vice versa.

Take a look at your numbers from the last step. How does your view on achieving the price tags for your dreams change based on your net worth? Do you have a ton of savings and a net worth that's higher than you expected so you're feeling more confident about how you're going to make up the gap? Maybe you're already at one of the wealth thresholds we outlined in Step 2 and breathing a sigh of relief? Or is there more work to do? Regardless, it's better to have an accurate estimate—*that* we can work with—than an over- or underestimate (that's likely just the mean girl talking).

MOVE YOUR ASSETS

The balance sheet template is an amalgamation of the ones used in accounting best practices. But it's not how we are going to organize this list moving forward. For starters, in an ideal world, you'd have nothing in the liabilities category. Now of course, not all liabilities, or debt, are created equal. "Bad" debt (the kind I'm always telling you to prioritize to pulverize) refers to credit card or other consumer debt that does little to improve your financial outcome. "Good" debt is the money you owe for things that can help build wealth or increase your income over time, like student loans, a business loan, or a mortgage (in some cases; more on mortgages in Step 9). So, if you do have some liabilities of the good variety, I'm not mad atcha. As for the assets category, I want you to aspire to an asset allocation that is more advanced in its breakdown than the initial list you just made—and that's where we're going to head next.

In Part II, I'm going to break all these components down to the smallest, most digestible pieces (there's a whole step for each section of your balance sheet). We are going to learn every possibility when it comes to investing your money. You will know how each one works and how they work together. By the end, you'll know where you're going and how to get there.

Many of the so-called millionaires next door aren't into flash but have the craziest cash stash and you'd never know it. Of course, we all go through flirtations with bravado and phases of trying to keep up with the Joneses or Kardashians or whomever. I certainly have. But being legit super rich and independent isn't about leading with your cash or ever looking like it. It's about *being* it, long after your working days are behind you.

Let's take these two women with different salaries, both of whom committed to saving automatically from each paycheck:

WOMAN 1

Starting salary: $50,000
Percentage automatically saved: 10 percent, $96 per week
Amount saved over lifetime of investing: $250,000

WOMAN 2

Starting salary: $30,000

Percentage automatically saved: 5 percent, $58 per week

Amount saved over lifetime of investing: $150,000

These scenarios are simplified, not accounting for a lot of things like increased salary, other income, or inflation, for example, but I'm using them to show you what happens when you save a fixed amount over time, even if it feels small. Both women have five years of Rich Enough salary saved up. This is not to say that the growth was magical, and they didn't have to put their money to work so it ultimately worked for them; they did. But once they took a few easy steps to set themselves up for success, they found it over time.

When I say "over time" (which I do, a lot!), I mean that rates of return are projected over long periods. The longer you have, the more your money will likely grow. It's not gospel or a sure thing, but that's what the data tells us. None of these projections are based on what you'll hear on the news of market hysteria—good or bad—but rather what happens if you take a business news time-out and don't touch anything, no matter how tempting it is.

"But, Lapin, what if I lose it all instead?!" you may be thinking. Honestly, you could. But that's a super small chance. And when you use tried and tested tactics, that chance becomes even smaller. As Warren Buffett, the world's most successful investor, once said, "Risk comes from not knowing what you're doing."[5] We will go through other risk factors that might impact your investments in greater detail—your time horizon being a biggie—but "not knowing what you're doing" need not apply.

For the sake of simplicity, I'm going to give you overviews for three basic time horizons—short, medium, and long. But don't forget that these change as you get older.

- *Shorty But Goody (shortest timeline, lowest risk)*: If you have a short time horizon for when you want to get your paws on your wealth, then you should be less risky with the steps you take with your Miss Independent Fund. Typically, shorter timelines can come into play when you reach an age you want to retire.

- *In Between-y (medium timeline, medium risk)*: If you have more than ten years to play with before you retire, then you can take on some moderate risk, because you have more time to recover if shit goes south.

- *Going Long (longest timeline, highest risk)*: If you're playing with twenty or more years before hanging up your work bag, then, girl, you can have a little more fun here while still allowing time to weather the financial storms that will inevitably be in the forecast.

Of course, if you're like, "Lapin, I'm only twenty, but I just cannot stand risk, it will stress me out and keep me up at night." Cool, then take the first path and get a good night's rest. Alternatively, if you say, "Lapin, I'm in my fifties but I have a lot of money to play with so I'm going to be super risky with half of it, because it won't matter if I lose every penny." Well, that's also great. Go wild.

There is no one-size-fits-all for investing. My goal is to show you the general patterns you can fit into as simply as I can, so that you can pick what works best for you. And you don't need to justify it to me or anyone else as long you're making your choices from a place of power.

If you're still assessing what percentage, what timeline and what level of risk feels best for you, consider this time value of money chart. This is what happens if you save $100 every month (compounded monthly), with different interest rates of return in five-, ten-, twenty-, thirty-, and forty-year periods.

INTEREST RATE	10 YEARS	20 YEARS	30 YEARS	40 YEARS	50 YEARS
1%	$12,731	$26,690	$42,117	$59,167	$78,010
2%	$13,406	$29,658	$49,508	$73,752	$103,364
3%	$14,129	$33,065	$58,626	$93,130	$139,705
4%	$14,903	$36,986	$69,929	$119,073	$192,386
5%	$15,733	$41,506	$83,998	$154,052	$269,548
6%	$16,623	$46,728	$101,580	$201,522	$383,620
7%	$17,578	$52,771	$123,637	$266,334	$553,671
8%	$18,603	$59,778	$151,406	$355,311	$809,071

INTEREST RATE	10 YEARS	20 YEARS	30 YEARS	40 YEARS	50 YEARS
9%	$19,704	$67,916	$186,485	$478,085	$1,195,226
10%	$20,887	$77,383	$230,935	$648,276	$1,782,570

I've always said that the best way to approach your finances is somewhere in between thinking you're going to die tomorrow and thinking you're going to live forever. The reason I'm so gung-ho about you filling up your Miss Independent Fund as early and as much as you can is because this is the accumulation phase of your wealth. Just like with any other aspect of time, you can't get these years back.

In order to make sure you are well fed in the future, you have to go through the planting, cooking, and eating phases. This is where you plant everything you could possibly want to eat later on. I don't want you to ever be hungry for money or anything else. Try to get as much stuff in the ground now, so you can watch it all grow, baby, grow—and reap the benefits later.

FEE FERTILIZER

Before you're well into growing season, make sure to protect yourself from the bugs that could eat into your crop early on. In the wealth world, those bugs are fees. From here on out, I will be on fee patrol for you. I'll flag specific ones to watch out for along the way, but for now just don't forget they are out there. While they could look too small to matter, they can be deadly.

Here's an example to illustrate that I'm not dramatizing this. Let's assume you and your two best friends invest $100,000 at 7 percent when you're thirty-five. When you're sixty-five and want to live your best Golden Girl lives, you compare your earnings.

You pay 1 percent in annual fees = $574,349 in earnings

Bestie 1 pays 2 percent in annual fees = $432,194 in earnings

Bestie 2 pays 3 percent in annual fees = $324,340 in earnings

If you're like me, you want all your friends to win, so don't let this happen to your friends. The whole "1 percent here, 1 percent there" stuff is "just" brutal when you look at what it does to your money over time. You may have heard the expression "death by a thousand cuts," which originates from a horrible form of torture during which the victim was cut, yes, a thousand times, slowly bleeding to death. In modern times, it's also featured in a Taylor Swift song, along with the lyric "I can't pretend it's okay when it's not." Well, it sounds morbid, but it's actually a pretty accurate way to describe how painful fees can be as they bleed out your earning potential.

Perhaps the biggest culprit of sneak-attack fees are mutual funds. We will talk a lot about mutual funds throughout the rest of the book because they are an important part of any investment portfolio.[6] They are usually the biggest component of retirement accounts, like 401(k)s and IRAs, which we will talk about in Step 8. Of course, it's in the best interest of fund managers to make these fees look super small, even if they're not.

Insiders call funds with excessive fees "fee factories," which, like the "farm factories" that value profits over the ethical treatment of animals, set you up for suffering before you even start. I mean, who actually calculates ahead of time to see how fees will impact their investments long-term? Miss Independents do, that's who. Someone who makes $100,000/year can end up paying about $300,000 in 401(k) fees in her lifetime if she's not careful. Seriously. Well, not you, sister. I'm not going to let you work the equivalent of three extra years in fees when you could retire in style!

THE SECRET

I started this step by asserting that it's never too late to start down the wealth road. Vera Wang, Toni Morrison, and Arianna Huffington all made their fortunes later in life at ages forty, forty-six, and fifty-five, respectively. It took me well into my thirties to finally get my own financial shit together, too, and to stop relying on my salary alone to grow my nest egg. If I can do it and if they can do it, so can you; and I hope you do it sooner.

The secret isn't luck or fate, but fear—and facing it. It's confronting exactly what it is that hurt you around money in the past and being really honest about where you are versus where you want to be. Say hello to your imposter syndrome. Give a wave to that scary debt of the past. Fist-bump it with the time you were told only to flush when it was number two to save on the water bill. You can give those past traumas a wink and then wave them goodbye, because we won't be seeing those bitches later.

Whatever you are afraid of admitting or talking about around money is exactly what you need to focus on, ASAP. You don't need to talk about it with others, at least not at first (although research and personal experience have shown that sharing your narrative works wonders for healing and personal growth) but you do have to confront it for yourself and your financial advisor. Only then will you not only be able to work effectively through the rest of this book, but feel truly empowered to implement the lessons you learn for the rest of your life.

I could say that I wish I had started working toward becoming Miss Independent earlier in my life, and that's why you should. But the truth is: I did. I started several times, but I stopped at this very point—facing my financial fears—and rolled over and quit. I wasn't ready to confront my past or speak my truth. Of course, no one is ever fully ready for any of the big things in life: buying a house, tackling a promotion, having a baby. But most of us jump in anyway. This time, I don't want you to just jump, hoping and praying for a net. I want you to fly and never stop soaring.

BOTTOM LINE

Conventional Wisdom: Only millionaires have a net worth.

Everyone has a net worth—you've just gotta take the time to run the numbers! I mean, hey, your net worth might be negative, but that doesn't mean you can't calculate it. You will never build your wealth until you know the foundation you're building it on from top to bottom. And if you're saying you're not a millionaire, then I would be sure to add "yet" to the end of that statement, missy.

Conventional Wisdom: The right asset allocations will make you rich.

There are infinite ways to allocate your assets, which just means figuring out the percentage you want to have of a particular asset class at any given time. There's no universally "right" way to do it; you have to find the sweet spot that makes the most sense given your time horizon and stomach for risk, and that means balancing "safe" assets with riskier ones. But one thing is certain: it's not the allocation that will make you rich, but the value of the underlying assets. And we'll tackle the many different types throughout the rest of the book.

Conventional Wisdom: There's no way to save when you're living paycheck to paycheck.

I know it feels that way. I know, because I've been there. But I'll say this: don't let perfect be the enemy of getting started. Sure, in an ideal world, would I love it if you started with ten grand or more in the bank? Yes. But, baby, this world is far from ideal. It's far from perfect and so are we. Think about starting small as a vital step to not living paycheck to paycheck in the future.

AUTOMATE YOUR WORLD

Get into a Rich Routine

f I weren't a financial person (and let's be honest, I've dealt with my fair share of imposter syndrome even after becoming a successful one), then I would definitely be an interior designer. I've never had a secret Pinterest account of engagement rings, but I always had one of faucets and sconces. I would rather online shop for knobs than pretty much anything else.

I've gone through a lot of home renovations, including designing my own dream home, which began as a dirt plot in the desert. I've learned quite a bit about architecture and decor, mostly through making very expensive mistakes—like, does Carrara marble really need to be *that* expensive? The biggest lesson I learned from being an amateur interior designer—which also applies to finances—is that while it's super fun (for some) to pick out the fabrics and fixtures, it's way more important to get the structure right first. Once you've built a solid foundation, the window dressing becomes easier. Bonus tip: it's less expensive because you won't have to worry about tearing it down to get rid of the nasty ass mold lurking beneath your pretty wallpaper.

So, before we go on with decorating your new Miss Independent life, let's get your foundation set up correctly. Creating a thoughtful system and process for your finances is like pouring the foundation of a house and watching it dry, so . . . slowly. Truth be told, it's my least favorite part of an actual home build. But once your foundation is solid and you start building the frame piece by piece, your vision board becomes reality in no time. In this step, I'm going to help you create a strong, well-made financial structure; one you can keep building on forever.[1]

PAY YOURSELF FIRST

If you take nothing else from this book, then take this lesson, please: *Always pay yourself first.*

No, you don't have to work for yourself to do that. You just have to prioritize your Endgame, a.k.a. your future.

Of course, you might think the first person to get paid when you do is Uncle Sam. That makes sense—and as I said previously in Step 3, I want you to consider the tax implications on your money at every turn. That dude takes about thirty cents of every dollar you make, then there's about five cents more to the state and then Social Security, unemployment, Medicare, and wabam! You're left with like sixty cents on the dollar![2] So, that $100,000 you are proud to make (six figures, baby!) looks more like $60,000 after the government gets its hands on it.

There are actually a whole bunch of perfectly legal ways to pay yourself before the government; for example, in pretax accounts like 401(k), 403(b), IRAs, and SEP IRAs. We will go over the whole shebang in greater detail in Step 8: Retire in Style. But for now, just know that you should set up a predetermined percentage of your monthly net earnings to automatically deposit into your main Miss Independent Fund, just like the government does with taxes, so that you can't get your beautifully manicured paws on it—and spend it now, instead of in the Endgame.

MISS
INDEPENDENT
TIP

CALCULATE YOUR BILLABLE HOURS

You don't need to be a lawyer to have billable hours. You just need to calculate what your hourly rate is. If you're already paid hourly, you know this number cold (and you should also have a strong handle on opportunities to make more money, like overtime or holiday pay). If you collect a salary, then take your gross (pretax) salary and divide it by fifty weeks (accounting for two weeks of annual vacation) and then divide that number by forty hours (or whatever number of hours you work per week). So, someone who earns $50,000/year would make $1,000/week or $25/hour. If you aim for my suggested Endgame target of 15 percent, that would be $150/week going into your retirement account. Yep, that means you worked six hours per week for you *and* your future self—a good feeling, amirite?

Unfortunately, most people save just a teeny percent of what they make, if they save anything at all. There is nothing wrong with nice things and fancy dinners, but not at the expense of your future self. One blowout today is the equivalent of ten in retirement. And if you're the person who pays for everyone else's drink before you pay your future self, stop. When you put others before yourself at your expense, then all the hours you are working benefit everything and everyone but you, the one who is doing all the work!

In *Becoming Super Woman*, I talk at length about why we should put our oxygen masks on first, like they tell us to do on the plane, before helping others. It's true. You must look out for yourself first, and that includes financially—or you'll never be able to help anyone else. It might feel selfless to be saving for your kids' college tuition before your retirement, but what happens when you show up to sleep on their couch, because you don't have any money of your own? Is that really helping them?

Instead, saving about twenty bucks a day (calculated using our earlier example of saving 15 percent of a $50,000/year salary toward your Endgame) for yourself will only benefit your kids long-term by giving them one less thing to worry about: *you*. I repeat: twenty bucks a day. That's it! Psychologists have a saying: "Neurons that fire together, wire together." The idea of rewiring your brain to recognize these incremental daily changes is nothing short of awesome, and makes the whole saving thing less scary. It's free but yields so much value (in this case, $7,300/year for Future You to retire in style—$7,320 in a leap year).

Once your brain feels good about the myriad benefits of paying yourself first, here's how to do it:

- **Open a special savings account.** We'll talk more about different places to stash your cash in the next step, but for now, let's focus on creating your Miss Independent Fund. This savings account can be at the bank you're already with or a new one. You can label it with a heart emoji or something aspirational—whatever does it for you—as long as you open it and start filling 'er up.

- **Fill the account.** Don't wait for some fat stack of cash to drop out of the sky to get started; it's not going to happen. You can start small with whatever you've got. Decide on a fixed amount or a percentage of each paycheck (10 percent, 15 percent, 20 percent of take-home pay) and stick to that. Does $150 a week still sound like too much? What about fifty bucks a week or seven bucks a day? I know you can manage *that*. That fifty bucks becomes $2,600/ year, and if you compound that over the next forty years, that would be far more than half a million bucks. And, hey, if you can manage more, do that. Start conservatively; the more you stick to it and see those numbers grow, the more you'll want to increase it.[3] Trust me.

- **Automate it.** Whatever the rule you set for how much you're going to contribute to your Miss Independent Fund, set an automatic deposit into that account from your paycheck or whatever other source of income you might have.

Pro Tip: If you earn a traditional salary, your employer should be able to set up a direct deposit into your Miss Independent Fund directly through payroll. Ask about a payroll savings plan, which is often included in employee benefit programs. If that's not possible, then your bank will be able to set up an automatic bank account transfer for a specific amount (just calculate what the dollar amount is from the percentage you decide on) from the account where your paycheck is directly deposited into your Miss Independent Fund.

salary → take home pay → Miss Independent Fund

We will automate more of your money trail from here, but for now, just make sure the money going into your retirement account is set up automatically. Just like you "set and forget" your bill paying so you never miss a payment, I don't want you missing a payment to your future self. If you're self-employed, think of yourself as the superstar contractor who must be paid first.

To be clear, your Miss Independent Fund is what is going to be feeding your future wealth. It's your foundation. It's not what you're using to buy groceries or book plane tickets for your next vacation. For simplicity, throughout the rest of the book, this is the money we are going to be playing with. This is going to be the hub from which a bunch of spokes will come to help you fly like I promised I'd help you do at the end of the last step.

Maybe you're saying, "There is no way I can save a single dollar. I'm living paycheck to paycheck and it's all Essentials and some Extras with no Endgame." Well, I hear you—this is hard work, no doubt about it—but I also promise that you can and will find $50 or more to save. This is for your dreams, your future. Cancel the random subscriptions you don't use, or crap from Amazon you don't need, and give some love to all the things you outlined in Step 2 that really make your heart beat.

Remember: *Rich people stay rich by acting like they are poor and poor people stay poor by acting like they are rich.*

NEW ROUTINE

The reason we are getting into a new relationship and routine with money is to essentially safeguard ourselves from ourselves. Yes, we all need that—even I do. Behavioral finance studies the principles of psychology that affect our thinking and actions as investors. Basically, we tend to be irrational, driven by fear and emotion. "Who, me?" Yes, you. And all of us.

Thankfully we're also thinking animals, so we are going to use this psychology to our advantage by protecting ourselves from the worst of our human nature, which can make us bad investors, including:

- Narrative Fallacy: We love stories, and we often let that love cloud facts and hinder us from making rational decisions.

- Loss Aversion: We have the tendency to avoid loss out of fear, rather than to optimize for gains.

- Herd Mentality: Our instincts tell us to follow the herd and copy what those around us are doing, rather than to trust our own independent analysis.

- Hindsight Bias: We often look back at events and lament that we "always knew" and should have followed our gut to a better outcome, as if we possess some special power or insight.

These are examples of behaviors and biases that all humans have but are in direct opposition to how successful investors should act: devoid of emotion, logical, and methodical. I've long argued that your intuition and EQ play a vital role in many areas of business—especially when it comes to the interpersonal skills required to get ahead in your career—and that remains true. But when it comes to investing, you have to check those babies at the door. I know it sounds harsh, but I hope that in saying this I can help you to skip past a lot of the mistakes that many novice investors make.

Investing and growing wealth hinge on reflective, not reflexive, decision-making. It doesn't require a high IQ. Warren Buffett says: "Once you have ordinary intelligence, then what you need is the temperament to control urges that get others into trouble." Even if that self-controlled temperament doesn't come to you naturally (it certainly doesn't for me), you can build it using the three Ps: preparing, planning, and precommitting.

SET IT AND FORGET IT

If you're like me, you have a calendar reminder for pretty much everything in your life (and maybe even multiple alarms too). If it's not on my calendar, I probably won't be doing it. I tend to batch entries, like entering all my therapy appointments at once or stalking my best friends on Facebook to make sure all their birthdays are in there. I've found the same concept to be super helpful for making regular financial moves, too, so that even when life gets crazy, I keep my money moving—and growing. Here are some of my favorite calendar reminders for you to set today:

- Pick one day per year to revisit your personal balance sheet and make any necessary adjustments. (I like the summer solstice, because it's a great use of that extra-long day.)

- Pick one day per year to increase your contribution toward your Miss Independent Fund. (I like the day before my birthday, because it makes me feel like a grown-up.)

- Twice a year, make sure you set a time to ensure your accounts are automated and running smoothly, including your bills, paychecks, and other direct deposits. This is also a good time to cancel any automatic memberships or subscriptions you're paying for, but not using.

- Once a year to once a quarter, depending on the major life events you have going on (new job, house, baby, and so on) check in with your financial advisor.

- If you have an accountability partner in your financial journey other than a professional—a friend, a sig-o, a family member— set a weekly or monthly check-in with them so they can keep you honest and hold you accountable to your goals.

NEW MINDSET

There has been a lot written about mindfulness in different areas of our lives, from eating to exercising to parenting. But little has been written about mindfulness when it comes to finances. Until now.

Being mindful with your money is not some fancy, hippy-dippy practice. It's about getting good at staying present and being aware of wherever you are and whatever you're doing rather than just going through the motions. Here's how that relates to your finances: to grow it, you must be intentional and aware of what's happening with your money.

We already started practicing mindfulness by pricing out our goals and taking an honest look at our current balance sheet. And before we move into the balance sheet of the future, it's important to get your mind right.

Money mindfulness is the opposite of what I did for the majority of my life. My first instinct was either to avoid thinking about my money altogether or to choose the path of least resistance. For example, if the default box on the 401(k) form was to go to mutual funds with 2 percent fees, I would do that without thinking twice (more in Step 6: Cash Is Queen about why that was a terrible idea). The thing I love most about mindfulness and any other emotional intelligence (EQ) practice is that it's a skill that can be learned. Your IQ (intellectual intelligence) is really tough to change, but about 40 percent of your EQ is within your power to change—and use for your benefit.

You may be saying, "Lapin, WTF does EQ have to do with getting rich?" Everything, my darling, everything. We will get to all the different investment vehicles, tricks, and formulas. I can tell you about that stuff all day—but if your mindset is off, it will just look like more of the same money gibberish that's turned you off in the past.

GROW YOUR MIND AND YOUR MONEY

Before we start getting into more of the number crunching and strategy, I want you to complete this sentence: "I am _____ enough to be Super Rich."

For those of you who put something along the lines of "good" enough, "smart" enough, or even "badass" enough, you're starting from a good place.

For those of you who allowed doubt to enter your minds and filled the blank with "not good" enough or "not smart" enough, it's time to take control of those limiting beliefs about money. Maybe someone, including yourself, has told you this along the way, and it's kept you from getting in a zen place with your money. Regardless, you are a grown-ass woman now, and the buck literally stops with you.

You and only you can change the narrative you tell yourself. You and only you can turn a fixed mindset (a.k.a. Poor Bitch Mindset) into a growth mindset (a.k.a. Super Rich Mindset).[4] I love this saying: Whether you think you can or you think you can't, you're right.

So, let's get it all out there. What are all the things or traits you don't have enough of to grow independently wealthy? Here are some common ones and how to start rephrasing them to yourself. Studies have shown it takes around twenty-one days to form a new habit, including a new mindset—so, your goal is to focus on this reframing exercise for the next three weeks. *Go!*)

POOR BITCH MINDSET	SUPER RICH MINDSET
I don't have enough money to start with.	I'm going to grow what I have.
I don't know anything about investing.	I'm learning about investing!
So-and-so is way better at finance than me!	I'm going to learn from so-and-so.
I'll never be smart enough to do this.	I'm training myself to learn a new skill.
I'm too old to get started.	Today is as good a day as any!

Now, let's complete the sentence again—this time with a little chutzpah! "I am _____ enough to be Super Rich." Yes, you are good enough, smart enough, capable enough, savvy enough, strong enough, and curious enough to be Super Rich. Baby, you are more than enough.

CONFESSIONS OF BEING
MISS INDEPENDENT

Nurse Martens

"I love your shoes," said a high-pitched voice from over my shoulder as I was trying to figure out my locker combination.

"Thank you so much," I said with a slight inflection at the end as I turned around to see two girls who could have been straight from Central Casting as the trendiest, most popular girls in school.

"Of course, where did you get them?" the other half of the popular-girl duo asked.

"Oh, um, I'm not sure. At the mall," I lied in another statement-question hybrid. I knew exactly where I got them. I got them at Payless ShoeSource. I got a lot of my shoes there or at the Downtown Los Angeles Fashion Mart, a.k.a way far away from where these Beverly Hills girls shopped.

"I didn't see them this weekend, and I went to Bloomies, Aldo, and Steve Madden. They must be so hot that they are sold out or a brand, brand new trend," bitchy girl #1 said.

"I'm not sure," I said, embarrassed and now catching on that this was an insincere compliment trap that really amounted to bullying. It could have been a scene out of an angsty teenage movie—but it was my first day at a new middle school.

"Well, they look like Doc Martens. Maybe they are 'Nurse Martens,'" bitchy girl #2 said as she stared me down. They both turned away, laughing.

Doc Martens were all the rage when I was growing up. But I didn't have a real pair; just a cheaply made knockoff version. The real ones were nearly $100! I never thought I would be able to spend that much money on anything, let alone shoes. But, of course, I dreamed of the day I would touch the yellow and black fabric tag on the back of a pair of my very own Doc Martens.

I wasn't the popular girl growing up. I went to school with a bunch of rich kids who gave one another Tiffany jewelry for their birthdays and bat mitzvahs. I had just started living with my immigrant mother after my father died, and there was no way I was going to see anything that resembled $100 combat boots or a chunky sterling silver chain in a little blue box.

I would have given anything to have what bitchy girl #1 or #2 did. I just thought that was never my destiny, because they came from good families and all sorts of generational wealth. Even then, I knew intellectually that the family cycle could be broken—but never actually believed I could do it. Perhaps my kids, the second-generation Americans, could do it. I wrote off the prospects of living in a house with a fountain in the driveway and a walk-in closet full of designer everything. I just thought it wasn't my lot in life—but, damn, did I want that knockoff-free life badly.

Well, bitchy girls #1 and #2, you should see my closet now! I have gone on to have more designer shoes than I ever imagined. They even have their own closet, full of brands that are ten times more expensive and exclusive than the Docs I once coveted. I don't say this to brag, but to reassure you that with some planning and chutzpah you, too, can break the cycle. I think of my "Nurse Martens" every time I add another pair of designer shoes to my collection. And, trust me, I've had to learn restraint over the years too. Once I could actually afford the brands I never thought I would have, I hoarded. I was starving for that tangible sense of wealth and security for so long that, once I actually could get a taste, I gorged myself. As I've moved through my own money journey, I've landed somewhere in the middle, treating myself to the shoes that I love without fostering an insatiable appetite for them. And that hard-learned lesson began on my first day of school, with that pair of knockoffs.

I've done a lot of work around telling my younger self that I have taken care of her, that she would always be enough and that she will always have enough. We all have deeply rooted traumas around money that have shaped our adult behaviors. It's taken me years to unpack where mine started, to learn from them, and then, finally, to articulate them to you in my confessions.

Where did *your* money traumas start? Maybe you were one of those trendy girls who picked on girls like me, with our knockoffs? Maybe you had a pair of Nurse Martens of your own? Or maybe you have a whole other variety of financial trauma with which I have no experience? We are all products of our upbringing, and to move forward we must try to address our past money triggers. You can get all of the doctoral degrees in economics that you want, but if you're still haunted by the Doc Martens the popular girls from middle school had, then that Doc has won. In this story, you win. We already figured out what you want back in Step 2. That number can and will change, of course, but it's tangible, quantifiable, figureoutable, and completely achievable. And, most important, *you* are the able one behind all the -ables.

I know you're probably getting antsy to get to the advanced wealth tactics. "Lapin, I'm tired of your financial foreplay," you may be thinking. Well, I hear you, but setting yourself up mentally and structurally from the beginning will bring on the happiest of financial endings.

FIND YOUR PERSON

I know it's hard to ask for help. I am the poster child for the "I got this on my own" mentality with a "Miss Independent" ringtone. But, even I, the Rich Bitch herself, have help with my own finances—and lots of it! (You'll meet my financial advisor, Rebecca, in Step 7: Girl, Get Some Bonds). Doctors have doctors. Shrinks have shrinks. Trainers have trainers. We *all* need help, even the experts.

BREAK UP WITH YOUR BROKER

The edge the experts have in picking another expert in their field is that they know where the bodies are buried and where the loops are holed, so to speak. And the biggest misconception about finding a financial advisor is thinking that your broker is one. Your broker is not on your team.

By definition, brokers work for financial services companies and are not required to do what's in your best interest. The only way brokers get paid is by selling you the financial products their company manages. They might talk a big game, they might act like your friend and send you holiday cards, but their only purpose is to get you to put your money into the financial products that are most profitable for them and their companies.

So, let me say again, brokers are not your friends. Several large-scale anonymous surveys have shown that brokers don't practice the advice they give when it comes to their own investments. In fact, about half of them don't even have a stake in the products they are pushing. That's like a shady baker who won't taste her own treats. Why not? The only reason could be that she knows they're made with nasty, artificial ingredients.

A BROKER BY ANY OTHER NAME . . .

. . . is still not your friend. Oftentimes "brokers" who are not acting in your best interest aren't actually called straight-up "brokers" but given euphemisms that mask who they really are. Other names for "broker" are:

mutual fund manager

registered representative

financial advisor

wealth advisor

vice president of blah-dee-blah at this bank or that brokerage

There are probably two hundred different names for financial advisors, many of which are not regulated by FINRA (the oversight body that watches how investments are pitched to potential investors). And, oftentimes, their "credentials" are pure puffery that aim to razzle-dazzle those who don't know the difference.

The only title that you should be looking for when sourcing a potential financial advisor is "RIA" or independent registered investment advisor.

These folks are fiduciaries. A fiduciary is someone who doesn't have any conflicts of interest (and if they do, they have to disclose them) and who puts their clients' needs first.

Not everyone who gives financial advice is a fiduciary. (In case you're wondering, yes, I am a fiduciary.) The financial services industry's—a.k.a. the brokers'—standard is to provide "suitable" financial advice. Think about it: Would you accept "suitable" food at a restaurant? "Suitable" coffee? "Suitable" friends? "Suitable" sex? I mean, I wouldn't. And I wouldn't want you to, either, especially when it comes to where you are putting your money.

One of the biggest differences between a fiduciary and others who might dole out financial advice is their fee structure. Fiduciaries charge a flat fee that is tax deductible, while nonfiduciary advisors charge a fee that you pay based on your investments, which aren't at all tax deductible.

Think of a fiduciary as being your stylist and a nonfiduciary advisor being the salesperson working on commission. You're likely paying the stylist a flat fee to make you look and feel good. Your stylist's reputation depends on you looking and feeling good, so while he or she has relationships with brands, ultimately that person's loyalty is with you. On the other hand, if you walk into a department store, the salespeople are only incentivized for you to buy stuff within their section, so that they can collect the commission on the sale. I get it, it's confusing when the gals at your favorite stores act like your besties. It may *feel* like they want what's best for you, but they don't. They just don't. They want your money—and theirs.

FINDING A GOOD FRIEND

My intention is not to bash all financial advisors. The truth is that, despite my warnings (which I hope you will take seriously), there are some truly all-star financial advisors out there who *do* have your best interest in mind, and having a trusted advisor who is not an RIA is better than not having an advisor at all. I just want you to know who your real friends are, and early on, when those friends can have a real positive impact on your bottom line. Finding friends isn't hard, but finding the *right* one for you and your money goals can be a little tricky.

Your search should start at CFP.net (the people who monitor Certified Financial Planner certifications) and the National Association of Personal

Financial Advisors.[5] These will give you a list of all the fee-only advisors. It doesn't mean they are all good or good for you. It's like searching through the list from your state's bar association to find a lawyer, or the medical board for a doctor; it's a good first step to know they aren't a quack, but it's certainly not the last step.

A good rule of thumb is to keep your investment fees to around 1.5 percent or less. That means around 1 percent in fees to your financial advisor and as little as possible in fees for your investments. (For reference, index funds that track the market can have fees that are less than 0.1 percent.)

Of course, you don't have to have anyone help you. If you don't, that means even more cost savings. You absolutely can read up and manage your investments on your own. Or you can treat your advisor like a personal trainer, from whom you get your fitness plan and then work out on your own, following the plan. But there is a lot of added value in continuing to work with a financial "trainer" as you strengthen your investment strategies and tax planning and portfolio management. It's also nice to have a buffer between you and all the news (or "panic porn," as I like to call it) out there about the financial world. Just never forget: not all advisors are created equal.

> You may have heard about the 2010 Dodd-Frank Wall Street **FYI** Reform and Consumer Protection Act when listening to or reading business news. This legislation was intended to reform Wall Street after the financial crisis of 2008. One of the reforms it proposes is the Fiduciary Rule, which requires financial advisors to act in the best interests of the client. That portion of the bill was supposed to go into effect by 2017, but, sadly, it was successfully challenged by then President Donald Trump and Congress. As of the writing of this book, the Fiduciary Rule has yet to be enacted.

I know the lingo can be overwhelming, especially when you're first learning it. So, as you are interviewing prospects to find your financial person, here's a basic script you can follow to make sure you are getting the answers you need:

YOU: Hey, Ms. RIA, before we chat further, can you please confirm if you are registered with the state or the SEC?

RIA: Well, yes, I am. I also have an investment advisor representative (IAR) who works with me and also abides by strict fiduciary practices.

YOU: Great! And how does your compensation structure work?

RIA: I take a 1 percent fee of all your assets under management.

YOU: Do you take fees for buying mutual funds? Or 12b-1 (marketing) fees?

RIA: No. Our 1 percent fee is the only fee, and we do not participate in any "pay-to-play" fees as compensation.

YOU: Wonderful. So, to clarify, you don't receive compensation for trading any stocks or bonds?

RIA: That is correct, and might I add, really great questions! Keep them coming!

YOU: This is really important to me, so I want to make sure I'm making the right decision. Only a couple more initial questions. Do you have any affiliation with a broker-dealer?

RIA: I don't. I know there are some fiduciaries who also sell products, so they get investment commissions as well, but that's not how I do business.

YOU: I really appreciate that. I find those RIAs who also are brokers offensive at best. And I assume you don't take my money directly?

RIA: That's right. I work with many reputable third-party custodians like Charles Schwab, Fidelity, and so on. You may choose whichever one you prefer and you will have access to your money and accounts through them at all times with regular statements going straight to you.

YOU: Thank you so much for getting the nitty-gritty out of the way. I would love to continue the conversation in greater detail so I can go over my specific goals and hopes for added value in my investments!

And, scene. Here's a checklist of things that should describe your financial person:

- Charge a flat fee for advice (ideally, around 1 percent of your assets under management, paid annually), which may be tax deductible.

- Is independent and not constrained by any one firm's financial products (for example, the financial person should not have an exclusive relationship with E*TRADE, Merrill Edge, etc.).

- Has the ability to access all products and services, not just those proprietary to the company for which the person works.

- Follows a fiduciary (not suitability) standard and is legally bound to disclose any conflicts of interest, such as performance-based incentives at the firm or building excessive risk into your financial plan in hopes of upping your assets under management—and the fee as a result.

- Uses a third-party custodian to hold your investments (such as Charles Schwab, Fidelity, or TD Ameritrade) and isn't the custodian of the investments themselves.

Even after you've found someone who checks all of these boxes, you still need to find someone with whom you have a legit connection. They all have access to basically the same information, but it's that *je ne sais quoi* that will make the most difference in getting you to your goals. You need to feel comfortable enough with your fiduciary to be really honest about big life decisions like a marriage, divorce, child, or move. These events are more significant to your net worth than whether you buy Apple stock or not, and you should absolutely feel comfortable to discuss them—and their impact on your finances—with your financial person.

NEW BALANCE SHEET

Without further ado, here are the asset classes you should aim for, as well as the corresponding steps that take a closer look at them:

YOUR FUTURE ASSETS	
SAFE ASSETS[6]	
Cash and Cash Equivalents (Step 6)	
Cash	
Checking Account	
Savings Account	
Money Market Account	
Money Market Funds	
Certificates of Deposit (CDs)	
Market-Linked CDs	
Investment Assets (Step 7)	
Treasuries (T-bills, T-notes, T-bonds)	
Treasury Inflation-Protected Securities (TIPs)	
Bond Index Funds	
Structured Notes (principal-protected)	
Fixed Income Annuities	
Retirement Assets (Step 8)	
401(k)s and/or Employee Savings Plan	
Profit-Sharing Plans and/or Pension	

YOUR FUTURE ASSETS	
Traditional and Roth IRA	
Private Placement Life Insurance	
Other (SEP, Simple, qualified accounts, etc.)	
Real Estate (Step 9)	
Your Home Equity	
RISKY ASSETS	
Investment Assets (Step 10)	
US Stock Funds	
International Stock Funds	
Emerging Market Funds	
Stock Options	
Commodities	
Currencies	
Cryptocurrency	
Corporate Bonds	
Junk Bonds	
Municipal Bonds	
Bond Funds	
Structured Notes (partial protection)	
Advanced Assets (Step 11)	
Real Estate	
REITs	
Trust Deeds	
Rent from Income Properties	
Other Real Estate (senior housing facilities, etc.)	
Tangible Assets	
Furniture and Electronics	
Jewelry	

YOUR FUTURE ASSETS	
Vehicles (car, boat, motorcycle)	
Other Goods (alternative investments like fine art, memorabilia, etc.)	
Funds	
Venture Capital Funds	
Angel Investments	
Life Insurance	
Current Liabilities	
Mortgage	
Student Loans	
Disputed Debt	

This is closer to where we want your balance sheet to be by the end of this book. (And, again, remember that it's totally fine if you have a bunch of blank spaces on your new balance sheet right now. In fact, I'd bet that most of you will! You can refer back to this list any time and add to it, or cross out categories that don't apply to your own portfolio or otherwise tinker with it.

You may notice the biggest difference between this new balance sheet and the one I outlined in the last step is that your assets are split between *safe* assets and *risky* assets. Of course, like everything in the world of finance, that distinction is not absolute but it's still an important one to make in getting your portfolio looking sharp.

If you think of an investment portfolio like one you would have for writing, modeling, or any other line of work, then you know it's intended to show a range, or diversification. The same concept applies here, where the types of pieces in your portfolio are assets (like published articles would be in a writing portfolio), with the asset allocation being how much of each type and style is displayed. And in order to get a winning portfolio set up, which we will do in the final step, we need to know what kinds of assets you may want to play with. For now, just look your destiny in the eye and give her a little wink, because you'll see her in a bit.

GET COMMITTED

I get it. It's not easy to commit to something in advance without knowing what's going to happen, especially with your hard-earned money. But you've done it many times before—with rent agreements, business deals, or maybe a prenup—and you can do it here. If it helps, sign a little agreement with yourself to uphold the appointments you've outlined on your calendar. Signing something has been shown to make us feel more serious about the commitment.

I, (your name), commit to making an automatic financial plan and sticking to it regardless of the scary news, intense peer pressure, or my glorious intuition. I am committing to my future self by adding a consistent dollar amount of _____ or percentage of _____ to my Miss Independent Fund every _____. I reserve the right to change the amount, percentage, or frequency as long as I am taking action to grow my wealth on a regular basis.

XO, _____ (sign here)

You can show this or give a copy to your financial advisor and/or your accountability partner. Heck, you can share it on social media if you want (tag me and I will repost it if you do!). I would personally rather see this on my feed than another food picture or overly edited mirror shot. I mean, hello, if you were building an actual house, you would probably announce it, right? And share regular updates of all of the pretty finishes you picked and the sweet firepit you installed and, of course, your tricked-out, walk-in shoe closet? Well, we are building our financial dream house now. We are the dreamers, builders, and designers of our own lives. So, let's nail the blueprints, get to work building, and then decorate the shit out of it.

BOTTOM LINE

Conventional Wisdom: Knowledge is power.

Knowledge is great, for sure. But book smarts aren't enough to become Miss Independent. Execution is the only way. And the best way to successfully execute something is by first actually doing it—and then doing it over and over and over again.

Conventional Wisdom: It's really important to have a financial advisor help you with your investments.

That I totally agree with. And I'd rather you start with high fees via some broker than not start at all. But, ideally, you would work with a fiduciary who is not pushing his or her own product but pushing you toward realizing your dreams and making the most money. Don't beat yourself up if you've already spent a lot on fees. You have done the best you could with the information you had. But now that you have more of it, it's time to do better.

Conventional Wisdom: I totally called a lot of the big economic ups and downs of the past, so I should really follow my gut here.

The most successful investors study behavioral finance and commit to precommitting to their financial plan to safeguard against any whims or emotions. I'm all for following your gut in relationships, in pursuing your passions, in sports fandom. But that bitch gives bad directions in your financial life.

PART II

STEP

6

CASH IS QUEEN

Maximize Your Safest Asset

Have you ever noticed that some of our most common colloquialisms use male terminology? "Big Brother." "Wing Man." "Cash Is King." Well, I've just started saying "Big Sister," "Wing Woman," and "Cash Is Queen." I might get a double take when I do, but I think the phrases are stronger this way. Obviously. Having cash at the ready is super important before getting into any more advanced investment strategies. You *need* cash around in case of an emergency; after all, you can't fix a busted furnace or cover a costly medical bill with money that's tied up in an index fund or other investment vehicle. And on top of that, you also want to have cash around in case the opportunity to make a big dream purchase comes a-knockin'.

Forget the proverbial mattress. That's no place for cash. (And neither is the safe under the sink, behind the maxi pads.) In this step, I will expand on the first section of "safe assets" on your balance sheet and show you how and where to stash your cash and cash equivalents to make them (safely) grow.

WOMAN UP

Savings won't get you rich on its own but it's one of the important foundational elements on which to build wealth. Surveys show that half of Americans wouldn't be able to come up with $400 if they needed it *right now*. If you're in the half of people who can, yay you—but when have we ever been satisfied with doing the bare minimum? And if you're in the half of people who couldn't come up with the emergency funds to cover, well, an emergency, that's about to change.

BREAK IN CASE OF EMERGENCY

An emergency fund is for just that, an emergency. But an emergency to you might not be an emergency to me. Here are some examples of reasons you may need to break into this fund:

- **Interruption of income**
  Issue with business
  Laid off
  Fired

- **Personal crisis**
  Death in family
  Health problems
  Taking care of loved ones

- **Unexpected life events**
  Unplanned move for family or employment reasons
  Loss of childcare
  "Oops" baby

- **Market and financial forces**
  Identity theft
  Spike in interest rates
  Stock market crash

- **Freak occurrences**
    Natural disaster: fire, flood, earthquake, and so on.
    Macro issue: pandemic, labor strike, and so on.
    Something weird/bad luck: four flat tires in a week, root canal,
        and so on.

If one of these things, or another issue you deem an emergency, happens to you, then you are going to need another way to eat and keep a roof over your head. Go back and review your Rich Enough budget from Step 2 for how much money you need to pay your basic expenses. The CFP (Certified Financial Planners) Board suggests having funds equivalent to three to six months of expenses saved at all times, but as with your stomach for investment risk, the number of months with which you feel comfortable is ultimately up to you. Some people are comfortable with having six months of expenses saved, while others insist on twelve months. It's all about finding that sweet spot where you have a solid buffer to handle any shit that might come your way (and it will) without tying up a ton of cash needlessly that could be put to work in other ways. Of course, you want to factor in the precariousness of your job, your family/health situation, and personal safety preference before making a decision.

Let's come back to that last one: personal safety preference. As we've discussed throughout this book, your personal traumas and baggage play a role in what it takes to make you feel safe. So, if you're like me, with no family safety net and an irrational fear of being broke and homeless, then having a good solid year of expenses in your "oh, shit" fund is the ticket to feeling secure. However, if you have a huge family or an inheritance or general over-the-top optimism, then six months might be your "comfy" number.

Whatever that number is, you should stash it in a separate savings account from your Miss Independent Fund. If your Miss Independent Fund is for growing your wealth and retiring in style, then your emergency fund is for making sure you arrive at that final destination in one piece. But just because we're saving doesn't mean we can't have a little fun with it. It's time to choose your own cash adventure.

If you already have the amount you want for your emergency fund, then follow the steps below to find the perfect new home for that money with a full, one-time transfer. Then, if you end up tapping into your emergency fund for any reason, prioritize refunding it before adding or going back to any of the other "spokes" off your Miss Independent Fund, which we will set up throughout the rest of the book.

Remember: Please don't shame yourself or suffer through crises because you are worried about "breaking the glass." If it's a legit emergency, break that sucker—that's what it's there for! Then, when you get back on your feet you can refund it all at once or with regular automatic deposits (which will become your new best friends in no time) until it's full again.

If your emergency fund isn't fully funded right now, then this is going to be the main place to funnel the money that's currently in your Miss Independent Fund. Set up the same automatic transfer from the account you set up in the last step to a new one that we are going to fund in this step. If you need to transfer all of the money that hits your Miss Independent Fund from your paycheck or other source of income until your emergency fund is, well, funded, then that's what you're going to do until it's full.

Remember those "Choose Your Own Adventure" books that you used to read as a kid, where, depending on which page you flipped to after each plot twist, you'd get a different story each time? Let's play now to explore some different options for how you might fill up your emergency fund.

CHOOSE YOUR OWN ADVENTURE

You make $5,000/month. You decide to save 10 percent of your income, or $500/month. You feel like you need five months of Rich Enough money ($2,500/month) in the bank, or $12,500.

- If you have nothing set aside yet toward that $12,500 goal, then you will set up an automatic transfer (into the account you pick after reading the options in this step) of $500/month for twenty-five months until it's full.

- If you have $10,000 saved so far, then you would set up a direct deposit of $500 for five months until it's full—and then redirect that $500 to some of the different types of investments we are going to explore in the next six steps.

- If you have the $12,500 set aside already, then transfer that into a savings account or cash-equivalent vehicle of your choice labeled as "Rich Enough Fund" or "Emergency Fund" or even the hammer emoji—your pick!—and then mosey on to put your money to work for you in other ways.

- If you have more than $12,500 set aside for emergencies, then I'll give you some fun options for what to do with the excess in the pages to come.

Income → Emergency Fund → Miss Independent Fund

I know you might want to just keep your emergency money in your Miss Independent Fund and skip the rest of it. Here's why that's a bad idea: it's too risky to keep your rainy-day fund near your spending money. Even if you have excellent self-control, if it's there, there's a chance you might spend it, and we're not taking any chances when it comes to emergency savings. And here's another big reason to keep the accounts separate: you are earning diddly-squat in interest if you leave your emergency funds in a regular ol' checking account. Presumably, you're not going to touch this money until you need it so you might as well let it grow the most, as safely as possible, in a high-interest savings account. If that account's in the same bank, you can transfer funds instantly to your checking account when that emergency hits, so you're never far from the money you need when you need it, but you're also not at risk of accidently spending it.

If you choose different kinds of cash equivalents to fund your emergency fund, which I will talk about in the rest of this step, then the combination of all of them would need to amount to your "oh, shit" number. So, let's use another example with easy math: You need $5,000 to be Rich Enough, and feel most comfortable with ten months' worth of those expenses in the bank. That means you need $50,000 in cash, fully accessible if you need it quickly. That amount can be spread out between different types of accounts or in one, just as long as the accounts are those we go over in this step only—nothing more advanced. That's because the types of accounts we talk about in this step are the closest to actual cash (albeit safer), which is what you need when you need it.

A friendly PSA in favor of financial advisors: this is where you can start to see the benefits of having one. Sure, you can keep track of multiple savings accounts on your own. You are organized enough. You are way more than capable enough. But it's really helpful to have someone monitoring them for you so that you can use that brain power toward executing your plans to make more money. And, of course, the more you make, the more you are able to save and the faster you'll be able to knock out your emergency fund and move on to more exciting investment strategies.

If you aren't ready to take that step, don't worry. You can track your accounts in one location using one of the free online tools available to do that exact thing. You would have someone there to ensure that you are maximizing financial opportunities, but you will be able to see all of your accounts in one nice dashboard. However, understand that nothing is completely free. Read the fine print and be aware of what they're doing with your data. If it's a reputable company, chances are it's nothing nefarious, but it's always good to know.

MISS INDEPENDENT TIP

MARIE KONDO YOUR SPENDING

I'm not here to pass judgment on what you spend. It's just not my approach, and there are plenty of other financial experts out there who will do that. I'd rather use the time you're giving me to help you make more money and then make that money make more money so you don't sweat buying your latte and other small—or even large!—indulgences in life. After all, a life you love and are proud of is invaluable. However, I do want you to think about which of your expenditures spark joy—and whether or not they *still* spark joy in the same way they used to now that you're finding the, well, *joy* in saving.

I'll start you off with a couple examples, then you can fill out the rest with your own:

EXPENSE (ITEM OR EXPERIENCE)	LEVEL OF JOY (1-5)	PRICE	FREQUENCY/ MONTH	MONTHLY COST (PRICE X FREQUENCY)	YEARLY COST (MONTHLY COST X 12)
Mani/Pedi	2	$75	2	$150	$1,800
Spin Class	4	$20	10	$200	$2,400

There's no hard and fast rule about cutting things out based on their joy rating. It's your money, and it's your joy. But extrapolating how much each expense amounts to yearly and then determining how much joy that yields will help you be more mindful and intentional about your extra spending.

Of course, the "Keeping Up with the Kardashians" pressure is something we all struggle with at one time or another. I'm not going to tell you to knock that off entirely, because I know that's not realistic. Instead, I'm going to suggest you take a step back to:

- Monitor those feelings, observe when they come up, and remember that you never really know someone else's backstory from what they post on social media.

- Marie Kondo that shit. Does lip gloss even bring you joy? So, why do you care if everyone is rushing out to buy Kylie's newest beauty trend? Take a look at the trends you've chased that are now sitting in your closet, gathering dust, and get real with yourself.

- Seek out different, more grounded examples of wealth and success. Yes, some celebs really *are* like us.

Carrie Underwood (who doesn't love that peach?) famously makes her own lunches to save money, and when she occasionally splurges on takeout for lunch, it's on an inexpensive option like a Subway sandwich. Ashley Greene of *Twilight* fame has openly talked about how she can't justify spending money on a first-class plane ticket and sticks to a modest standard of living so that she doesn't stress about money when she doesn't have an acting job lined up. Tiffany Haddish has never forgotten her days of sleeping in a car, and says she still rocks a fake Michael Kors handbag. As for the real ones she's been photographed with? She says: "I haven't paid for these bags. They are gifts. The last bag I bought for myself was a Madden Girl backpack that's really cute. And it was on sale for forty-five dollars!" After all, just because you *can* spend the money doesn't mean you *should*. These leading ladies are clearly ready to embrace the true Miss Independent lifestyle. Are you?

GO SHOPPING . . .

. . . for the best rates! I know, I know. If you've looked at interest rates lately, they are super low (which is great when you are borrowing money, but crappy if you're trying to earn it). You know, this wasn't always the case. Interest rates were at about 12 percent in the 1990s. Then they went down to 7 percent for a while, and then to 1 to 3 percent in the early 2000s, and all the way below 1 percent by 2020.

Are they going to go back up? I have been reporting on this question for the last decade, and they haven't budged much. I'm no betting woman, but there seems to be only one way for them to go from here—and that's up. Regardless of where they are right now, interest rates fluctuate a lot, daily even.

Banks take their cue from the federal interest rates, but ultimately, they are competing with other banks for your business. Some banks are more competitive with savings rates, while others focus elsewhere. Don't assume that your bank has the best interest rate or the best account options. Think about bank shopping like car shopping. Just because the dealership is down the road doesn't mean you can't get a better deal at the dealership on the other side of town for the exact same thing. When you're in the market for the best interest-bearing account, you'll have to go through the shopping process to get the best deal.

MONEY MARKET ACCOUNTS

I would begin shopping around by looking for a money market account (MMA), which typically offers slightly more interest than straight-up vanilla savings accounts. Hey, I'll take "slightly" any day when we are talking about percentages of interest (a.k.a. APY, as you remember from Step 3: The Big Things Make the Biggest Difference) on my cash. I've seen the difference be as much as 0.01 percent interest on a savings account compared to 1.6 percent in a money market account. So, it's not nothing. Historically, MMAs were looked at as vehicles only for the already wealthy, because the minimums were as much as $10,000 to get going. That's no longer the case, with many starting at around $1,000 and some banks even letting you open them for a buck.

The first place to look for the rates offered by different banks and brokerage firms for money market accounts would be a site like bankrate. com or ratepro.co. You can also look at *Barron's, Investor's Business Daily*, or *The Wall Street Journal* for comprehensive lists of current options. In addition to the highest rate, here's a checklist of other factors you should consider when shopping for an MMA:

- The minimum required to invest.

- If an automatic investment program can be set up so money is transferred out of your checking account on a regular basis. This can be as low as $50 a month. Oftentimes, if you have an automatic deposit set up, the minimum to invest will be lowered, so be sure to ask.

- Whether the financial institution is federally insured. This may be noted as FDIC insured for banks, SPIC for brokerages, or NCUA insured for credit unions.

- What check-writing and ATM capabilities does the facility have. Even though you're not touching this money often, it's good to know in case you have a "break the glass" moment and need to. Many MMA accounts set a threshold of monthly withdrawals before imposing fees so you don't want to treat this account as a regular savings account. You want to make sure you are intentional about taking money out of the account, hence emergency fund.

- If there is a penalty for carrying a low balance.

- If there are any other fees.

The biggest factor is going to be the interest rate you're getting. Honestly, most of the big, reputable, FDIC-insured banks and brokerage houses are very similar. The one you pick for your money market account can likely hold some of your other investments, too, which might be helpful if the rates and privileges are strong across the institution's other products, but they don't have to be in the same place. I don't work with any of the following companies, nor am I endorsing them, but if you're stumped on where to start, here's a list of some options[1] to get you going:

- Fidelity Investments

- Vanguard

- Capital One

- Charles Schwab

- Barclays

- TD Ameritrade

- Edward Jones

FYI Where do I get this stuff anyway? And what the heck is the difference between a bank and a brokerage anyway? Your bank is where you do the everyday financial stuff, like withdrawing cash, depositing a check, or contributing to your savings accounts. Personal loans, debit cards, credit cards, or home mortgages also flow from a bank. On the other hand, a brokerage firm, or simply a brokerage, is a financial institution that handles transactions involving the trade of stocks and bonds. So, if you wanted to buy a stock in company X or put some money into mutual fund Y, you would need a brokerage to help you do that. One key difference is that most bank accounts are federally insured whereas most brokerage accounts are not.

If you know you want to take out a loan for a business or mortgage, for which of course you'll want the lowest rate possible, then it typically helps if you are already a customer at that bank—they know you, they trust you, and you're "in the family" already, so to speak. Plus, as we saw during the pandemic, business owners who were looking to apply for a Paycheck Protection Program (PPP) loan got better and faster help from the banks where they already had money. In order to build your bank relationships *and* maximize optimal interest rates, consider a savings tripod: online, traditional, and credit union. Let's explore the advantages and disadvantages of each.

ONLINE BANK

Online-only banks, like EverBank, CIT Bank, and Ally Bank, or app-based banks like Aspiration tend to have slightly higher interest rates because they don't have the overhead of brick-and-mortar locations. Many of the app-based brokerages like Betterment and Wealthfront are also getting into the savings game with high-yield savings accounts. The biggest difference between a money market account and a high-yield savings account is the access you'll have to your money. High-yield savings accounts don't often come with a checkbook but might give you more interest in exchange. For that reason I wouldn't have 100 percent of your savings in a high-yield savings account, but you could have a majority of it there.

There is an ever-growing cast of companies in the fintech (financial technology) space, which of course makes my heart happy. I would treat these as a fun way to gamify savings—like the dessert of your online savings meal, not the main course. Some notable ones that aim to make saving money fun are: Acorns, Simple, Digit, Qapital, Long Game. These companies are different from regular online banking because they use innovative and fun technologies to deliver financial services and products and encourage you to save. But, because they exist outside of the traditional banking system, they don't come with the same perks or security, so keep that in mind. Online banking, on the other hand, *is* still tied to the traditional banking system—including its perks and security—only accessed online and mobile instead of walking into a physical bank. Which, let's be honest, do you even know where your bank branch is? Take the extra money.

TRADITIONAL BANK

The benefits of having an online bank make all the sense in the world these days. You don't really *need* to go into a physical bank branch for something you can do online or on the phone. Except . . . when you're traveling. As a self-professed passport stamp collector, I will say that having an ATM card from a bigger bank—like Bank of America or Chase— has helped me to get cash when I needed it on more than one occasion. You can use a traditional bank for your checking account for day-to-day spending instead of for savings, and that's just fine too. But I would suggest having access to some of your money with a traditional bank in some capacity.

CREDIT UNION

Because of the community vibes of a credit union, you'll often get a more favorable decision for credit and a better rate if you're part of it already. Credit unions have all the same offerings as other banks but are backed by the National Credit Union Administration for up to $100,000 (unlike the FDIC, which insures banks up to $250,000). They aren't in the banking game for a profit, just to cover their costs, so those savings and good will often come back to you in the form of higher rates for saving and lower rates for borrowing. (Plus, you are technically an owner of the bank, which is kind of cool!) However, credit unions don't usually come with the same bells and whistles as larger banks (like nationwide ATM locations or an easy-to-use mobile app), so I wouldn't recommend putting a ring on only them.

Some savings accounts have fees. Even though they are relatively low—sometimes a monthly maintenance fee is ten dollars or less—you don't want to pay them. There are plenty of savings accounts without fees. But, still, I've said it before and I'll say it again: I want you to get in the habit of waging your own personal war on fees of all stripes. On the surface, fees might seem like little things—what's 1 percent here or 1 percent there? Short answer: a shit ton over your lifetime. The longer answer is that because of the power of compound interest (which we now know and love), fees can add up to thousands if not millions of dollars over time, depending on how much you invest. Paying excessive fees on your investment and retirement vehicles can cost you 50 to 70 percent of your future nest egg. Yes, you read that correctly; no, it's not a typo; and yes I'm officially the fee police. It was shocking to me when I found that out too. From here on, we are going shopping for a lot of financial products. And while I'll flag the biggies as we go along, I want you to be on the lookout for the fees associated with each and every one.

CERTIFICATES OF DEPOSIT

Certificates of Deposit, or CDs, are an investment vehicle where you put your money for a certain period of time—three, six, nine or twelve months or a multiple of years up to ten—without touching it at all in exchange for a slightly better return than other savings vehicles when you go to take it out. The longer you leave your money in a CD, the more interest you will get. Just like I wouldn't put 100 percent of your emergency fund in a high-yield savings account, I wouldn't put all of it in CDs either. But they are another good option for keeping your principal safe while getting some additional bang for your buck. Note that some CDs go into auto renewal mode, automatically signing you up for another CD when the first term is over. Luckily, you already know the best way to avoid that pitfall: set a calendar reminder for the day before your CD term ends to either withdraw your money or re-up the term . . . on your terms. Conventional CDs will penalize you for taking money out earlier than the maturity date. Many CDs will charge a penalty of six months' interest if you take your money out early. Some will even require you to pay to take your money out of the account. So, while these are great ways to make some extra money, you need to be able to handle an emergency without solely relying on those funds.

There are "liquid" or "no-penalty" CDs out there that will not penalize you for early withdrawal, but they also come with a lower rate of return. While CDs are typically considered pretty straightforward investments, there are a few interesting flavors to consider:

Market-Linked CD: This type of CD tracks the market, so you don't have fixed rates of return. If the market goes up, you could make more than you would with a conventional CD—but if the market goes down, you won't. Market-linked CDs have longer terms (think years instead of months) and higher penalties if you take the money out early, meaning that once you stash your cash in there, it's going be tied up for a while. They are also taxed at higher rates than regular CDs, and as interest instead of as capital gains (which you remember from Step 4 have a more favorable rate than your income tax rate). Also, you have to declare interest each year of the term, not at maturity, so you may be paying tax before you even make money from them. Still, if you want some market exposure without the risk of losing your initial investment, market-linked CDs might be a good option for you.

Brokered CD: These are offered by a broker or middle(wo)man who buys CDs in bulk for better rates and then sells them to institutions and individual investors. These can be bought or sold on a secondary market before their maturity date, but the rules are much more complicated, so if you want to go this route definitely discuss it with your advisor first.

Jumbo CD: These require at least $100,000 as an initial deposit but offer a higher rate of return. Dream big, girl!

MONEY MARKET FUNDS

Not to be confused with a money market account, money market funds are actually mutual fund investments that invest in cash and cash equivalent securities, not accounts where you can pull out money if you need it. YES! This is your most advanced option yet, but don't worry—we are still in the safe zone.

Money market funds (MMFs) are often offered in short durations, up to about thirteen months. If you need your money out before then, you will need to make a request to redeem your shares, which the broker must do within seven days. These funds are not FDIC insured, so that means your principal isn't 100 percent protected like the rest of the options in this step. Still, the investments within these funds—including government bonds like Treasury bills (which we will talk about in the next step) and CDs—are generally considered safe. Higher risk MMFs might invest in corporate bonds or foreign currency CDs.

If you have a super "shorty but goody" timeline or are looking for another place to park some cash, MMFs don't carry much risk and often give returns that are slightly above inflation. That's a much lower average return than more traditional mutual funds, which is why MMFs are in this section and not later in Step 10: Index Funds and Chill. If you have a long-term investment horizon, want to grow a fat retirement account, and rock an overall killer portfolio, MMFs will give you safety but not the growth you are looking for.

Scan this code with your phone to see what $12,500 can become:

$12,500 EXAMPLE QR CODE

DECODING PERCENTAGES

There's another money basic you need to nail before we go any farther: percentages. You may be thinking, "Lapin, I learned what a percentage is in middle school, thanks." Well, maybe, but I doubt that your seventh-grade curriculum explored the significance of fractions of a percent when your money is tied to it (although it should have!).

Wall Street has a very fancy way of talking about what's to the right of a decimal point: basis points. The more you get into this world the more you will hear people talk about "getting 2 more basis points at XYZ bank" or "interest rates that increased 20 basis points." Sometimes they will say "bips" or "bps," which is shorthand for the same thing. So, what are 2 basis points or 20 basis points, anyway? Well, think of a basis point as a hundredth of a percent:

2 basis points = 0.02 percent

20 basis points = 0.20 percent

200 basis points = 2.00 percent

Why can't they just say 2 percent instead of 200 basis points? Partly to look cool and partly to quickly relay the exact percentage in a world where every hundredth of a percentage point can be big money. There's a world of a difference between 2 percent, 0.2 percent and 0.02 percent over time. So, start seeing—and appreciating—the significance in these seemingly miniscule differences.

BETTER TOGETHER

We've talked about the importance of having a financial accountability part- ner already, but beyond leaning on a trusted friend or family member, there are more formal ways to do this. Your journey down the Miss Independent road usually starts as a solo one, and a true commitment to yourself. But the road trip to wealth will be way more fun if you've got someone riding shotgun and others in the car.

GO CLUBBING

Some banks and credit unions have accounts called "savings clubs," which allow you to easily save toward a certain goal. "Christmas club" accounts are one example of this type of account, where you can save for the holidays in a systematic (and often strict) way. If you sign up for these, you're basically safeguarding yourself from any temptations not to stick to your goals. There are requirements for regular contributions with penalties like interest rate loss for failure to do so and conditions that prevent early withdrawal. These rules are helpful if you know you're likely to fall out of healthy habits quickly because they help automate better behaviors.

"Social savings clubs" are also a thing. There's no velvet rope or bottles popping, and they're not backed by a bank in any formal way; just some folks in your circle who are trying to up their savings game together. Essentially, you pool your money with other people under mutually agreed-to rules. This set up might come in handy if an extended family is planning a big vacation, so each person has to put in a specific amount, say, every month and all agree to take it out at a certain date. In addition to the peer (or familial, which is often more intense) pressure, oftentimes you'll get more interest in a big pool because that collective money may qualify for a higher interest rate than your money would on its own.

Some online savings accounts like Smarty Pig have a social network component that allows you to announce your financial goals, network with other savers, and ask family and friends for help. Twine is an app that lets couples save together. And eMoneyPool is another app that allows you to be part of a larger savings cohort where each participant pays into it regularly and gets the whole pot of money once the schedule rotates; if timed correctly this can help fund larger expenses, when you need a big chunk of money without taking on debt.

CONFESSIONS OF BEING
MISS INDEPENDENT

Susu Who?

"Everything I learned about money, I learned from Sue Sue," my friend Judy from across the hall said as we brushed our teeth in bathroom of our dorm room.

"That's cool . . . I didn't have someone like that. I guess I'll do more of those science department studies so that I can save up for the concert. Hopefully they don't get too weird," I said, picking up my toiletry caboodle.

"Well, if you want, I can map it out on the whiteboard in the common room tomorrow and we can all do it together. There's strength in numbers, you know?" she said as we walked back to our rooms.

"Even if we don't actually have numbers in our bank accounts!" I said, cracking what could have been my first (and worst) finance joke.

"Think about it. I'm here for you, Lapin," she said as we hugged good night.

Long before I was Miss Independent myself, I was a hungry college student. I guess you could say I was pre-pre-rich. And like a lot of college students, I took fancy economics classes with obtuse ideas but knew zilch about actual personal finance. My friends and I were trying to save up to go to a Dave Matthews concert, and I was paying my way by signing up for the scientific studies that were advertised on bulletin boards around campus. (And before you're too weirded out, these mostly entailed filling out surveys. There was only one weird one where the students put a cap on my head with some sort of gel inside? Whatever, it was college, okay!) I made about fifteen bucks, cash, an hour—a rate at which I surely wouldn't have enough for a ticket by the time the concert rolled around.

"OK, so what did Sue teach you? Is that your mom's name?" I asked Judy a few days later when I saw her in the dining hall.

She laughed.

"What?" I said. "Do I have something on my face?"

She laughed harder.

"Something in my teeth? Urgh, I knew it . . ." I tried to see if there was anything using the reflection of my knife.

"No, no, you have nothing in your teeth . . . but maybe something in your ears!"

I was so confused.

"There is no Sue!"

I was even more confused.

"This whole time I've been saying "susu" as in the name of the savings club we have back home," she said, still catching her breath from laughing so hard.

Judy was from Ghana, where a "susu" or "sou sou" is a type of lending circle in which a small group of people chip in cash at different intervals and then take turns at taking the whole thing until everyone gets back what they put in. These clubs are especially common for women who don't have access to traditional financial institutions.

"Say what?!" I said, about to learn more about finance over rubbery lasagna with Judy than I would in four years of lecture halls at Northwestern.

"Okay, Miss Los Angeles . . . let's say you, me, and those three people at the other end of the table put in $10 every weekday," she explained, taking one of the little salt packets from her tray, one from mine and three others from our new friends at the other end of the table and placing all five on the table between us. "So, $10 . . . in the form of this beautiful salt packet . . . from five people for five days or $50/day is our 'susu' money pot."

"So, then, what happens to the money pot?" I asked.

"Well, whatever we want to happen . . . this is our money pot and our rules. Let's say we each take $50 one day a week for ourselves but put $10 in every day. We aren't earning more money overall but it incentivizes us to all save by trusting and incentivizing each other."

"So, like, if I really need $50 on Thursday for the concert, I could be the one to take the whole shebang that day, even though I only put in $40 so far, and I'd put my outstanding $10 the next day for someone else to take the pot?" I said, using the salt packets to demonstrate.

"Yes!" she shouted, legitimately excited to be teaching me and the little crowd that had now gathered around us. "And you won't have the temptation to spend the money you get from the science experiments you are doing, because we are all counting on you for your $10 that day—including, you!"

And she was right. If Judy was counting on me, I wouldn't have spent the money I got that day on a croissant and hot chocolate on my way back from the science center. But, as soon as I got my (cold . . . hello, Chicago!) paws on that cash it burned a hole in my hand, and I had to spend it right away. I never did end up seeing Dave, but I'll never forget Judy introducing me to Sue.

Savings clubs go by many different names around the world. In the Caribbean and West Africa, they are called a "susu" or "sou sou"; a "tanda" in Latin America; a "tanomoshiko" in Japan. The ideas are similar. They are run informally, transparently, without fees, and cost no money to run. While there's no interest, it's a wonderful contrast to the terms and conditions page for your standard credit card.

Of course, clubber beware. Scammers have long exploited the savings club concept and turned it into an illegal pyramid scheme that is sometimes called a "blessing loom," "circle game," "money board" or even a "sou sou," stealing the credibility of legit sou sous. These scams become more prevalent during economic downturns, when people are in the most dire situations, and sadly tend to target those at the lowest socioeconomic levels.

FYI While it's important to be vigilant to spot unhealthy and dangerous financial forces around you, it's also important to pay attention to the ones that may come from within. I am a big fan of twelve-step programs (QED).[2] If you feel like you need more of a support system for financial addictions or compulsions, look into Debtors Anonymous and Underearners Anonymous, the two formal organized recovery programs related to money.

The most important takeaway here is that there are all sorts of tricks and tactics to save money and find support. There's no single path for everyone. Therefore the most important one is whatever works for you.

There is no elevator to becoming Miss Independent; for those of us who weren't born into money, we have to take the stairs. Watch out for the supposed "opportunities" that make it seem like it's possible to skip too many steps. Every year, the average American spends more than $1,000 on lottery tickets.[3] Seriously. After reading this step, I'd love to see what you'd do with that cash instead. After all (mom joke alert!) the only quick way to double your money is to fold it in half.

BOTTOM LINE

Conventional Wisdom: My emergency fund is comfy-cozy in my checking account.

Nope. Hard pass. Not only is the temptation there to spend it on something that's, um, not an emergency but it's also not growing until you need it. While the vehicles outlined in this step aren't going to give you some earth-shattering return, they offer more than you'd get with a checking account. I mean, wouldn't you want to have the money in your "oh, shit" fund be at least a little more than what you put in when you need to take it out? Hard yes.

Conventional Wisdom: Interest rates are crap for savings accounts.

For some, sure. But, you can also find the hot guy at the ugly party. There are less crappy options for savings or cash-equivalent vehicles if you do a little homework and check in with new rates on the regular. This is a type of comparison shopping I can get down with. Nothing lasts forever: the good, the bad, and the rate of interest. When they are low, you may get less in savings accounts but it's "cheaper" to borrow money (like with a mortgage, which we will talk about in Step 9: Get Real About Real Estate) and vice versa.

Conventional Wisdom: Finance is a solo act; you can't trust anyone else.

Well, your trust issues are beyond the scope of this book, but there are legit ways to incorporate community into your goals to help keep you on track. If you don't have anyone in your circle you want to talk about your savings with, then you might not need more options for ways to do that—you might need more options for friends.

7

GIRL, GET SOME BONDS

Safe Assets Just Got a Little Sexier

hen someone says "my word is my bond," they mean that you have their promise. It's the idea that someone's spoken vow becomes their sacred commitment. In the 1500s, this concept allowed merchant traders to make contracts legally binding before the advent of written agreements. In the 1800s, the London Stock Exchange made its motto: *dictum meum pactum* (my word is my bond). And, of course, it was famously used by queen Michelle Obama during the 2008 Democratic National Convention.

Now, let's talk about what a bond is in our modern-day financial world. Let's say you buy a bond from me; I'm giving you my word that I'll give you your money back with a certain interest rate after a certain period. For certain.

You've likely heard that healthy financial diets include bonds. That's because they are more reliable than some other types of investments, which we will get into in later steps. In this step, we are going to figure how to include bonds in our own portfolios.

LADIES PREFER BONDS

Bonds (and, more specifically, government bonds) are the only kind of investment you will find on your balance sheet under the "safe assets" section. You'll notice that corporate bonds (which we will get to in Step 10: Index Funds and Chill) are under the "risk assets" section because those are, well, more risky. That doesn't mean there is zero risk to the government bonds we will talk about in this step, but it's pretty low.

A bond is essentially a glorified IOU. When you buy a bond, you are promised a rate of return and the return of your initial investment. So, in exchange for letting the government use your money—say, to finance a road or a bridge—you get your money back with a little something extra. The riskier the issuer of the bond is, the more of that extra somethin' somethin' you get back. The less risky it is, the less you'll get back.

Now, the promise is only as trustworthy as the government behind the bond. Think of it as lending a friend money. We all have friends who are better and worse with managing their money, but I'll give you two fictitious examples: Bad Bonnie and Good Greta. If Bad Bonnie, who is terrible with her finances, wants to borrow $100, you're going to want a little more "extra" back to cover your risk of losing it. But if you lend Good Greta money, you know it's pretty likely you'll get it back, so you won't need as much incentive (in other words, interest) from her as you did when lending to Bad Bonnie.

The same thing happens with governments. If the United States or Germany issues bonds, you can be pretty sure that you'll get your initial investment back, since those countries are economic powerhouses and very unlikely to go under. Therefore, they don't have to pay as much interest (that becomes your profit) because there are a lot of investors like you who would take that bet. However, if Portugal, Italy, Ireland, Greece, or Spain (known as the PIIGS countries of the European Union, or the ones whose economies are struggling) asks you to give them money, it's less likely you'll ever see that cash again, so you'll want more of a return to take on the risk.

The best way to assess the risk level of the issuers of the bond is by looking at their credit rating. There are a few internationally recognized ratings agencies, including Standard & Poor's and Moody's, that rate the creditworthiness of the bond. It's like the credit check you get when you apply for a credit card or mortgage, but for the government (booyah!), and using a different scale. Credit scores for us range from 300 at the lowest (poor credit) to 850 at the highest (great credit). For bonds, credit ratings range from D at the lowest (meaning the government is in default) to AAA at the highest (the country is economically rock solid). The lower the rating, the more interest you'll be promised in exchange for your investment. Anything lower than BBB is considered "sub-investment grade" or "junk bonds." Sometimes they are referred to as "high-yield bonds," which sounds awesome—but remember the yield (interest) is high because the quality is crap.

Before we go any further, let's make sure we have some of the most important bond jargon down:

- Fixed income: Bonds are also known as "fixed income" investments because you get a fixed rate of return (that is, interest after a fixed period). The CDs that we talked about in the last step would also be considered fixed income, but they are technically savings accounts, whereas bonds are loans to a government or company.

- Paper: Bonds are essentially sold as debt. That's so national and local governments can pay for those big projects I mentioned before, like roads and bridges. On Wall Street, debt is known as "paper." (Unlike in rap songs, where "paper" means money. I wish!)

- Yield: This is a fancy term for the profit you get back for lending your money.

- Price: This is how much the bond costs. The value and the yield move in opposite directions. Think of it as a seesaw. When yields go up, the price goes down to adjust and vice versa. The easiest way to explain why is that bonds are constantly adjusting rates on the open market. If a $100 bond is at 10 percent, and the next day the rate goes up to 20 percent, then the price on that bond needs to go down so that it's fair to the folks who just bought in at a higher rate. Otherwise, no one is incentivized to choose the bond with the lower interest rate when there's a shiny new one available at a higher rate.

- Coupon payments: This is the profit you're making on the bond on a regular basis as it matures.

- Maturity date: Of course, in addition to your profit in coupon payments, you get your initial investment back when the bond reaches the end of its term, or its maturity date. The duration for a bond is generally three months to thirty years.

Quick check-in: There is going to be more and more jargon in this step and as we move through more advanced investing tactics through the rest of the book. Don't freak out. There's no need to brace yourself or hyperventilate or skip over the parts with jargon. In fact, please don't, because I want you to harness these words and make them work for you (and your money). If you need to, go back and reread the list above or revisit the dictionary at the back of the book a few times until you feel more comfortable with these terms. There is no shame in that game. This is not happening *to* you, it's happening *for* you. You got this.

Okay, back to business: the bond market in general is considered a "leading" indicator for the economy, meaning that it's a good predictor of what's going to happen in the future. (In contrast, "lagging" indicators point to a trend that has already been happening, like unemployment rates, which typically reflect pains in the economy in the preceding months.) So, understanding how bonds work will help you understand—and even predict—major moves in the economy.

That's why I don't want your eyes to glaze over when we talk about interest rates or, gasp, inflation. Paying attention to how those indicators are moving will give you the power to make informed decisions about the timing of your goals. For example, in a low interest rate environment, you'll likely get a better mortgage but shittier returns on bonds or savings accounts.

The trick to using bonds to gauge where the market is going is using the "yield curve," which is simply a chart with all the different rates of return on all the different lengths of maturities on bonds.[1] The rates of bonds change every day, so the shape of the curve changes accordingly. In a recession, you'll typically see shorter-term bond yields be higher than longer-term ones, because there is more short-term risk for investors during less secure economic times, which means the curve is inverted.[2] Remember how we talked about higher rates signaling crappier issuers? Higher in the short term means investors are thinking shit is going to hit the fan. Knowing that will help you make better investment choices.

BOND FLAVORS

Many of the smartest, richest investors out there swear that the safest bonds are US Treasury bonds because they are backed by the US government. And while, sure, there's a chance the US government is going to default, there will be bigger problems than not getting the principal back on one of your bonds if that happens. So, for that reason, investing in Treasuries (that's what you'd call them for short) is a good way to make your overall portfolio more secure. During times of economic uncertainty, you'll hear business news talking heads going on about a "flight to safety." That basically means a ton of people are flocking to buy bonds, because other stuff is too risky. But not all Treasuries are the same, and not all of them are even called bonds. Stay with me . . .

T-BILLS

The reason there are different names for different Treasury bonds is to denote their term. Those with the shortest term (shorter than twelve months) are technically called Treasury bills, but are more commonly referred to as "T-bills." They come in increments of weeks: four, eight, thirteen, twenty-six, or fifty-two. (That's one, two, three-ish months, six-ish months, and a year for those of you who haven't had kids and don't speak in weeks.) There are also super short-term ones that come due in just a few days, called Cash Management Bills.

T-bills pay out slightly differently because they are shorties but goodies. There is a face value on the T-bill—like $1,000, $5,000, or $10,000—which is referred to as "par value." That value is not what you actually pay. You pay a "discount rate" and then get the full amount back at the end of the term.

So, let's say a fifty-two-week T-bill has a face value of $1,000 and a discount rate of 2 percent. That means you would pay $980 up front, and then at the end of the term you get the full $1,000 par value back. You're getting a profit in the end, of course, but there aren't coupon payments like there would be with bonds with longer terms.

With shorter terms come lower entry points. So, if you have $100, you're going to get more back with a T-bill than in a savings account for not much more risk. There are two ways to purchase T-bills. The simplest way is through a noncompetitive auction process on treasurydirect.gov. (By the way, it's called an auction, but the T-bills on offer are pretty much at a fixed price, and there are no paddles involved.) If you opened up your savings or any other account in the last chapter with a brokerage like Schwab, Vanguard, or Fidelity, then you would purchase T-bills through that platform too.

T-bills are sold in increments of $100. What's cool about helping the government pay for stuff is that you don't have to pay state and local taxes on the money you make. (You do have to pay federal taxes though. Boo.) And there's no penalty for taking your money out early—although you'll likely get dinged with some sort of transaction fee by the bank or brokerage you're using, so early withdrawals should still be avoided if possible.

T-NOTES

Treasury notes (T-notes) are the intermediate term of the T-crew (that's not a technical phrase, I just made it up) and mature between two to ten years. You can buy them in these increments: two, three, five, seven, and ten years. They offer interest payments every six months.

T-notes are often used as the basis for general long-term interest rates. In bad economic times, the Federal Reserve, the body that sets the interest rates for the entire country, will lower interest rates. That's to incentivize investors to take on riskier investments (and for regular folks to buy cars and homes) and therefore stimulate the economy. However, in times of high interest rates (which usually go along with a sluggish stock market), T-notes are actually really good investments, because they pay a higher yield than many other investments.

T-BONDS

Technically, all of the investment vehicles we're discussing in this step are bonds, but the Treasury only calls the ones that mature from ten to thirty years "T-bonds." They pay interest every six months like T-notes. You have to hold on to a T-bond for forty-five days at a minimum, but after that you can sell it on a secondary market. Just call your brokerage if you need to liquidate or cash it out.

T-bonds have the highest rate of interest of all the T-crew because of the risk you are taking, not that the country might go under but that there will be higher interest rate bonds available later on, which, as you remember from the seesaw, will lessen the value of *your* bond.

CONFESSIONS OF BEING
MISS INDEPENDENT

Don't Tip Your Financial Advisor

As I stepped off the elevator for my first meeting with my financial advisor, I was sweating. A lot. Like, a lot lot. So much so that I bought maxi pads from the little coin-op machine in the firm's bathroom to stuff under my armpits.

"Ms. Lapin, it's so wonderful to have you aboard. I'm Rebecca," my advisor said, extending her hand for a sweaty handshake.

"Oh, um, call me Nicole . . . or do you want me to call you Miss . . . ?"

She laughed, then said, "Don't even think about it."

Rebecca wasn't at all what I expected a financial advisor to be. I imagined she would be some old, pantsuit-wearing troll who hid out in a dark closet with a calculator and stacks of paperwork all day—but no! She was about ten years older than me, had a young family, and sported a bouncy blowout. She actually *was* wearing a pantsuit, but it was so stylish that I asked her where she got it.

"It's from Express," she said warmly. "They have some great workwear."

Well, yes, they do, Rebecca. *"Is my financial advisor . . . cool?"* I wondered in awe as I walked into her tasteful West Elm-y office. *"Yes. Yes she is."*

We went through all of my bank accounts, bills, and credit card statements, fine-tuning the automation behind it all. The process was relatively painless, and as the meeting went on, I realized that maybe the maxi pads had been overkill, after all.

"Let's talk about growing wealth, shall we?" she asked.

"Absolutely. I'm making a good six-figure salary, and I'm on track to keep increasing that, so my wealth should be growing."

"That's awesome," she said. "But even an increasing salary won't grow wealth. In fact, even if you save more, you're actually losing money over time in regular savings and checking accounts like you're currently doing."

"Why? Are banks not safe now?" I asked, with the trauma of someone who had recently lived through—and reported on—the financial crisis of 2008.

"Well, they are much better capitalized and regulated now. Your money is insured up to $250,000 per bank and if the ones you're banking with go under, we've got some bigger fish to fry. So, no. It's not that. It's inflation."

I kinda knew about inflation but was still confused. I smiled and nodded.

"Think about it," she said, sensing (correctly) that I needed more explanation. "Historically, inflation rates go up by about 3 percent a year. If you're making 1 percent at the bank a year, then you're actually losing 2 percent in purchasing power in the future; the rate of inflation would still be more than what you're earning."

"Oh, I see. That sucks. So, does that mean I should try to make even more?"

"Making more money at work is always great if you can swing it while still maintaining some personal balance," she said, sounding like a protective big sister. "But you should have your money make money for you to at least cover that pace of inflation. Have you heard of TIPS?"

"Yes, of course, I'm really good with tips," I said, trying to figure out if she was asking me to tip her.

"Oh, excellent. Then that's a really good way to protect yourself."

Welp. I guess she was. And maybe I'd get better tips from my financial advisor if I, well, tipped well?

"So, what's customary? Like 15 percent?" I asked, having clearly missed this section from Emily Post's *Etiquette*.

"No, that's a lot. It's the rate of inflation, and thankfully the United States is not in the inflationary environment of Argentina," she said with giggle.

Shit. I had no idea what the rate of inflation was, but I figured I would just look it up when I left. "So, could I do it next time?"

"Sure, whenever you're ready. I just want to make sure you know that there are options out there, and I'm happy to help you with it," she said.

"Sounds good. So, would you just add it to the bill or is this a cash thing like at the nail salon?" I asked, getting up, assuming we were done talking until the tip happened.

"Well, no," she said with the patience of a doctor responding to the stupidity of a patient's medical question. "You would just buy the TIPS through the Treasury or the brokerage we set up, and they pay back enough to cover whatever happens with inflation, because we can never know."

What. The. F?! Clearly I had missed something. "So, wait—this is not a tip to you for more financial tips??"

"Oh, my goodness, no!" she said, almost falling out of her mid-century modern office chair. "That's hilarious. No, I'm talking about Treasury Inflation-Protected Securities, or TIPS, for short. They are bonds you can buy that protect you and your money. You *never* have to give that to me, not for inflation or anything else!"

This exchange became a running joke between me and Rebecca, and one of my favorites to pass along to other women. The best sport is laughing at my former self. I stopped hating on that girl long ago; she was doing the best she could. But I'll never forget what TIPS stands for (and Rebecca won't let me live this one down, anyway).

Tip your waitress. Don't tip your financial advisor.

MY TIPS ABOUT TIPS

Treasury Inflation-Protected Securities, or TIPS, are mainly used to protect your money against fluctuations in inflation. When you buy TIPS, the principal (or, again, par value) rises and falls and comes back to you in semiannual payments as the consumer price index (CPI), an index that tracks inflation, rises and falls.

For example, if you buy $1,000 in TIPS and the interest rate is 1 percent, you get $10 in interest payments. If inflation stays the same then nothing happens. But—this is my favorite part—when inflation goes up, say, 5 percent, your bond is then worth $1,050 and your payment then goes up to $10.50. I know fifty cents doesn't sound like a lot, but if you own more TIPS and inflation gets nutso, then that's real money.

"WTF is inflation anyway?!" you might be thinking. I'm so glad you asked. Inflation happens when the cost of goods is more expensive than it used to be. It's why movie tickets were five bucks when we were growing up and they are fifteen bucks now. The good is the same, but the cost is higher. This is what the CPI tracks: it looks at a smattering of different staple goods (think transportation, food, medical care) and tracks their prices over time to determine if inflation exists. Conversely, deflation is what happens when stuff costs less than it used to. Yes, that can happen; it did during the Great Depression and even a little in the Great Recession. While it sounds great to have things cost less, it's a pretty bad thing for the overall economy, as falling prices lead to lower consumer spending. Inflation and interest rates move together. When we are in inflationary times, interest rates usually go up. When we are in deflationary times, interest rates go down.

Investors who think we are headed for inflationary times will typically buy a lot of TIPS to take advantage of the increase in inflation, and corresponding increase in their return. Just as TIPS can adjust up with inflation, they can adjust down during deflationary times—which we don't want. It's tricky to predict inflation, so the best way to balance these forces is to:

1. not hide from them, and
2. balance the amount of TIPS you buy with traditional Treasuries (our T-crew of T-bills, T-notes and T-bonds).

Why? I know you know the answer, but I'll tell you anyway to bring everything I've explained full circle. When interest rates go up, inflation typically goes up, too—causing TIPS to go down and traditional Treasuries to go up. No one really knows what will happen with interest rates or inflation, even with all the charts and curves and analysis in the world. But if you have *both* in your portfolio, you're fully protected from any inflationary situation.

FYI

You may have heard of people buying savings bonds for their kids. My parents weren't into that sort of thing (cash was the only form of money in our household), but I wish they had been. Now, as an adult, I buy my friends' kids stocks or bonds instead of onesies. It's a way better investment—truly the gift that keeps on giving as they grow up!

You can only buy savings bonds through Treasurydirect.gov, and they mature in thirty years (must be held for at least a year). There are two kinds:

Series EE pays a tiny interest rate, like 0.1 percent.

Series I protects your money against inflation with a combination of a semiannual inflation rate and a fixed interest rate (that could be 0 percent) so, when you take the money out, it's adjusted for the value of the original money in present-day value.

And here you thought the perfect baby shower gift didn't exist.

All these varieties of Treasuries are part of any stable portfolio, because when the market is down, these slow and steady investments save the day. Typically, the rule of thumb is to make your age a percentage and then have that percentage of your portfolio in bonds, with the rest going in stocks.[3] So, if you are thirty, you would put 30 percent of the money you want to invest in bonds and 70 percent in stocks. The logic behind this rule is that the older you get, the less risky you should be with your investments.

So, the way you divvy this up really comes down to your timeline. What did you say your timeline was back in Step 5? Shorty but goody? In between-y? Going long? Based on that, you can find the duration that works best for you and your goals.

MUNICIPAL BONDS

Just as the federal government issues bonds when it needs money to build stuff, so do states, cities, and counties. When a city or state needs to build, say, a big park or a mass transit system, it will often issue municipal bonds, or "munis" for short, to pay for it. The interest it pays back is usually exempt from federal and potentially state taxes, which is another added hookup for hooking your state up.[4] So, if you're in a higher tax bracket, a lower-paying, tax-free bond of, say, 4 percent might have the same benefit as a taxable bond at 7 percent. The tax benefits alone make munis worthy of a closer look.

Remember how the riskier the government behind the bond is, the more interest you get back? Same goes for cities and states. Within the United States, there are some cities that are more at risk fiscally—like Detroit or Chicago—than others. The ones in the worst financial straits offer more interest in exchange for lending them money. Some US cities and counties have even gone bankrupt, like Detroit did in 2013. When that happens, muni bondholders get screwed. But, that's unusual. Cities often have the ability to tax their way out of trouble (by taxing their constituents, not the bondholders themselves) and ultimately pay back their debt.

There are two main kinds of muni bonds:

1. General obligation bonds for things like upgrading a school system; they are tied to projects that don't inherently make money, but improve the area they serve.
2. Revenue bonds are issued for projects that make revenue once they are established, like toll roads.

BOND INDEX FUNDS

If you want to scream "uncle!" at me with all these different flavors of bonds, I get it. If you're overwhelmed by choice and think you'd be good with any of the bonds I've introduced so far, then a smattering of all of them might be your best bet. Bond index funds spread out your risk and give you exposure to different parts of the bond market, while taking the guesswork out of assembling the perfect combination of bond investments for you.

The main upside of bond index funds? Instant diversification across all the bonds the fund owns. The fund might own dozens or even hundreds of bonds, from which they pass on interest rate payments to investors, less expenses. Because the fund is a pool of a bunch of people's money, it allows you to get into expensive bonds for much less than you would be able to on your own.[5] Downside: they can have potentially high, recurring management fees. And there's no guarantee that you'll get your initial investment back. The fund's price fluctuates, so you get the price it happens to be when you sell it. My suggestion: find a low-cost, low-fee bond index fund that matches your timeline.

I'm not going to recommend specific bond index funds in this book, because they change all the time. Rather, I'm going to give you the key things to look up or ask your financial advisor when you're ready to pull the trigger on your bond girl gun. The biggest thing to dig into—and this should come as no surprise by this point in the book—is the fees, even when they seem tiny.

Generally, bond mutual fund fees will be lower than equity (stock) mutual fund fees. For high-yield bond funds, the average expense ratio is around 1.35 percent. International bond funds (which we will touch on next) also hover around 1.35 percent, which is considered to be on the high side compared with those that incorporate the safer bonds we've talked about and hover around 1.07 percent.

When researching bond funds, I would first filter by those with the lowest fees, ideally something below 50 basis points (which we now know is 0.50 percent). That's because the fees come directly out of the profit you're getting and are looked at as a direct deduction of interest. That means if the fund earns an average of 6 percent, but the expense ratio is 1.5 percent, then the net yield to you is 4.5 percent; whereas with a 0.5 percent expense ratio, you'll get 5.5 percent. Over time we know how impactful that 1 percent can be.

Next, I would consider:

- Thirty-Day SEC Yield, which is how much investors got in the last month (this is not fixed like it is when buying the bond itself)

- Types of bonds included (government, municipal, corporate, etc.)

- Credit quality of the bonds (remember AAA is the best)

- The average term to maturity, or duration, of the bonds in the fund

The duration of the maturities within the fund also matters for the timeline of your personal goals. Short-term bond funds hold bonds of maturities of less than four years; intermediate-term bond funds hold bonds with maturities between four and ten years; and long-term bond funds have bonds with maturities of more than ten years.

A bond ETF is a newer version of a bond fund. ETFs (exchange-traded funds) trade like stocks and have lower fees. Remember, there's no guarantee with either a bond ETF or a bond mutual fund that you get your full principal back at the end like when buying an individual bond. You still get regular interest payments, but it never fully comes to maturity like an individual bond does, so you ultimately get back what someone else will pay for it. You can sell mutual funds once per day after the stock market closes, but you can sell any ETF (we will talk about the stock kind in Step 10) anytime during the day as you would any stock.

The biggest risk to these bond funds is interest rates. As you remember, the price and interest rate work like a seesaw. So, when interest rates go up, the price goes down. The funds with longer maturities tend to have more interest rate risk, which is also known as market risk. (So, say you have a coupon of 5 percent that was redeemed, and now you can only get a 4 percent rate. As we've seen with that "just" 1 percent difference again and again, it will eat into your earnings big time long-term.) The number you want to look at to get a sense of this is the duration. Duration is different from maturity. There's a whole bunch of nonsense math to it but all you need to know is that the longer it is, the more volatile that bond fund is likely to be. The shorter the duration, the less volatile it is likely to be. It's worth a look if you're getting serious about being a bond girl, because it gauges the greatest risks you'd face.

MISS INDEPENDENT TIP

DON'T MOURN PAPER LOSSES

Go into the investing world knowing that stocks, bonds, funds, home prices, and so on, go up and down. A lot. That's what markets do. One of the first rules of investing is: *Don't mistake volatility with risk.*

You haven't lost until you sell. You only lose money when you actually liquidate an investment, not when it looks lower on "paper." Start getting into the habit early of not getting sad when something in your banking portal looks like it's in the red.[6] Unless a return is guaranteed, an investment is only worth as much as someone else will pay for it.

You haven't gained until you sell. If you're like me, you may look at your account, see a massive number, and start Googling five-star hotels in Tokyo. But, just as you only lose money once you've sold, you only gain money once you've sold. The market is ever shifting, and tomorrow that giant number could look very different.

The most important day is the day you sell. The rest is noise. (Noise-canceling headphones might be a good investment.)

PREMIUM FLAVORS

So far in this step, I've offered an overview of the plainest flavors of bonds. I am not going to go too far into the top-shelf stuff in this book, but I want you to know some of the options out there for when you feel ready to explore. One of the many things that pisses me off about most of the other books out there that claim to help you grow your wealth (aside from the fact that they tend to be mansplain-y) is that they generally leave out some of the more premium investment options available. Not here, ma'am. We are not about that "shrink it and pink it" life. This shit is not over your head. You might not be there yet, but I want you to have a full picture so you can make an educated decision for yourself based on where you are—and where you want to be—in your financial journey.

Scan this quote with your phone for more advanced information on bonds:

BOND CALCULATOR QR CODE

STRUCTURED NOTES

Structured notes are a hybrid investment comprising a bond from a bank paired with a riskier component, like derivatives, commodities, or currencies (we will talk about these exotic beasts in Step 11: The Riskiest Business). Here's my early disclaimer: the Securities and Exchange Commission (SEC) has issued warnings about structured notes. I don't think that means you need to stay totally away from them; it just means that you need to be warned about some potentially risky downsides.

Structured notes are issued by banks, and they are all very different. The reason I'm mentioning them at all is because oftentimes there are "principal protected" notes, where your initial investment is protected. If it is (and you must make sure that all of it is, not just a portion), then the worst that could happen with the investment portion is that you don't get anything more back than what you put in. Structured notes also have the ability to protect you against downturns in markets by backstopping the amount of money you lose. The other reason I'm including them here is because they can allow you to dip your toes in the waters of more complicated markets.

Here's how the best structured notes work: you lend the bank money (as opposed to the government in the case of Treasury bonds) for a certain amount of time (term), and the bank promises to give you the greater of your money back after the term or a percentage of the gains it accumulates with the riskier investment component. That means when the market is down, you are breaking even. When the market is up, you might not get all of the gains, but you get most of them, in exchange for the insurance if the opposite happens. The percentages will fluctuate depending on what the product is and the risk you want to take.

The best principal-protected structured notes often get gobbled up by ultra rich investors, but a solid fiduciary can sometimes find access for us mere mortals to get in the game. And if that happens, just make sure you are very careful about the terms you're signing up for. As with any other investment vehicle, there are some shitty structured note offerings out there, and there are some incredible ones. I can't pick for you, but I can introduce you to the concept so that you can grab the ones that work best for your financial goals and timeline.

It should go without saying that you should choose a reputable bank[7] for structured notes because, like the other bond products we've talked about so far, the bond is only as good as the issuer. You've already become a fee-spotting ninja, but it's extra important that you spy the other ones that might pop up here, like underwriting fees and distribution fees. Last, while I'm all for not being scared of the right exotic investments if you have the money and time to pursue them, just make sure you don't get too wild, too fast.

INTERNATIONAL BONDS

I alluded to international bonds a little bit earlier in this step, so I wanted to make sure to circle back on them before we leave bond land for now. I really don't recommend dabbling in international bonds for a novice American investor. The biggest reason is because they are traded in a foreign currency,[8] and the currency risk against the American dollar is tricky to track. For example, the interest rate could look like it's rocking, but if the currency denomination the bond is in is faltering against the dollar, then it's not really rocking at all.

If you want some exposure to other parts of the world (and don't we all get the travel bug?) then here are some *DOs* and *DON'Ts*:

DO try to find international bonds in bond funds to start. There are "dollar hedged" funds[9] that use tools to safeguard against currency fluctuations of the foreign bonds in the fund.

DON'T go for emerging markets like Indonesia, Malaysia, and Kenya, unless you happen to be an expert on those places.

DO stick to developed countries like the United Kingdom, France, and Germany.

DON'T forget our Canadian friends, whose banks rode the Great Recession hurricane out like a boss. They are technically international but just as safe, if not safer, than buying homegrown Treasuries.

To grow your wealth for the long term in a healthy, sustainable, and successful way, you need to not just invest in bonds but also to understand how the bond market functions. It's only once you fully grasp the concepts in this step, including those that used to make your eyes glaze over, like inflation and interest, that you'll not only be a real player in the investment world, but really playing for keeps.

You have my word. And you know what my word is.

BOTTOM LINE

Conventional Wisdom: If you want more money, you have to make more money.

Sure, making money is really important—but being truly wealthy means that you don't just work for your money, your money works for *you*. People who've made the most money haven't necessarily been the ones to keep the most money. In many cases, it's harder to keep it and grow it than to earn it in the first place.

Conventional wisdom: Bonds are a ho-hum investment.

Bonds are not the shiniest investments on Wall Street, for sure. But the lower reward you may receive is balanced by the lower risk you take on as well.

Conventional wisdom: Inflation will eat away at any investment.

The risk of inflation is real. But there are specific investments that protect you from inflation, including Series I Savings Bonds and Treasury Inflation-Protected Securities (TIPS). There are also other assets, like real estate (which we will talk about in Step 9) that can hedge against inflation.

RETIRE IN STYLE

Take Care of Your Fabulous Future Self

By now you know my style. I'm sassy for sure, but generally pretty chill when it comes to so-called scary financial concepts. I don't want to add more scare tactics onto what's already a scare fest. That is, until we start talking about retirement. Then *I'm* the one who's scary.

Because I'm typically not dramatic (when explaining complicated money topics), I hope you pay attention when I do sound the alarm bells. And this is the step where I will be pretty worked up because the whole construct of retirement straight up pisses me off. The way the system is set up truly scares me—and I don't scare easily about anything finance-related anymore.

The misconceptions about retirement and retirement accounts actually keep me up at night. Here's the biggest issue: Millennials like myself are the first generation to come into retirement without guaranteed income like pensions, and likely without Social Security. Most of the accounts we know about or currently have open are now tied to the stock market, which has also never happened before. We are brainwashed into thinking that we can put away 3 to 10 percent of our income for thirty years and expect that to last for a thirty-year retirement. As you saw when we ran your Rich Enough numbers back in Step 2, that's just impossible. And if you are from another generation, you probably aren't in much better shape anyway as the government has chipped away at social services for decades, and inflation has been stacked against your retirement savings from the get-go. In this step, I'm going to help unwind the misconceptions about retirement and help you embrace what *is* possible.

YOU CAN'T BE OLD WITHOUT MONEY

One of my favorite playwrights, Tennessee Williams, said it best when he said, "You can be young without money, but you can't be old without it."[1] I think we all know what the former is like. I don't want you to have to know what the latter is like.

HOW OLD IS "OLD"?

Back during the Great Depression, when the concept of Social Security was developed, the life expectancy for an American was sixty-two years. And Social Security was to kick in at sixty-five. So, that meant 1) not a lot of people were getting the benefits, 2) if they were, they weren't getting them for long, and 3) people were basically working till they died.

Nowadays, I know many sixty-five-year-olds who are in better shape than I am and are nowhere near their deathbeds. Of course, life expectancy has changed a lot. Someone retiring at sixty-five these days is then expected to live for about twenty more years. That means twenty or more years of retirement. Women are also living longer than men. At sixty-five,[2] women are expected to live sixteen years more, whereas men are expected to live eleven years more.[3] Well, yay us for living longer. But living longer means paying to live longer. And living your *best* life for a long time takes a lot of money.

That's money not a lot of people have. I'm sure you're not surprised to hear that three out of four Americans will have their savings and assets disappear before they die. And it's clear to see that Social Security is basically bust, and we can't rely on it anymore.

WHAT'S YOUR NUMBER?

I'm not suggesting that you'll want to stop working, ever. Interestingly, some of the richest people out there are also the ones who work the longest. Half of the people making more than $750,000 a year say they will never stop working (yours truly included). Part of being an OG Rich Bitch is loving what you do for more than the money—because otherwise it's just paper—like these women:

- Oprah is sixty-seven years old

- Martha Stewart is eighty years old

- Hillary Clinton is seventy-three years old

- Helen Mirren is seventy-six years old

- Betty White is ninety-nine years old (and my imaginary best friend, because she is so cool)[4]

I'm not here to glorify working till the grave, but it is important to think about what your preferences are now and what money you will need if those preferences change (and they likely will) later on.

I told you that being a statistic is not cute, and that I wouldn't let you become one. That's why we already started to map out your number back in Step 2. Flip back and revisit what your numbers were for each year with the different standard of living classifications: Rich Enough, Pretty Rich, and Super Rich. When we were thinking about your life and lifestyle goals in that step, the numbers we came up with were meant to reflect how you want to live in both the near and far terms. But you can use that same yearly burn number for your retirement calculations in this step as well.

This is where you get to choose what happens next on the road to becoming Miss Independent. There is no right way to determine your number for how you want to live now or how you want to live when you retire, or if you want to retire at all. The only wrong way to do this is to not think about it at all. Your plans can and will change but having a realistic idea of what you're aiming for is the only way you'll be able to figure out how to get there.

There are a lot of calculators out there[5] that can help you get morbid and figure out your life expectancy. But if you're healthy and younger than fifty, a good assumption is that you will live for twenty years after you retire, so start figuring out your retirement number by multiplying your burn rate of choice by twenty. So, if you want to be Super Rich and that calculation as of now is $100,000, then you will need to aim for around two million bucks to live out your days in the (Tuscan) sun.

MISS INDEPENDENT TIP

TWO MORE TRICKS TO CALCULATE YOUR RETIREMENT "NUMBER"

If the way we broke down your burn rate in Step 2 doesn't resonate, or you just want to run the numbers for a second opinion,[6] here are some other formulas that are commonly cited:

Multiply your salary by 12

Multiply 80 percent of your current burn rate by 25

Whichever methodology you use, you need to entertain inflation (hooray for already thinking about that in the last step). To get an accurate estimate of what the yearly amount will be in tomorrow's terms, multiply the salary or burn rate you feel most comfortable with by 1.03 raised to the power of how many years until you retire. The easiest way to do this is to Google it. Yep. For example, if I decided $50,000 was the number I needed and I planned to retire in ten years, I would type "50,000 x 1.03^10" into the Google search bar. That will give me around $67,000—the amount I will need in ten years to buy me the equivalent of $50,000 today.

The number you get probably feels really big. And it should, because it likely is. The only way to make it feel smaller? Start getting savvier with the rest of this step as early as you can.

WHAT'S YOUR PROBLEM, LAPIN?!

Another big issue I have with retirement is that even of the roughly 50 percent of Americans who are "covered" by a traditional retirement plan (yep, almost half of Americans are not), most are covered by investment plans that are not awesome, like Ye Olde 401(k). Not only are they risky, but many have high fees. And the kicker is that the way they've been marketed to us over the years has made most people believe that they are going to be enough for retirement. Financial news flash: *A 401(k) is not going to be enough to cover your retirement.*

You read that right. We've been fed the idea that if you just max out your 401(k), you'll be all right. To understand why that's not true, I'll give you another history lesson. The 401(k) was actually born the same year I was (so, it's obviously very young!)—1984. It provided a way for more people than just the ultrarich and big institutions to participate in the stock market. It was never, ever intended to replace a pension. But it was cheaper for companies to run 401(k) programs than pensions (guaranteed income replacement), so companies went after it. And so did employees.

Workers were fed the idea that they could get rich with a retirement plan linked to the market, so naturally most chose that rather than a boring (but steady) pension. Remember, the stock market was rockin' and rollin' in the mid-1980s, so this seemed like a super attractive offer. But why was it rockin' and rollin'? Because there was an influx of investments from all of the companies feeding their 401(k) plans!

We are a country built on freedom, and the 401(k) represented the freedom to invest as people chose (even though most had no business making those choices). It was also cheaper for employers to offer a 401(k) than other types of pensions. So, our workplace-based retirement programs went from defined benefits plans to a whole lot of freedom, a.k.a. undefined, unclear, and unstable benefits. As I write this, we are experiencing the first wave of people to retire depending solely on their 401(k)s—and it's not pretty.

The system just doesn't work. For it to do what you've been led to believe it can, you would have to save 7 percent of every dollar starting in your early twenties. If you waited until your fifties, that would be 30 percent of every dollar. Then make sure you earn more than inflation on your investments by picking the best fund options at the lowest price and never take the money out even if you have a crisis. Finally, you have to account for the huge chunk taken out for taxes when you withdraw your money (unless you are fortunate enough to have a Roth 401(k) option, always choose that), and then somehow time your withdrawals to make sure that money lasts you until the day you die. That's nearly impossible, especially before you started getting smart about your wealth.

Before you freak out, know that you have options and there are some simple things you can do so that you're not left financially abandoned by your 401(k), if you already have one. But before we get to solutions, we have to accept the reality. Straight up, no chaser. Here goes:

- More than half of Americans are at risk of not having enough money for retirement.

- A third of working folks in the United States have less than $1,000 saved for retirement.

- Nearly two-thirds have less than $25,000[7] saved for retirement.

That's not a brown-rice-and-beans diet, my friends; that's a cat-food diet. So, what gives? We know in theory our future selves would totally thank us if we put even just the money we were going to blow on another pair of jeans into an account that would compound over time. But, in practice, we have a block. It feels so daunting.

If we get to the heart of the internal block against saving for retirement that so many of us have, we see that a lot of it has to do with the overwhelming choices we have. It's been scientifically proven that when we have too many choices, we freeze. We either stick to whatever is chosen for us (for example, the default plan offered by our employer) or worse, do nothing at all. It's not that we are lacking information, but that we have too much of it. Plus, we're the #YOLO generation. Getting old, dying, and all that is no fun to talk or think about, so we ignore it and just hope it never happens. Baby, I love you, but you're not going to live forever. As spiritual guru Ram Dass said, "We are all just walking each other home."[8] Let's make it an enjoyable stroll, shall we?

MORE IS MORE

The retirement number you come up with is just an estimate, albeit an important one that you should know. There's no way to predict, well, anything in the future much less when, exactly, you are going to retire and how long you are going to live after that. But an estimate gives us a good North Star toward which to travel.

As we build up our retirement savings, I want you to remember two main things. First, whatever you choose, automate it. There's no need to be ruminating over retirement every day. Look through your options, weigh the tax implications, and "set it and forget it," at least for a year until you want to reassess. Second, the more investment options, the merrier. Exclusivity can be for the person you grow old with, but it has no role in growing the funds you'll need to live your best life.

401(K)S

I know I've been knocking 401(k)s so far, but that's because there are a lot of misconceptions about them out there, and I want you to have a realistic picture of what you will actually need in retirement. As always, I want you to rethink conventional financial wisdom as you start to think about your own financial future for yourself and what's right for *you*. The truth is that 401(k)s are not bad—they're just *one option* of the many retirement vehicles out there. So, let's get to know the 401(k) a little better.

What is it? A 401(k) is the most common retirement program offered through your employer.

While a 401(k) is the most common type of retirement account offered by employers and purchased by solo business owners,[9] 403(b)s[10] offered by nonprofits and schools, or 457 plans offered by state and local governments operate very similarly with minor distinctions.

Should I do it? You should do it as long as your company matches,[11] for sure, and max it out if you can and you like the options being given. If you want to be a more active investor, take a close look at those options and decide if you can get a better return investing on your own.

What's the limit? $19,500 per year[12] (with $6,500 more if you're older than fifty); the combined you+employer match has a $57,000 annual limit ($63,500 if you're older than fifty).

Also, 403(b)s have an added bonus of allowing you to contribute an additional $3,000 per year until $15,000 if you have been with the company for more than fifteen years.

When can I withdraw without penalty? Typically, at age 59.5, but there is the Rule of 55, wherein the IRS lets you withdraw money without penalty if you leave your job in the same calendar year you turn fifty-five and beyond.[13]

What's the tax sitch? You don't pay taxes on the money now, so it grows "tax deferred"—meaning you still have to pay it, and all of the money you earn in that account, later on. Oftentimes people think they have a huge amount in their 401(k) but don't realize that in some cases that can be eviscerated by taxes when they want to take that money out. We don't know what taxes are going to look like in three years, much less thirty years, so we don't actually know how much will be left over for our old lady selves to spend. But, don't worry, we'll talk about some ways to minimize taxes.

Who the heck is Roth? The darling of retirement funds is the Roth 401(k). If you have this option available to you through your employer, you are one lucky girl. This account is just like a traditional 401(k) with one key distinction: you pay taxes on the money now.

Wait, Lapin, why would I want to pay taxes now? You may be thinking. Well, with a traditional 401(k), you have no idea how much the tax rate will be when you retire and taxes don't have a habit of going down, but on top of that, you will have to pay taxes on the money you earn in the account, also. But, with a Roth 401(k), you've already paid the taxes. When you go to pull that money out of your account, the money you have is the money you get. No more taxes.[14]

FYI At most companies, you are required to be vested before you can keep the money you earned when they matched your contribution. "Vested" simply means that you have worked for the company for a minimum amount of time, usually two to five years. Sometimes companies have vestment schedules that allow you to earn a percentage of the money if you leave before the date when you would be fully vested.

I know, I know: I am now the chief of the fee police. Here's the thing though: 401(k)s are notorious for having high fees, so much so that the Department of Labor has cracked down big time on businesses offering plans with excessive fees. Class action lawsuits against excessive fees have been settled for millions of dollars with corporations like Caterpillar and even financial institutions themselves like Bank of America and Fidelity. The reason these fees get out of control is because the investments within the plans (like mutual funds) have fees of their own, plus the 401(k) plan has its own fees like communication expenses, recordkeeping and administrative expenses, investment expenses, or trustee expenses. Fees on fees on fees.

If you think your fees are too high,[15] you can always go to your company (if it's a bigger one, go to the human resources department) with a reminder that it legally owes it to you and your fellow employees to have a plan that's competitive in terms of costs. If you're not getting very far with that, you might want to mention that the company could get fined if it doesn't comply.

A quick note about fees in tax-deferred accounts like traditional 401(k)s or IRAs, which we will talk about next. While this sounds like an awesome benefit, it's often not actually more beneficial. The tax costs in tax-deferred accounts are swapped out with "plan administrative" fees, which are around 1.1 percent. Those fees come in addition to everything else you're paying. And how much are tax costs in a taxable account like a Roth 401(k) or Roth IRA? Wait for it, wait for it. About 1 to 1.2 percent! So, sometimes tax-deferred accounts are basically the same or even more costly. This is just another example of not letting the finance euphemisms like "tax deferred," which sound really positive, get you. Of course, there *are* positives for tax-deferred accounts, because they allow 100 percent of the money you put in to work for you and give you a tax deduction now. But "deferred" or growing "tax free" doesn't mean "tax free" forever. Resist the financial gaslighting.

IRAS

While employer-based retirement plans offer some wiggle room with what you can do with them (I'll discuss those in a bit), an Individual Retirement Account (IRA) gives you the most freedom to choose what goes in it. The "individual" part of this type of retirement account means that it's under your name and portable. If you buy IRAs outright, the contribution limit isn't very high—but they can be used as rollover vehicles from other accounts or just as a nice addition to another retirement plan. Let's break down the IRA:

What is it? A traditional IRA is your portable retirement account that follows you wherever you go and whatever company you work for. You can continue to use and contribute to it even if you work for yourself or take time off from working altogether. If you work for a smaller company, you'll likely have different options like a SEP IRA[16] (limit is up to $55,000) or a SIMPLE (limit is $12,500).

Should I do it? You might have an IRA already, even if you just got it as a method to rollover previous accounts. If not, yes, please, get one. If you're a gig worker and you have no retirement plans whatsoever, an IRA is a great place to start and really easy to set up with the banks you forged relationships with starting back in Step 6.

What's the limit? $6,000 ($6,500 if you're older than fifty).

When can I withdraw? At age 59.5 for traditional IRA (the Rule of 55 doesn't apply to IRAs). If you need to take any money out of your retirement account early for a crisis that extends beyond the emergency fund and cash-equivalent investments we set up in the last couple steps, you should start with the money you contributed to Roth accounts penalty-free. If you take your profits out, then you'll face a 10 percent penalty and income tax.[17]

What's the tax sitch? Traditional IRAs work like 401(k)s in that you pay taxes when you take the money out.

Who the heck is Roth? The Roth IRA works like the Roth 401(k) in that you pay tax on what you put in now, but never again. However, you can't make more than $139,000 single or $206,000 if you're married filing jointly.

PROFIT-SHARING PLANS

Oftentimes, companies who try to recruit sought-after talent for big jobs lure them with enticing profit-sharing plans. It's like offering swag to a star athlete you want to recruit to your basketball team. But what is profit-sharing, anyway?

What is it? Only your employer contributes to a profit-sharing plan; you can't contribute even if you want to.

Should I do it? Definitely, but just make sure you understand the vesting schedule, because if the benefits require you to be at the job for two years before they kick in, for example, then you get zilch if you leave before then.

What's the limit? $57,000.

When can I withdraw? You can typically take a loan from profit-sharing plans, but to withdraw, you have to wait until age 59.5 or face a 10 percent penalty fee.

What's the tax sitch? Usually the money isn't taxed until it's distributed.

Variations? A money purchase plan is a hybrid between a profit-sharing plan and a defined benefit plan (which I will talk about next) and requires employers to put a certain percentage into an account every year regardless of profit, whereas other profit-sharing plans allow employers to be flexible. Sometimes a profit-sharing plan is added onto a 401(k) in lieu of a match. There are three main types of these plans:

1. Pro rata, where everyone in the plan receives employer contributions from the company at the same percentage.
2. New comparability or cross-testing lets owners get more of the profit, while other employees go into a separate benefit group for a lesser amount. This typically happens at companies or firms that have older owners and a younger employee base.
3. Age-weighted plans give more to those employees who are closer to retirement, which can act as a good retention tool for companies hoping to keep talent up to retirement age.

DEFINED-BENEFIT PLANS

Defined-benefit plans are basically pensions, because the amount you get is "defined" and not at the whim of the market. This concept is the opposite of a "defined-contribution" plan—like 401(k)s and 403(b)s—where the contribution (the amount you put in on a regular basis) is defined but the benefit is not. Defined benefit plans are quickly becoming the most popular out there. Let's find out why:

What is it? A defined-benefit plan is basically a private pension.

Should I do it? If you've maxed out everything else (401(k), IRA, and so on) and you have a high income or solo business (preferably family-run), then yes. You could also have this as another retirement plan option through an employer.

What's the limit? Up to 100 percent of your compensation, up to $220,000.

When can I withdraw? At age 59.5, but you can choose if you want a one-time lump sum payment, a single life annuity payment (a fixed monthly payment and nothing more after you die) or a qualified joint and survivor annuity payment (a fixed amount monthly and then a payment to a surviving spouse until he or she dies).

What's the tax sitch? You get a tax deduction for what you put in. This is not an easy-peasy setup though. You will need a third-party administrator to write the plan document and then work closely with your accountant to make sure you're filing everything correctly.

Variations? Cash balance plans are quickly becoming popular because they act like a hybrid of a defined-benefit and defined-contribution plan. They guarantee a lifetime payment, but are held in individual accounts and are usually based on a percentage of your salary.

MISS
INDEPENDENT
TIP

MAKE SURE YOUR BENEFICIARIES BENEFIT

I love it when people create a living trust to protect their estates. Just don't fall into the trap that some do by including your retirement plans in the trust; otherwise, you'll be leaving your spouse with a potentially ginormous tax bill if you die. If that does happen, your surviving spouse can use what's called a "spousal rollover" to transfer the account into his or her name.[18] Also, if your retirement plan is in the name of the trust, then whatever money is in the retirement account goes to the trust and therefore becomes taxable. If you're single with kids, skip this option altogether because it might impede their ability to get the tax benefits from your account.

PLAYING NICE IN THE SANDBOX

Over the span of their careers, most people (and especially millennials) move around, switch jobs, end up working for themselves—and all of the permutations in between. In *Boss Bitch*, I say that the cliché career "ladder" is dead. A career looks more like rock climbing than a ladder these days. Along the way, you may have picked up different kinds of retirement plans and aren't sure how to have them all play nice in the most advantageous way for you. Here are some common issues I get asked about along with my solutions for each.

ISSUE #1: WHAT SHOULD I DO WITH OLD 401(K) PLANS?

Miss Independent Solution: You can leave them with former employers, if those companies are still in existence, or you can have them rolled over into an IRA. I prefer the latter. By rolling your old plans over into an IRA, you have more control over what happens to them and aren't beholden to the options your previous employer had selected for the plan. Plus, you're protected should your former employer fold, because your money follows *you*. Rolling over a plan takes just a few minutes through your bank.

ISSUE #2: WHAT IF I MAKE TOO MUCH MONEY FOR A ROTH IRA?

Miss Independent Solution: I love getting this question because it means that you're making more money! Here, you can actually do in two steps what you can't do in one, which sounds odd but I didn't write the tax code. And, yes, before you ask—this is all legal. I would put money into a traditional IRA and do a "Roth conversion," which lets you pay tax now, and then let your money grow tax-free.

ISSUE #3: CAN I ROLLOVER MONEY FROM MY 401(K) WHILE I'M STILL WORKING AT THE COMPANY?

Miss Independent Solution: Yes, if your employer allows it; this is called an "in-service" distribution. If you decide, for instance, that the fees are too high (good for you!) and you want to take more control of your retirement options with an IRA, this is what you ask for. Remember: you must be vested in the company or you will lose the money from your company match.

Another reason for having different kinds of retirement vehicles in your corner is the diversification of tax exposure. Tax benefits are a big part of each of these retirement plans. If you're not sure if taxes are going to go up or down or you can't even begin to imagine which tax bracket you are going to be in later on, I get it. That's why having exposure to both kinds of plans—those that you pay taxes on now and those that you pay taxes on later—will hedge your risk against whatever happens.[19]

You might also be starting to feel like, "Damn, Lapin—I've got a lot of accounts going!" Well, welcome to the big leagues, my dear. But also consider that back in the day folks relied on a three-legged stool of retirement savings: Social Security,[20] pension, and personal retirement savings. With the first two essentially going gonzo, you have to come up with other ways to hold your old-lady booty up on that stool. Would you feel nostalgic for the Blackberry? No, you'd just learn to type work emails on an Android or iPhone. So, let's not cry over Social Security or pensions and instead learn how to use all the other retirement options out there.

WHAT THE HECK IS IN THERE, ANYWAY?

It's one thing to diversify the *types* of investment vehicles you have; it's another to diversify *what's in* those vehicles. The specific vehicle—whether a 401(k), 457, IRA, Roth IRA, SEP, SIMPLE, and so on—is just that: a vehicle for the investments. We now have to go shopping for the actual investments themselves. Get excited. This is our first real foray into asset allocation.

A lot of women I talk to want to be conservative with their retirement plans (women tend to be conservative investors in general, but we will tackle that in the steps to come). I get why you would think that. After all, it's retirement; it's not meant to be sexy, so you should go after only boring, basic investments, right? Well, first of all, who says retirement isn't going to be sexy?! I for one am planning on having a compound with separate little bungalows for all my real-life Golden Girlfriends so we can party our last days away together in style. Second, unless you're planning on retiring in the next five years, then you have to go for growth in order to beat inflation and make money beyond that. So, that means no more Miss Playing it Safe.

"Playing it safe" means you have too much of one type of asset in your portfolio, in fixed-income options, like the ones we talked about in the last step. (In financial terms, a safe portfolio is overweighted in bonds.) Bonds of all varieties, bond funds, and fixed-income annuities,[21] which are technically insurance products but act similarly, are investments within retirement plans, too, as are equity or stock investments (which we will dive into along with more risky investment categories throughout the rest of the book). The most common equity investments within retirement accounts are mutual funds, target date funds, and your company's own stock.

MUTUAL FUNDS

I've already sounded the alarm bell on the hype around mutual funds since they often have high fees (I break the fees down in Step 10) and often don't beat the market even though they are "professionally" managed.[22] But, that's not the only catch with mutual funds. Every quarter, mutual funds pay dividends that are taxed at the end of the year. Since mutual funds are designed to be set up and forgotten, my suggestion is to keep these long-term, dividend-paying investments growing inside tax-deferred accounts like a 401(k), IRA, defined-benefit plan, annuity, and so on, so that you're letting them compound in a tax-free environment (or a future, tax-free environment in the case of Roths) to minimize the blow.

TARGET DATE FUNDS

If you have a company retirement plan, it's highly likely that you have a target date fund option. If your plan is run by one of the biggies—Vanguard, T. Rowe Price, TIAA-CREF, or Fidelity—you'll have some strong options to choose from. These are technically mutual funds that are actively managed based on your target retirement date. If you don't know when you want to retire, you can probably guess within a five-year range. But don't go all Tracy Flick (Reese Witherspoon's character in *Election*) and sign up for multiple target date funds to have extra hedging and diversification. Let me say, I like where your head's at, but that's overkill. You can always change your date or the age you want to retire. Before you pick, make sure you know the fund's "glide path," a.k.a. its investment strategy. Some glide paths end once the target date is hit and others continue after your retirement age. If possible, you want the latter, because you'll likely live past that date by a few decades.

DON'T GET HIGH ON YOUR OWN SUPPLY

If you work for a publicly traded company, your employer will likely allow you to invest in company stock. As a rah-rah employee, I'll bet you want to put your money where your mouth is by investing in the company you work for. It can also feel enticing to put a lot of your money into your own company after hearing the stories of those who have worked at Google or Facebook and made a killing by doing that. But for every Googler you talk to, make sure you also hear from someone who worked at Lehman Brothers or Enron. Both of the latter companies went under and so did the investments of their shareholders, including those who also happened to be employees. Remember, you can still be the company's biggest cheerleader without putting too much of your retirement fund in its stock. You are already putting a lot of your financial future into what happens with that company when you work for someone else, so, where possible, take some of your risk elsewhere.[23]

For the most basic asset allocation, you can go back to the "pick your age in bonds" strategy we already talked about. In Step 12, we will get to more options that you can use for your overall portfolio and for the investments in your retirement accounts. But for now, I would suggest to KISS: keep it simple, sister. The most important thing you can do as you build your assets, allocation, and rebalancing skills is to get comfortable getting more aggressive. Then, make sure you understand what options you have so that when you go over them with *your* Rebecca, you are ready to rock.

RETHINKING RETIREMENT

I know that my run-through of most of the retirement plan options under the Wall Street sun was pretty dense, but I promise there won't be a quiz. Just use it as a cheat sheet the next time you're taking a closer look at your retirement accounts. Now, let's get creative with what your retirement path *could* look like by thinking outside the alphabet soup options we just went through.

MINI RETIREMENTS

Who said you need to retire at a certain age? I certainly didn't. And who said you need to work, work, work, and then take the rest of your life to chill? Not it, either!

Saving up with all these tricks and tactics can be stressful, to say the least. But what if you didn't work for forty years to try and save a bundle for some grand finale? What if, instead, you added an "s" onto "retirement" and took several smaller retirements instead?

CONFESSIONS OF BEING
MISS INDEPENDENT

That Time I Retired and Didn't Realize It

The first time I put an "out of office" automatic reply on my work email account was after I turned thirty-three. Seriously. I had started working in my teens and never had a true vacation until then. Sure, I would "go away" for a week or so and loved collecting passport stamps, but even while "on vacation," I would always end up in the hotel business center or with my laptop by the pool.

So, I was pretty proud of the message I crafted, which people would get if they emailed me, when I finally took that first real vacation at age thirty-three. It read, simply: "In case of emergency, call 911."

"Another piña colada, *señorita*?" the waitress asked.

"*Sí*. It's an emergency," I said, and we both laughed.

I had taken myself to Cabo San Lucas, Mexico, to make up for missing that particular rite of passage in my teens and twenties. During those "prime" years, I was busy raising the career bar while other girls my age were busy dancing on it.

"Frozen, extra cherries, and extra rum this time," the waitress said sweetly as she handed me an Instagram-perfect coconut filled with luscious piña colada goodness. (My Cabo trip was a little more luxe than the typical spring-break version, for sure. One benefit of taking the trip later in life.)

"*Muchas, muchas gracias, cariña*," I said in my broken Spanish, reaching for my phone to take a picture. "Oh, never mind, I forgot I don't have my phone. On purpose."

"That's okay, Miss Lapin, mental pictures are the best kind," she said, smiling and miming taking a picture of the drink.

"Yes! *¡Sí!* A mental picture, the best way to enjoy . . . everything," I said, reminding myself to be more present.

As you may have read in *Becoming Super Woman*, I had just gotten out of the hospital after being admitted to the psych ward following a mental, emotional, and physical breakdown that stemmed from severe burnout—and had just started my journey to recovery.[24] Hence, the long overdue vacation.

"How long are you with us, miss? Are you enjoying no phone and no work?" she asked me.

"Oh, I think I've been here a week, maybe a week or two, or more . . . maybe a year! And I've worked really, really hard, so I'm trying to enjoy not working for a little while, *sí*," I said, not realizing at the time that I would go on to take a yearlong break from working.

"It's *jubilación!*" she said, almost singing.

"A jubilation? Sure! It's like my own little party," I said, air cheering her with my coconut.

"*Sí*, a celebration for *jubilación!*" she said as she called her colleague over and asked her, "*¿Cómo se dice 'jubilación' en inglés?*"

"That's 'retirement' in English," the colleague said, looking at me with sheer joy on her face.

"Retirement? But it sounds like a celebration!" I said, equally confused and amused by this fascinating new Spanish word I had just learned.

"*Pero sí, señorita*. That's because it—retirement—is a celebration! That's how we see it here."

Cheers to that!

Because you know I love breaking everything down into baby steps and then those steps into even tinier steps, you might not be surprised to know that I like breaking down retirement goals as well. I've decided that, for the rest of my career, I'm going to aim for several mini-retirements of one or two years each. That way, they are not only more manageable to plan for, but I can go back to work part-time or full-time feeling reenergized—without being totally out of the loop. I reserve the right to change my mind, but I know I'll be bored in full retirement mode with no end (er, besides death) in sight. Plus, mini retirements can help to stave off burnout.

If you've been thinking of burnout as a mental issue and not a money one—well, you couldn't be more wrong. Few things drain money and resources faster than burned-out employees. The stats are sobering:

- Burnout costs upward of $190 billion every year in healthcare costs.

- Workplace stress accounts for 8 percent of national spending on healthcare.

- Burned-out employees cost their employers 34 percent of their annual salary.[25]

When you're disengaged, everyone loses: our healthcare system, your employer, and, most of all, *you*. Think of all of the opportunities you're leaving on the table because you can only go after them half-speed. You can pick up *Becoming Super Woman* for way more on this topic, but suffice it to say: nurturing your wealth and your well-being not only should, but *must*, go hand in hand.

FIRE MOVEMENT

FIRE stands for "Financial Independence, Retire Early." This became a popular movement in the 2010s when young people would save aggressively—like 50 to 75 percent of their earnings—so that they could retire by thirty-five or forty.

Yep. Saving half your income. (Now the amount *I* want you to put toward your Miss Independent Fund doesn't seem so bad, does it?)

I love and downright admire the laser focus of these young people. It shows us that saving and investing aggressively *is* possible if that's your biggest, most overarching goal that you are determined to reach by all means necessary, even if that means eating oatmeal for every meal and rarely leaving the house. But I'm not the biggest fan of any extreme or crash diet, even of the financial variety. I created a spending plan for you in *Rich Bitch* that allows for small indulgences—like the latte that other financial experts yell at you for buying—because I believe that if you don't allow yourself the occasional treat you'll just end up binging on something else later on. It's the equivalent of having a Hershey's kiss instead of going on some fad diet that allows for no fun, so you don't end up noshing on a big ol' hunk of chocolate cake in the middle of the night because you feel so hungry and deprived. I think the same concept applies to the FIRE folks. A bunch of deprivation for a retirement promised land seems likely to, well, backfire.

GO ABROAD

Just as you might have an idea of how you wanted (or want! or don't want!) your wedding to look, I'm sure you've pictured something for that little old lady you to be doing during her retirement days. That doesn't mean you need to have a Pinterest board for it, but chances are you've pictured the broad strokes: Beach house? Mountain cabin? Airstream living?

I would like to throw another possibility into your retirement daydreams: going abroad. Entertain the idea of an exotic location where you'd want to retire. If you don't have a lot saved, your money could go a lot further in places like Mexico, Costa Rica, Cambodia, and Thailand, where the cost of living is much lower than in the United States. You could live a pretty baller lifestyle on what you may consider an average amount of money here. In Guatemala, for example, you can get a full-time staff, including a house-keeper and a gardener, for about $300 a month as well as a live-in nurse, should you need one, for about $500/month (the average in the United States is about $4,000/month). How do you say "queen" in Spanish, again?

ANNUITIES

I mentioned before that annuities can be options within a retirement account, but you can also purchase them on your own. Annuities have gotten a bad rap in recent years, and for some of them, that's for good reason. But just as not all structured notes are bad, as we discussed in the last step, not all annuities are, either.

Annuities are contracts with insurance companies where you pay a premium (think of that as the money you invest) in exchange for a guaranteed payout. The first phase of the contract is an accumulation phase, and the second is the distribution phase where you get regular payments back. If you get the right annuity, it can act similarly to a personal pension. Before you consider that, know the difference between the types of tax-deferred annuities you can buy:

- Fixed annuities date back two thousand years. Seriously. Julius Caesar used them in ancient Rome, and they have been utilized as a safe, steady investment option ever since. They work similarly to CDs where the principal is protected, but tend to have higher rates, longer terms, and different payout schedules. You can structure them so that you set yourself up with a consistent paycheck later in life.

- Fixed index annuities (FIAs) are also principal protected, but your return is based on what happens in a particular index or benchmark of the market, like the S&P 500. The "fixed" part of FIAs is that you don't get the full return of what that index does, so if it goes up, you only get a predetermined percentage. But you also have a backstop from significant losses, similar to structured notes or market-linked CDs.

- Variable annuities are *not* principal protected, and they consist of insurance contracts wrapped (in an "insurance wrapper") around a mutual fund or investment of your choice, or a subaccount. Your return is not fixed, so you get the upside and downside of what happens in that subaccount. I am not a big fan of variable annuities because of all the uncertainty. I'm mentioning them so you know the subtle differences between each of these options.

Ultimately, any annuity is only as good as the insurance company you're buying it from, so make sure you're certain about the quality of the company. In some cases, you are handing money over to an insurance company for decades, so make sure you understand the ratings of the companies themselves. Insurance companies are not FDIC insured if they go under (although your state will likely give you some of the money back if they do). And fees vary widely, so find out about all the internal fees, backend surrender fees, and sales charges.

I know that "retirement" sounds like a scary word (in most languages besides Spanish!). But just as monsters are only scary when you can't see them, retirement is only scary when you ignore it. Yes, there are elements of the system that scare me; I'm not going to lie. But they are totally tackle-able once you slay the monsters inside your head, turn on the light, and have a *jubilación*!

BOTTOM LINE

Conventional Wisdom: I'll be in a lower tax bracket after I retire, because I'll be making less income than when I was still working, so that's why I should load up on tax-deferred plans.

Maybe, but if I'm more bullish on your earning potential than you are, consider this: you'll likely have paid off your mortgage by then, and your kids will be long out of the house. That means you won't have big mortgage or dependent deductions, and therefore you'll have more money in the bank.

Conventional Wisdom: I'm maxing out my 401(k), so I'm good.

Well, that depends on what your definition of "good" is. If it's that you're going to eat cat food and crash on your kids' couches until you die, then you're "good" with just a 401(k) for retirement. But if "good" means living an independent and comfortable life, then a 401(k) where you contribute 3 percent for thirty years is not going to be enough to carry you through your golden years with dignity. Better to invest in a variety of retirement vehicles to get you there.

Conventional Wisdom: I don't have enough saved for retirement, and there are days I don't think I ever will.

We all have shitty days where the mean girl inside our head tells us that we suck with money. I still have her pop up in my head from time to time! Do the best you can to ask her to take several seats as you think of alternatives for yourself, whether that's a few mini-retirements or investigating your options abroad. When I catastrophize a situation (and that's often), I try to entertain the worst-case scenario. I try to think about what would actually happen if I didn't have enough saved. As soon as I run through alternative possibilities, even if that includes sleeping on a friend's couch, then I know that I'll be okay.

STEP

GET REAL ABOUT REAL ESTATE

Build Out Your Safe Assets from the Ground Up

O ver the years, I've found that the biggest ruffler of *Rich Bitch* readers' feathers has been the unconventional advice I give when it comes to home buying. I don't say *never* buy a home. But I don't say *always* buy one, either. Homeownership isn't for everyone, and it's especially not for people who don't have the rest of their financial lives in order.

Sacrebleu! It's true. Although homeownership is often touted as one of the main components of financial well-being, it can make you sick if you're not ready for it. I have seen far too many women skip far too many steps in their financial journeys and end up house poor, which is the situation that happens when you put all of your money into buying a home before slaying your debt or building up savings. You have a roof over your head, but not much else—and if that roof springs a leak, you're screwed. One of the biggest financial misconceptions out there is that buying a home is a good investment. Don't get me wrong, it can be; but it's not a given[1] like many tend to believe and then use to justify step-skipping.

I think you get it: I'm not about skipping steps to get you to your dream house (although you can skip up and down the stairs and slide down the banister all day long once you get there, of course). So, with the assumption that you've completed all of your previous financial steps and you're exactly where you need to be in building out your safe assets, let's get real about real estate. In this step, I'm going to help you buy a home the right way, and come up with a plan to pay it off.

TO BUY OR NOT TO BUY

I get it: A house is way more than just talk of mortgages and investments. It's your nest. It's your haven. As someone who comes from a broken home, I've always longed for a stable, safe, and beautiful home of my own.

As I've gotten older, however, I've realized that my home is wherever I am and that my surroundings don't have to be straight out of *Architectural Digest*. Having moved around for the majority of my twenties and early thirties, I came to imagine that I carried the idea of "home" with me, like the shell on top of a snail. As much as I longed for stability, I also knew that a bunch of bricks wouldn't afford me that. In fact, because I was moving around so much, I wouldn't have been able to afford buying and selling those bunches of bricks each time I hopscotched across the country. And the only thing I wanted more than the security of what I thought a permanent nest would bring me was the freedom that comes with financial security.

Another disclaimer before digging into real estate is that if you think you are going to be moving around a lot, like I have—whether it's for your job or your family or simply because you like to—then buying is probably not right for you. People will often say that you should only buy a home if you intend to own it for five years or more, more on that later. There is no shame in the renting game. Let me repeat that: *There is no shame in the renting game.*

Actually, depending on what's going on in your life, there are many benefits to renting. First and foremost, the big down payment that you need to fork over to purchase a house is a big hunk of cash that you could invest instead, in the market or in yourself. Missing out on the upside of that is your "opportunity cost." There are tons of really rich and/or really famous people who could absolutely afford to buy a home but choose to rent, because it cuts back on the costs[2] and hassle of buying and selling whenever they need to relocate (which is often), and it allows them to play with a good amount of money that would otherwise be tied up in bricks (or wood, or stucco, whatever). (Not only do really rich/famous people rent, but, according to 2019 US Census data, 36% of Americans do. So while you think you might be alone, you have about 45 million others right there with you.)

FIVE CELEBS WHO CHOOSE TO RENT THEIR HOMES

1. Beyoncé[3] and Jay-Z rented a Holmby Hills mansion for $150k/month
2. Caitlyn Jenner rents her Malibu house for $14,500/month
3. Rihanna rented a New York apartment for $40k/month
4. Lady Gaga rents her Bel-Air mansion for $25k/month
5. Lindsey Lohan rents a Beverly Hills house for $9k/month

The houses these stars are renting sell for millions of dollars. In the case of the one Mrs. and Mr. Carter were renting, it sold for $35.5 million. Even a modest down payment for that home, at 20 percent, is $7.1 million. Sure, that amount of money may just be a rounding error for Queen Bey, who could buy it in cash from her $400 million net worth before even tapping into her hubby's. But it's still a good amount of money that they have available to invest or do whatever they want with. Ideally, whatever they did with that chunk of cash instead of using it as a down payment would make more money for them than the profit[4] from the sale of a house.

The secret is that the higher the home value is, the lower percentage of the mortgage you will have to rent it for. That means if you own a $200,000 home, your monthly mortgage could be $1,500 and you may be able to rent it for $2,000, which is, of course, a premium and your profit. But, if you own a $2,000,000 home, you likely wouldn't be able to rent it for $20,000 a month, because there just aren't a lot of renters in that price range in most areas. So, you'd likely have to rent that very expensive home for less than your mortgage, and you would not make a profit. From a property-investing standpoint, which we will talk about in Step 11: The Riskiest Business, the owner may be willing to take less in hopes of making up for it in the sale price. But for a Miss

Independent investor at that level, it likely makes more sense to rent a $10 million pad at $25,000 a month and not deal with maintenance and upkeep (air conditioning, plumbing, landscaping, all expensive stuff that requires cashflow) versus pay double in mortgage payments. From a pure cashflow perspective, if you have a situation where renting and buying monthly is the same, renting puts you in a stronger position.

This is an important concept to remember and might feel like a revelation: your house is not a true asset until it is paid off. And even once the mortgage is paid off, and you own your home in full, you're still paying property taxes, insurance, and regular maintenance costs. Your house is an expense, forever. This concept was first popularized in Robert Kiyosaki's *Rich Dad, Poor Dad*, the bestselling money book of the 1990s and 2000s. The idea—which really upset financial planners and middle-class real estate brokers at the time—is that rich people have investments that increase cash flow, like rental properties or other investments, whereas a mortgaged home doesn't do that. Instead, it takes cash out of your pocket every month.[5]

MISS INDEPENDENT TIP

DON'T JUST GUESS

When confronted with a big decision that can cause me to feel emotional, I love returning to the data. And home buying can be just that. If you are debating renting versus buying, consider these metrics:

1. **Price-to-rent ratio** (or rental price ratio) is a formula that is used to determine if a particular housing market is overvalued or in a "bubble." To calculate the rental price ratio in your desired area, divide the median home price by the median rent in that area. If the number you get is between 1 and 15, it's probably better to buy than to rent. If the number is above 16, then the area might be in a bubble, and you should strongly consider renting until it goes down.[6]

2. **The Five-Year Rule** is another go-to benchmark, and says that you should expect to live in a house

for at least five years before selling so as not to lose money. Very little of the closing costs, taxes, interest, and maintenance[7] you pay during the first years of a mortgage go to the principal or real value of the house. Only after five years or so will you have a surplus to make buying more beneficial than renting.

I know it's not easy to quantify flexibility versus stability, but rely on the available tools and data like these—and check your emotional baggage at the door—when making a high-stakes money decision.

I would never discount the intangible, emotional value that can make the decision to buy a home complicated. We've long heard that owning a home is part of the "American Dream," so it's no wonder it's deeply ingrained in our psyche, along with other life events like getting married and having kids, as something we have to do to be considered successful members of society. All of that can be heavy and cloud our best judgment. To cut through that, you have to keep rethinking convention and ask: Am I a nester or investor?[8] I can't answer that question, but I think you know who can.

There is one reason to buy a home that I can't argue with: Simply because it makes you happy—*and* you have the rest of your financial house in order. Whether you're just dying to decorate to your heart's delight, to create a warm environment for your family, or to soothe past trauma, it's totally legit to believe that a home will make you happy. As long as you acknowledge *that* is why you are buying a house, and not to make money, then *that* can be as good a reason as any.

SO, YOU WANNA BE A HOMEBUYER?

If you've considered all of the facts and data I've laid out so far and come to this conclusion, then yay. Now I'm going to help peel back this crazy onion for you so you can save some of the work (and tears). The first thing you should know is that being able to live in a house without paying for it monthly is pretty freaking amazing. But the only ways to do that are to inherit it, win it (haven't seen an Instagram contest for one yet but I'm sure it's coming), or buy it.

For the remainder of this step, I'm going to assume that you're buying your home with a loan. I'm also going to assume that you're *not* hoping to be the star of the next HGTV home-flipping show. And, last, I'm going to assume that you are hoping to pay it off as quickly as possible. After all, the point of homebuying, at least within the scope of this book, is about accumulating more assets, not more liabilities. So, by taking out a loan to buy your home, and then paying that loan off,[9] you are raising your asset base and in general increasing your overall wealth position while also likely taking advantage of low interest rates[10] and some sweet tax advantages.

> FYI
>
> Don't let real estate agents or bankers razzle-dazzle you with the "scarcity tactic" hard sell, pressuring you to lock in all-time low interest rates. Quiet the "buy now, it's a once-in-a-lifetime opportunity because they aren't getting lower" pitches and remember that those people get paid when you buy or originate a loan. Locking in a low interest rate can't be the *only* reason to get into a thirty-year commitment for something you should not buy in the first place, even at a zero-percent interest rate. It's a much more extreme example of "just because it's on sale at Target doesn't mean you should buy it."
>
> In fact, if you think interest rates are going to go up, it may be better to wait. When interest rates go up, housing prices go down. Sure, you may have a slightly higher interest rate, but when those rates go down again, you can refinance. You can never renegotiate the price you pay for the house, just the interest rate.

Of course timing matters—both for yourself and the world. There's no way to fully "time the market" and buy your home under market value, but we can use the tools and data that exist to make the most informed decisions. And by "tools and data," I don't mean anecdotes from friends or family about your Aunt Sally who bought a house in Poughkeepsie for $250,000 and then sold it for $400,000, "so the market is hot." First of all, no one totally knows where the market temperature is, and it changes all the time. Second, you are not Aunt Sally, you are you. Third, a house is ultimately only as valuable as what someone will pay for it.

STAY IN YOUR ZONE

Where most people go wrong is that they buy houses that are more expensive than they can actually afford. They are just barely hanging on when some unforeseen event happens—a death, a divorce, a global pandemic—that kicks their ass(ets) and makes them "house poor." Bottom line: you need liquidity during bad times, as well as credit. If you are overleveraged—in other words, your debt-to-income ratio skews toward debt—then you won't be able to get either. And if you don't have cash or access to untapped lines of credit, then you end up thrust into a fire sale of distress. Miss Independents are not damsels who take uncalculated risk that can land them in distress, we are queens who rethink conventional financial wisdom, think ahead, and handle it.

A good general rule is that your safe zone for monthly housing expenses is about 30 to 40 percent of your gross pay. So, if you make $100,000 a year, then your gross monthly income is about $8,300, which puts you in the $2,400 to $3,400 range. Another way to look at it is with your front-end ratio, or mortgage-to-income ratio, which is a percentage of your yearly gross income that can go to PITI: principal, interest, taxes, and insurance. Usually lenders like to see that lower than 30 percent of your gross income.

As for the down payment on a house, I've said it a bunch of times already and I'll say it again: *Do not put all your savings into a down payment.* I know it's likely the biggest bill you'll ever pay but clean out your savings for a down payment, and you're more likely to end up at the cleaners.

Generally, people can afford to finance a place that is 2.5 times their gross annual income. Using the $100,000 a year example from above, you would aim for a $250,000 home. Again, these rules and calculations are just one way to look at this. I know these are all conservative guidelines when it comes to how much you should be spending monthly and on your down payment, but I would rather them be conservative than the alternative.

PREPARE FOR PAPERWORK HELL

The mortgage route comes with piles of paperwork on all sides. Going into it, you should have your side of the street cleaned up as much as possible. You will be asked many times along the way for your assets (and if you are self-employed like moi, you'll be asked to verify even more), so pull together these documents ahead of time and keep them in a drive or folder on your laptop for easy reference:

- W-2s for two years, tax returns for one to two years, and copies of pay stubs if you work for someone else

- Names and addresses of employers for two years

- Signed tax returns and year-to-date profit and loss statements if you work for yourself

- Bank statements for two to three months

- Any other income information: Social Security, pension, disability, child support, alimony, bonuses, and so on

- Information on debt, including student loans, car loans, and credit cards

- Investment account information: stocks, bonds, retirement accounts, life insurance

Remember that prequalifying for a mortgage is not the same as qualifying for a mortgage. During the prequalification process, the bank (or online mortgage provider like Quicken Loans) runs simple formulas to ballpark the amount you could spend on a home. But when shit gets real and you want to make a formal offer on that home, they will scrutinize everything. Oftentimes they will not count income that you included in your prequalification numbers for all sorts of reasons. They are particularly hard on self-employed Boss Bitches, because the income might not be as consistent or predictable. (Or so a friend told me.)

WHAT KIND OF MORTGAGE SHOULD I GET?

The short answer is a fifteen-year fixed-rate mortgage at the lowest interest rate possible. Your interest rate can vary from about 2 percent to 9 percent and how much your initial deposit is depends on your credit score. You don't need a perfect score (850); less than 2 percent of the population has that anyway. I would aim for 775 or above to qualify for the best rates. Before you start the mortgage process, make sure your credit is in tip-top shape by doing the following:

- Dispute any credit report errors[11]

- Don't apply for new credit and limit big purchases

- Ask for a credit limit increase[12]

- Get added as an authorized user on the account of someone with flawless credit

- Look into a credit-builder loan[13]

Once you've done as much credit hygiene as you can, request a rapid credit rescore. This entails submitting proof of positive account changes to the three major credit bureaus: Experian, Equifax, and Transunion. The process can lift your score by 100 points or more within days when erroneous or negative information is cleared from your credit profile, as opposed to the months it usually takes for your credit score to reflect positive account changes.

These two factors—your interest rate and your down payment—are extremely important to nail by every basis point possible. A slightly higher interest rate could mean thousands of dollars over the lifetime of the loan, and the amount you're putting down determines how much cash you have free to use to generate returns elsewhere.[14] Conversely, a higher deposit could mean a lower interest rate because lenders like to see that you have the discipline to save a bigger amount.

The strategy you take on the down payment depends on your overall financial picture, but everyone can agree that the lowest interest rate possible is ideal. If you're having trouble in a traditional loan application process, getting a mortgage broker isn't a bad idea (obviously check to make sure that person isn't sketchy). I used one who found the best deal for my needs, and the lender paid the commission. If you're a first-time homeowner, then also make sure to look at your state's bond loan programs.[15]

THE SHORTER, THE BETTER

I'm not going to mince words here: try your best not to get a thirty-year mortgage. I think they are one of the scams of the financial world that are made to look innocuous but are actually cancerous to your finances.

Okay, I'm calm now. Look at the numbers. If you get a thirty-year, $300,000 mortgage at 4.5 percent, then your monthly mortgage payment is $1,519.98. Do you know what that amounts to at the end of thirty years?! $547,200. You've basically paid double for your house with all the interest over time. The alternative is a fifteen-year mortgage, which has a slightly higher monthly payment of $2,295 and would total $413,000 at the end of the term. Paying more than $100,000 over the original price for your house is not awesome, but it's not as bad as $250,000.

"Holy shitballs! But I already have a thirty-year mortgage!" I hear some of you say. Keep it. One of the things that doesn't suck about them is that you have a lot of flexibility. That means, you can turn the thirty-year mortgage you likely got suckered into a twenty-five-year or twenty-year or even fifteen-year mortgage (really, any number of years you want) simply by upping your monthly contributions.[16] If you can get ahead of your payments, even by $100 a month to start, and shorten the length of the term, please do. Make sure you call your lender and let them know you are doing this, and that you want that money applied to your *principal*, not the interest.

The philosophy behind going for the shortest mortgage duration possible is that we are trying to build assets, not get dragged down by debt. The thirty-year mortgage is no way to sprint to wealth. It's not even a jog. If anything, it's a crawl.[17]

ONE OF THE GREATEST MORTGAGE HACKS

Sharing this hack with you makes me very happy, because it's so simple and makes a world of a difference. Make biweekly payments on your mortgage, rather than monthly (so, divide your monthly payment in half and pay that amount twice per month). In the $300,000 home example I just mentioned, you would save more than $40,000 in interest just by paying biweekly. That's because, paying biweekly, you would make twenty-six payments over the fifty-two weeks in a year—which amounts to about thirteen regular monthly payments, instead of the traditional twelve. This scheduling shifteroo can knock years, and tons of interest, off your mortgage. Have the bank set up your biweekly payments to deposit automatically. Some banks or credit unions use a third-party processor for biweekly payments with high fees, so if that's the case you can DIY this by basically picking a month to pay twice. But you can't just mail in more money. You have to have this conversation with your lender first:

> **You:** Hi there. I would love to set up biweekly payments for my mortgage.

> **Lender:** Great, we can set that up for you.

> **You:** Will those extra payments go toward my principal?

> **Lender:** Yes, I can help you with that, but we will need a letter specifically saying that you want your additional payment to go toward your principal, as our default procedure is to hold extra payments in a noninterest-bearing account.

> **You:** I'm so glad I asked! Do you have a form letter stating this that I can just sign? Electronically would be even better!

> **Lender:** Sure thing, look out for a secured email from the bank and follow the instructions to sign and submit.

And, scene.

Another strategy is to prepay half of next month's principal, which cuts your payments in half in the long run. Millions of Americans dutifully pay their mortgages every month without knowing the power of pocket-change prepayments, even if they have the money to do it. Paying off even a little extra of the principal (not interest) of the loan early can save you from the astronomical interest you wind up paying on your mortgage. It hurts my heart when a half-million-dollar home ends up costing you a million bucks after interest payments—and my guess is that it hurts yours too.

DON'T GET FANCY

Our new favorite acronym, KISS (keep it simple, sister) applies to mortgage flavors as well. Stick with fixed-rate, period, the end. I know adjustable-rate mortgages might be tantalizing. I know interest-only mortgages might be calling your name. I know negative amortization loans might sound sexy. I know 'em all—and I don't like any of 'em. These creative mortgages are just fancy window dressing for subprime loans (you know, the ones that sank the economy back in 2008). These loans aren't just risky; they're downright nasty and can increase dramatically overnight or even leave you paying more than you signed up for. I like a lot of fancy things in life, but mortgages aren't one of them. I want you to keep this fixed and consistent. If you can't qualify for a traditional fixed-rate mortgage, then revisit the joys of renting until you can. No exceptions.

CONFESSIONS OF BEING
MISS INDEPENDENT

Ticked Off

"Wait, wait, is this for real, Erik?" I texted my badass real estate agent in Los Angeles when he sent me a listing for a new house by the beach for $700,000.

"Let me investigate but I thought of you, Sarah, and Tracy when this one popped up, LOL," he wrote back. He was referring to my longtime dream of one day living (and dying, as morbid as that sounds) with my best girlfriends on the beach with our own little bungalows, so that we can each have our own space but spend a ton of time together too.

"I mean, I'm not ready to live out the Golden Girls just yet, but 1) I love you for remembering my dream, and, 2) are the other two houses next to it available for the same price?" I asked.

"I will find out but it seems perfect and a steal," he wrote, likely thinking what I was thinking: this was too good to be true.

I wasn't looking to buy a place per se, but I love looking at real estate porn, and I love having an excuse to riff with Erik. I was shocked to see three brand-new bungalows that looked the same (that is, cuuute), but each had its own little lot right by the beach—and priced way, way lower than the comps of other properties for sale in the area. If everything checked out, I was mentally prepared to make the biggest online purchase of my life, bidding for my bungalow sight unseen because I couldn't get out there to see it in person. If it was legit, the competition for it would likely be intense, and mama doesn't lose.

"So . . . it's a TIC," Erik wrote with the emoji that could either be rolling its eyes or thinking "uh oh." It ended up being a little bit of both.

"Say what?!"

"TIC stands for 'tenancy-in-common.' It's a loan that's getting more popular in California, kinda like a co-op in New York City with a dash of communism. It's a little funky, LOL," he wrote.

And by "funky," Erik meant this: a TIC is a fractional loan where you're basically the owner of a share of the larger property with the other people in the condo (or the plot of bungalows in this case). Even though you have exclusive rights to your condo, you don't technically own your place. The terms that come with TICs are typically super strict to make up for the low purchase price: a high minimum down payment and only adjustable-rate offerings. Plus, few banks want to deal with TICs, so you can't really shop around for your loan to get a good one.

"So, that means all my Golden Girl hopes and dreams are now crushed?" I texted.

"Well, drama queen, no. But I'll say this: No one goes in looking for a TIC. They fall in love with a spot and the shockingly low sticker price and thennnnn find out it's a TIC. So, your dreams aren't crushed, but maybe deferred."

"BOO!" I responded, pretty ticked.

TAX TIME

Homeowners love, love, love to brag about claiming extra tax write-offs on their mortgage interest. This is true: you can deduct the cost of interest you pay on your mortgage (up to $750,000) on your taxes; so, the government gives you a huge incentive to become a homeowner. If you're in the 30 percent tax bracket then the government is essentially paying a third of your mortgage payment. This is helpful in the early years because, as I mentioned, most of your monthly payment goes to interest (grrr). You also get to deduct property taxes (up to $10,000).

However, while a wicked smart tax strategy can be a killer tool for saving significant amounts of money, never make a decision based on taxes. Don't let the tax tail wag your whole financial dog(ma) so to speak. Spending a hundred bucks in interest just so you can deduct it on your taxes is one of the craziest pieces of financial advice I've ever heard. That's basically saying you should take on more expenses to save a fraction of them.

You should 100 percent be informed about any and all tax implications with every Miss Independent move you make in life, but it shouldn't work the other way around. Admittedly, talking taxes still gives me hives. It was the last piece of financial fear for me to get over myself. Thinking about them or talking about them might not be most people's favorite thing to do, but getting savvy about them will save you money that you can then use to do all your favorite things.

Whenever I come across diehard, buy-a-house-at-all-costs people who want to tell me all about their tax deductions, I remind them of the lovely capital gains taxes they may have to pay on the profit when they sell their house. Normally, they tell me about how you only pay capital gains beyond $250,000 (if you're single, or $500,000 if you're married), which is when I fill them in on all the exceptions when that's not the case, like if you didn't live there for at least two years. Sometimes they bring up their "secret" (not-so-secret) 1031 Exchange, which is basically where you can defer taxes from the sale of a house if you buy another one instead. Of course, that's tax-*deferred*, not tax-*free*. Hey, it might work out awesome for you to kick some taxes down the road—or it might not. Don't take anything as gospel and, especially when buying a house, consult a tax wizard first.

REFINANCING FUN

I know I've been warning you about all the possible pitfalls in financing your home, but one awesome thing about a mortgage is that you can refinance if interest rates go down. And awesomer still is that if you have a fixed-rate mortgage, which you should, and interest rates go up, it's not your problem; your rate remains fixed. That is a huge deal. That gives you extraordinary power compared to banks.

DOS AND DON'TS OF REFINANCING A MORTGAGE

DO interview lenders like you would a doctor or lawyer whom you plan to use. Not all lenders' programs are the same and not all fees are the same. The first thing you should find out is whether the lender is a broker, able to sell multiple mortgage companies, or they are "captive" and can sell only their company's mortgages. Next, ask these basic questions of each lender you are considering: Which refinancing options are available for me? What would an estimate of my monthly payments be in those scenarios? What are the upfront costs? What are the fees for appraisals, credit checks, escrow, and anything else associated with my mortgage? Can I buy points?

DON'T be unrealistic about the value of your home; it just stalls the process. And I hope this goes without saying but don't bribe the appraiser, *ever*. If you have upgrades or improvements to do on your house that would increase its value, do them before you start the refinancing process.

DO ask if you have to pay a prepayment penalty for paying your current loan off early.

DON'T go for a "float down," which lets you take advantage of a lower rate if interest rates fall by the time the refinance goes through (thirty to sixty days). It's a good option to have when buying the home, but a "lock-in," which locks whatever rate you had agreed to even if rates go up, is usually what you need in a refinance. If rates happen to go down a significant amount and you want to take advantage of that, you can always cancel the refinance and go elsewhere and start over. (The original lender probably won't be stoked, but it's business, baby.)

DO understand and calculate your break-even point. It gives you an estimate of how much time it will take to recoup the costs of the refinance to start seeing any difference/benefit to you. For example, if you paid $5,000 in closing costs and save a hundred bucks a month from refinancing, it would take you fifty months (more than four years) to break even. If you save $50 a month after refinancing, then it would take you eight years to break even.

DON'T blindly accept what your lender comes back with. Look closely at both the rate (this is usually the biggest focus) *and* the term. Calculate whether the new package actually helps you before you sign.

Generally, you should knock at least 75 basis points off your rate to make a refinance worthwhile. More expensive homes can justify smaller rate reductions because the savings are so much greater. Also, don't get greedy here or addicted to refinancing. I've seen people do it too often to try and chase rates lower and lower without accounting for the 3 to 6 percent of the loan balance they will have in closing costs. If you refinance too often, your costs will build up and bloat your principal balance to a point where you're not actually helping yourself financially—not to mention that you're expending a ton of time (and causing a lot of headaches). While I am always a proponent of doing your homework and being proactive, compulsively chasing interest rates also comes with opportunity costs. I'd rather have you refinance once, the right way, and then spend the rest of your extra time on making smart investment decisions—and more money.

As a migraine sufferer, I can tell you that I would take a few more basis points in my interest rate than suffer unnecessarily. I want to prevent that as much as I can for both of us. So, don't jump to take advantage of every offer and possibility that exists if you don't have to, especially if the ROI (return on investment) isn't strong.

To that point, many people use a mortgage refinance to borrow against their home equity for renovations or other big purchases. That may seem like an attractive way to borrow money at low rates,[18] but when you cash out too much equity it leaves you vulnerable to falling home prices. I know you want to make history on this earth, but don't be a part of history repeating itself in a bad way. One of my favorite sayings is: nature doesn't make a storm that lasts forever. As goes nature, so goes the housing market; trying to keep up with the weather patterns can be exhausting. There are going to be beautiful days and nasty days. That's just something we have to accept.

We will talk about investments in the stock market in the next step, but money to invest there should not come from your house (as some pundits, unfortunately, suggested during the major housing crash of 2008 that led to the Great Recession). At the end of the day, you can't cook dinner inside an index fund. You do that inside your home, so don't treat it like an ATM.

Now that we have rounded out the rest of the safe asset category, we are 75 percent done with our Miss Independent journey. In the last four steps we have covered important themes: 1) asset allocation 2) diversification 3) tax efficiency 4) lower fees 5) automation. These are some of the strongest forces in finance that will bring us the biggest returns. We will continue to use these concepts as we mosey on over to our risky assets.

BOTTOM LINE

Conventional Wisdom: Renting is flushing money down the toilet.

Hello, there is a cost of living. Do you think eating food is flushing money down the toilet (even though that's where it literally goes)? There are some things we pay for in life that are plain old expenses and not investments, and that's a-okay. What's not a-okay is not knowing the difference between the two. Some people see housing as just another line item in their budget—and they are still rich. With fast-paced, ever-changing industries and lifestyles, renting and being Miss Independent are not mutually exclusive.

Conventional Wisdom: I'm for sure getting a thirty-year mortgage when I buy a house because it gives me a long time to pay it off and I'll likely sell my house before then anyway.

First off, the length of time is not free. The longer a mortgage drags out, the more interest you pay on it. Second, if you're thinking about selling your home before you even buy it, then you should rethink buying in the first place.

Conventional Wisdom: Your home is your best investment.

No, no, no, no, no. Get the whole "I'm going to make money off my primary residence" thing out of your mind. A house is a home. A house that's not paid off is an expense. A house is not an investment.

10

INDEX FUNDS AND CHILL

Time to Get Risky

riting this step brought me the greatest joy because it covers topics in the stock market that I never, ever thought I would talk about—much less teach others about. Whenever anyone asks me about investing or getting into stocks for the first time these days, I basically verbally vomit all the information I wish I had known earlier, but didn't, on them. I am totally a stage mom cheering all the market newbies on.

One of the mistakes people make when starting to invest for the first time is not knowing what they want. Heck, that's an issue that comes back to bite us in many aspects of our lives (read: love life). The best way to clap back? Answer the damn question. I know, thank you Captain Obvious.

The good news is that you already figured out what you want and your timeline to get it throughout the earlier steps of this book. And that roadmap serves as a plan against which you can execute your investing moves. In this step, I'm going to introduce you to the wonderful world of Wall Street. As we have done when exploring all of the assets to come before, we will make our way from least risky to more risky investments. If your investing timeline is shorter, you will want to hang out in the shallow part of the stock pool. But if you have more time to play, then meet me in the deep end.

TAKE A WALK DOWN WALL STREET

Before we start our stroll, here's one thing you must understand: The sidewalk is not even. This shit gets bumpy and hilly and sometimes the sidewalk ends altogether, forcing you to cross the street. So, either know and accept this now, or don't set out on the walk at all. Seriously. There are other ways to grow wealth that don't involve stocks. Of course, I would really love for you to come along, but, if you do, we can't stop in the middle. I mean, we can take pit stops and whatnot, but we can't quit walking all together no matter what happens along the way.

Since its inception, the stock market has recovered from 100 percent of the dips and recessions it has had. And there are going to continue to be dips, recessions, and maybe even depressions; that's how this thing works, so don't be surprised by it. I'm always, well, surprised when people are surprised that the market is down. Like, this is what they signed up for, and maybe someone should have spelled that out for them as explicitly as I will for you. This is my big disclaimer before we get going so that you don't DM me when the stock market tanks asking me if you should sell. (I would likely respond by saying to buy *more* stocks during those times. Seasoned investors "buy on dips" because equities—that is, stocks—are on sale.)

There is one and only one truism on Wall Street: "Buy low, sell high." Everything else is rooted in someone else's opinion and is just one of many, many ways to analyze the market. Don't take anything else any pundit or analyst says as gospel beyond "buy low, sell high," because none of them are right all of the time. Their best guess to try and predict the market's future is ultimately just that: a guess.

The issue with "buy low, sell high" is that no one knows exactly where the low is and where the high is. However, there are ways to hedge for trying to time the market correctly. The most common one: dollar-cost averaging. This is basically where you put parts of the total amount you want to invest into action little bits at a time instead of all at once. For easy math, let's say you have $12,000 you want to invest in the stock market. Because you don't know if the day you enter the market is the lowest point or the highest, you hold off on putting all $12,000 in on the same day. Instead, you put in $1,000 every month for a year. The average of where you buy in every month will likely average out to split the difference between the high point and the low point.

Dollar-cost averaging has core elements that align with the tactics we've talked about so far: automation and consistency. I'm not promising you that it will *definitely* work out, but it will give you the best shot at success—and that's all we can really ask for in anything we do on Wall Street. The zillions of variables will do their thing, from weather systems that wipe out orange crops in Florida, messing with the futures market that we will talk about in the next step, to a shortage in semiconductors that screws up the NASDAQ, or a terrorist attack that throws off everything. You are never going to have total control. The most successful investors know that, which is why they aren't DMing me in the middle of a crisis.

WHERE ARE YOUR HANDS?

Start by asking yourself this basic question to figure out the best way to proceed with entering the stock market: Do you want to be a hands-on investor or a hands-off investor? Not sure? Here's a breakdown of what each means:

INVOLVEMENT TYPE	
HANDS-ON	HANDS-OFF
Monitors and reviews account performance	Doesn't check
Monitors and reviews account performance regularly	Doesn't check on accounts on the reg
Picks and chooses investments	Uses a premixed portfolio
Miss Independent, does it solo	Picks actively managed investments
Discount brokerages	Full-service brokerages

This is the first fork in the road. Whichever road you choose, you don't have to be on it forever, and you can always take a detour. But let's start by figuring out where your hands want to be because that's going to determine which brokerage will hold your investments, if you don't have one already.

For you hands-on ladies, you'll want to go with a discount brokerage. There are many of them out there, including: Merrill Edge, E*TRADE, TD Ameritrade, Interactive Brokers, TradeStation, Ally Invest, and First Trade. Some of them, like Charles Schwab, Vanguard, and Fidelity, have their own investment offerings. People constantly ask me which I prefer, and I always say the same thing: Honestly, they are all pretty similar. It really comes down to a matter of preference—truly whichever one you like and will actually stick to is the right one for you—and weighing their features:

- Account minimum/minimum balance

- Commissions on trades (they should have none)

- Promotions

For you hands-off ladies, you'll want to go with a full-service brokerage. Examples of those would be: Merrill, CitiFinancial, Morgan Stanley, UBS, Wells Fargo. The advantages of a full-service brokerage include having extensive research, personalized recommendations for you and your goals, updates on market trends and tax laws, and access to initial public offerings (IPOs). Of course, you'll have to pay for these perks, and there are much higher minimum balance requirements. Some of the features to look for here include:

- Cost per trade

- Annual service charge and maintenance fees

- Exclusive investment access

If your brokerage charges for trading or has account fees, you should look for a new one. There are plenty of brokerages that don't have either of these.

Think of these different types of brokerages like the self-service and full-service lanes at a gas station. Both options give you the same gas to drive off with; it's just a matter of who's filling the tank. Same here. For the most part, both types of brokerages are selling the same kinds of investments, which I'll walk you through in this step.

You have no obligation to be loyal to any one company for your whole life, although there are some benefits to having many of your assets at one establishment because companies generally treat their top customers the best. If you don't have a lot of money to invest, discount brokerages are a great option for you. If you do have the money but not the time to be actively reading up and rebalancing your investments, then a full-service brokerage might be worth a closer look.

If you aren't tech savvy, full service is the way to go. However, if you are, then a robo-advisor might be a good option. Robo-advisors are sort of a hybrid between full-service and discount brokerages. You get some of the qualities of a full-service brokerage, like automatic management of your assets, but it's done by an algorithm and basic investing principles rather than a truly tailored strategy by an actual human. Because of the use of technology, these companies have lower overhead than full-service brokerages (which employ, um, humans) and you get a discounted fee. Some robo-advisors are: Betterment, Wealthfront, and Robinhood. Some of the bigger banks are getting into the robo game, too, like Charles Schwab's Intelligent Portfolios, Vanguard's Personal Advisor, and Fidelity Go. Again, you should look at a fee comparison when you're choosing, and note that oftentimes fees go down with the more money you put in. It's also a good idea to download the app and play around with the interface to see how you like it before committing. You might find that one feels more intuitive to you and that's a great reason to choose a particular company; an easy-to-use interface will help to keep you motivated to actually open it and engage with all of your beautiful growing investments.

GIRLS JUST WANNA HAVE FUNDS

"Lapin, I wanna have funds, but where do I start?" I got this question all the time during quarantine, when most people (a.k.a. most novice investors) were freaking out about the market. At one point this step was called "Index

Funds and Chill" because that's my general advice when someone asks me what to invest in when they are just starting out.

WTF ARE INDEX FUNDS?

Warren Buffett said the greatest investment investors can make is putting money in low-cost S&P 500 index funds. And when the greatest investor of all time speaks, we listen. So, let's unpack that.

For starters, because you are pooling your money with a bunch of other investors, an index fund is technically a mutual fund but it's a lower cost option because it's not actively managed where a human is actually picking the stuff that goes into the fund.[1] That's right; as you've probably caught on to by now, there are a gazillion varieties of mutual funds out there, and an index fund is a stock-based mutual fund that tracks an index passively, no human input involved.

And WTF is an index, you ask? An index is a collection of different stocks by a certain set of parameters. So, when you hear stock market reports saying, "the Dow is at blah-blah, the S&P 500 is at blah-blah, and the NASDAQ is at blah-blah level," they're talking about the three main indexes. The Dow Jones Industrial Average (or just "Dow"), for example, tracks the thirty biggest stocks in the United States, including Apple, Microsoft, and Disney. The S&P 500 is made up of 505[2] different large-cap companies, or companies with a value of more than $10 billion. All of the Dow companies are in the S&P 500 plus 475 more, making up 80 percent of the US stock market by capitalization, or value. The NASDAQ is an index that tracks mostly technology and internet-related companies. There are 3,300 companies in the NASDAQ, including Facebook, Alphabet (parent company of Google), and Amazon.

While these three indexes track large US companies, there are other indexes that track smaller companies, including the Russell 2000, Wilshire 5000, and the S&P small cap 600. You can track international stocks with the MSCI EAFE and MSCI Emerging Markets indexes. Those are just a few of the most popular ones. Remember we also talked briefly about bond funds in Step 7, which are technically index funds. An example of those would be the Bloomberg Barclays Global Aggregate Bond (try saying that ten times fast!).

When you buy an index fund, you are basically buying a little bit of all these companies without buying the actual company. Buffett and I (we are besties in my mind) both like index funds because they are 80 percent less expensive than actively managed mutual funds. You also get diversification built in, since they include small slices of lots of different companies from different industries; they are less risky because if one company fails within the index, you have all the others to prop it up. There are real tax advantages, too, because there isn't a lot of active trading, which can trigger capital gains. The fund managers aren't doing much unless there are stocks added or dropped from a particular index, which is rare.

Not that you should follow my investment strategy, because my goals are different than yours, but I personally like to use a discount brokerage without having to put a ton of research into stocks all the time. That's why I own a lot of index funds: I can automatically invest, month after month, ignoring the ups and downs, confident that over time my investment will grow in step with the overall market, which has only gone up if you look at the levels over long periods of time. Generally speaking, few investors—even the most lauded fund managers—beat the market. And the ones who do put an awful lot more time into their investments than I do or would even like to (if I did, I wouldn't be able to write these books!). So, after my own cost-benefit analysis (cost being the time I spend managing my investments compared to the benefit of money I get from them), index funds are my go-to investments.

WTF IS AN ETF?

Exchange-traded funds (ETFs) are similar to index funds in that they can track an index[3] (there are thousands), but they are traded like stocks[4] all day instead of for a set price at the end of each trading day like an index fund I hope you're not savagely buying anything at noon and selling it at 2:00 p.m. so that shouldn't matter as much as their ease of entry. ETFs can have a lower-cost option that lets new investors get into the game, often for less than $100 per share (or even fractional shares via a robo-advisor), whereas there can be minimums of more than $1,000 to invest in index funds. Generally, ETFs are less risky than buying and selling individual stocks, because there is also built-in diversification.

WTF ARE TARGET-DATE FUNDS?

The darlings and the fastest growing segment of the mutual fund community these days are target-date funds, sometimes called lifecycle funds. We already touched on them back in Step 8, but they aren't just for retirement; you can buy them on their own. Essentially, you give your brokerage a target date of when you want to take your money out, whether it's your retirement age or your honeymoon or some other date that you choose. Then the brokerage works to figure out the right balance of stocks to go into that fund.

Target-date funds sound pretty perfect, but there are some hangups that many experts won't tell you about because they think either a) you're not smart enough to understand or care about more than the basics, or b) target-date funds are good enough, and certainly better than the alternatives of investing everything in your own company's stock or doing nothing. The number one thing that pisses me off about how the financial community educates people about this product is that they don't explicitly say that this is a target for a *date*—and not for the *amount* you get on that date. According to a recent survey, more than half of the people thought they wouldn't lose money in these funds and that they would magically get exactly what they wanted when they wanted it when their date arrived. I know, it sounds crazy when I put it that way, but it's true. *There is no guarantee of what you will get on your target date.* There is absolutely no guaranteed rate of return. Additionally, not all rates of return are the same on all funds.

My second biggest issue with target-date funds is that they operate on the assumption that you need more bonds than stocks in the mix the closer you get to the target. Generally, bonds are a safer investment than stocks, so that makes sense on the surface—but if you double-click on that concept you'll remember our talk about how bonds move back in Step 7. Remember the seesaw? Bond prices tank when interest rates go up. The assumption with target-date funds is that the seesaw is stocks and bonds. That is not correct all of the time. For example, during the 2008 recession, *both* stocks and bonds fell, which means your ass would have been on the floor if that was your target date.

I get why someone telling you to "pick your date and we got the rest" is alluring, for sure. Just know that target-date funds are more expensive than mutual funds (with fees of as much as 2 percent, which is unnecessary in my opinion) and more volatile than the marketing makes you believe. It's like what I say to people who get a financial advisor who is not an RIA: it's not ideal, and you can't lose sight of the fact that advisors from big banks and brokerages are hawking their own products and books,[5] hard stop. But, it's better than having no financial person at all. Same situation here. If choice freaks you out or you honestly just don't want to deal with your own allocation over the years, then target-date funds are a better choice than doing nothing at all. But, they are basic. Their assumptions are for the "average" person. We are many things, but basic and average aren't two of them.

WTF ARE MARKET CAPITALIZATION FUNDS?

Another way to break down funds is by market capitalization. There are five main buckets.

- Large-cap value funds invest in companies like those in the S&P 500 that have a total market value of $10 billion or more. The "value" part refers to the quality of those companies. "Value companies" are ones that are selling at low price-to-earnings (PE) ratio, which means they are strong companies that are trading below their book value. Typically these funds offer consistency and lower volatility.

- Large-cap growth funds are companies that don't pay dividends but rather reinvest their earnings back into the company. You guessed it, on Wall Street the opposite of "value" would be "growth." That doesn't mean the companies need it or are hurting but rather that they want to grow certain areas of the business and are hoping to use the cash they generate to make more money for shareholders in the future. For large-cap growth companies, we are talking about the likes of Facebook, Apple, Amazon, Netflix, and Alphabet.[6]

- Medium-cap funds invest in, you guessed it, medium-sized companies. By the way, medium-sized for Wall Street is still

$2 to $10 billion. These funds see a lot of volatility, because the companies in them are still hitting their stride, but there's also a potential for higher returns.

- Small-cap funds are made up of small companies, or companies with a market value of $250 million to $3 billion. (You know, those young pups with their measly $3 billion . . .) These are companies that have just recently gone public, so investing in them is more of a gamble.

- International funds which, obviously, invest in companies abroad. These are different than "global funds" which invest in the whole world, *including* the United States (about 40 percent of global funds fall into this category of having some US exposure). I like the idea of investing some in the global economy because it allows you to capitalize on the growth of other markets; plus, it forces you to at least somewhat pay attention to what's going on outside of the United States. There is a Wall Street saying, however: "When America sneezes, the world catches a cold," meaning that there is a ripple effect abroad if US markets tank.

It's important to understand the difference between the kind of funds out there and how they are categorized as you are taking your walk down Wall Street, especially if you're not just window-shopping. In the last step, we will talk about asset allocation and diversification. But you can also keep this in mind as you are going along so that you're not lopsided or in finance speak "heavily weighted" or "under weighted" in one particular investment or type of investment.

DON'T GET F-ED BY FEES

"Lapin, you sound like a broken record. I get it, check out the fees." Well, you're right—and I'm sorry I'm *not* sorry for drilling this into your head! It's for your own good.

Mutual fund fees are a special breed of fees, which is why they deserve a special callout here. It would be one thing if mutual funds were the best investment on the planet. Maybe then, I wouldn't need to specifically shame them? Or, just maybe then would their fees be worth it? Well, they are not. And far from it.

Nearly all (96 percent!) of actively managed mutual funds don't beat the market. That's right. These are the ones that are rated on Morningstar, the most popular service for evaluating mutual funds, where you can read all about the track record of the dude (sadly, it's mostly dudes) who acts as the puppeteer of the fund, picking what's in it. They spend a lot of time researching the perfect smorgasbord of offerings. But it's all a lot of hot air once you dig into the data.

FYI The Morningstar rating, which is on a scale from 1 (worst) to 5 (best), is a make-or-break for mutual funds: 75 percent of investments go to 4- and 5-star funds. A good rating is so important to mutual fund companies that they often do some behind-the-scenes ninja tricks when one of their funds fails, essentially dropping the crappy ones and riding on the track record of the good ones. It's not breaking news that many online reviews are fake. So, it shouldn't be breaking news that mutual fund companies, who have a lot more money on the line than the restaurant down the street does with their Yelp reviews, pull out all the smoke and mirrors to keep starry-eyed investors coming back for more.

DECODING FEES

Just like a magician, many mutual funds try to misdirect your attention to "something shiny over here" instead of what's actually happening, a.k.a. them charging sneaky fees that eat into your return. You may think that your "expense ratio" is low or even that you have "no load" mutual funds, making you a good bargain shopper. Don't believe that for a second.

I'm not going to make you read a hundred pages of fine print to figure these fees out. First, you need to know what types of fees you currently have on your existing investments. Sites like personalfund.com or bankrate.com can help you decode those fees as well as fees associated with additional investment vehicles you might be looking into for the future. Next, you need to know what those fees mean. The "expense ratio," for example, is the sticker price of funds, and it's usually between 0.5 percent and 1.5 percent, with an average of 1.3 percent—about the equivalent of tax on a hotel room. And just like hotel rooms have their cleaning and resort fees and other sneaky add-ons, there are additional costs lurking.

Here's a cheat sheet of the five most common additional fees to look out for:

Expense Ratio: This includes marketing (12b-1), distribution, and administrative fees. Many funds try to keep this in the 1 percent range.

Transaction Costs: These are costs associated with buying and selling within the fund itself. Remember, mutual funds do a lot of trading. And they're not doing that work out of the goodness of their hearts; it's how they make a living. The size, scale and frequency of brokerage, market impact costs and spread costs make the transaction costs the steepest fee in mutual funds (even more than expense ratios) at an average of 1.4 percent.

Soft-Dollar Costs: This is like an expense account for fund managers to pay for extra stuff like research and reports. The fee is usually only tenths of a cent, though they do add up.

Account Fee: These are maintenance fees just to keep an account open. Some funds also have exchange fees or redemption fees as part of your account.

Sales Charge (Load): This charge is either paid when you purchase the fund or when you exit it. It's usually expressed as a percentage of your investment.

A quick note about fees in "tax-deferred" accounts like traditional 401(k)s or IRAs: while this sounds like an awesome benefit to have growth compounding in that environment, it may not actually be more beneficial to your bottom line all fees considered. The tax costs in "tax-deferred" accounts may be swapped out with "plan administrative" fees, which are around 1.1 percent. Those fees come on top of everything else you're paying. And how much are tax costs in a taxable account like a Roth 401(k) or Roth IRA? Wait for it, wait for it . . . about 1 to 1.2 percent! So, these accounts can be just as or even more costly than regular taxed accounts. Remember, "tax-deferred" doesn't mean tax-free. You still have to pay taxes when you take the money out! This is just another example of not letting the finance euphemisms fool you.

So, instead of getting caught up in the ratings, fees and hoopla of actively managed mutual funds and their high fees, you could be putting your money into passively managed ones, à la index funds, which come out with the same if not better performance because they "track the market." The "market" is what most fund managers can't beat. Let's say another recession happens like back in the early 2000s, and you lose a decade of stock market gains seemingly overnight. Now, if you have a low-cost, low-fee setup, that would suck—but not as much as if you have, say, 3 percent in fees. If you put $100,000 in at the start of the decade and paid "just" 3 percent in fees, then you would be down $30,000 in fees alone. Regardless of what happens to the market, the fund managers win.

But, remember: in this story, *you* win. You are the heroine. And a Miss Independent heroine doesn't spend her precious time trying to beat icky odds.

STOCK IT TO ME

"Nicole, should I buy Zoom?" "Thoughts on buying Peloton?" "Netflix is killing it now with everyone stuck at home watching it (at least, during the pandemic), should I buy stock?" asked every person on Twitter ever at the start of the pandemic. (Okay, that's an exaggeration, but many of them slid into my DMs and asked me about buying these "hot" stocks.) To all of those who said it was their first time getting into investing, I said "no" and repeated the original title of this step to them: *Index Funds and Chill*.

If, on the other hand, you are a day trader[7] and trade all the stocks all day long, then go for it. If you have a particular affinity to a company or you follow a certain sector really, really closely, then you have my blessing to put some—not all—of your money in there and leave it there for a long time (likely long after the pandemic is over).

CONFESSIONS OF BEING
MISS INDEPENDENT

Better Than a Bracelet

"I'll take as many shares as $300 will get me of the stock with ticker symbol TIF," I said to the representative at my brokerage over the phone.

"Yes, Ms. Lapin. That would be six shares."

"Thank you . . . you know what? Double it and please debit the amount from my high-yield savings account," I said, trying to catch my breath in the crisp October air.

"Of course, and what would you like to do with the dividends?" she asked.

"Reinvest them," I said, without skipping a beat, as I stood on Fifth Avenue amid the usual New York City bustle.

An hour earlier, I had received an email that made my heart sink. It wasn't from any of the CEOs or politicians I was interviewing or any of their people. It wasn't from my boss or agent. It was from *her*—my childhood bully, the same one who had teased me for my "Nurse Martens" all those years before. Here's what she wrote:

> *Dear Nicole,*
> *It's been a while! I was watching TV with my mom the other day and I saw your face pop up. That's amazing—it's so exciting to see one of us make it big.*
> *I'm living back at home until I figure stuff out, working at Bloomies part-time. If you have some time, I'd love to get*

some advice from you about how to get on TV. You know
I've always wanted to be on the screen since we were kids.

Xoxo,

Her

I had just moved to New York and started appearing more
on the *Today* Show and MSNBC in addition to my anchor role
on CNBC. Getting a note like this should have spelled V-I-C-T-
O-R-Y! Well, it has since, but on that day, scrolling through my
Blackberry (I know, I know) and seeing her name pop up made
me feel like I was twelve years old again. I immediately felt small
and scared. The truth is that, no matter how much we accom-
plish, or how much money we make, we all have that vulnerable
little girl buried deep within us who comes back to life when
triggered just so.

And I was triggered. Soon after I opened the email, I hopped
into a cab, telling the driver: "Fifth Avenue between 56th and
57th, please."

My palms started sweating, my chest started thumping, and I
got flashbacks to her teasing me for my knockoff boots and not
having trendy clothes or a sterling silver Tiffany bracelet with a
dangling heart like all of the popular girls at my school did. Wow,
did I want that bracelet. I know the grown-up thing to say would
have been that I was over it and who cares about a stupid bracelet? I know that; but it's not how I felt at that moment.

"Right here in front of Tiffany is great, sir," I said as I ran from
the cab to the foyer of the jeweler's flagship store.

It was my first time visiting the store, and I stopped to take it
all in. It was more magical than I had imagined it to be, with high
ceilings and wood-paneled walls and that Tiffany blue everywhere, outshone only by the bling, also everywhere. I slowly
walked around the store saying "I'm just looking" to all the prim
and proper salespeople who asked.

"Actually," I finally had the nerve to ask one salesperson, "Where would I find the chunky silver bracelet with the heart that says 'Tiffany & Co.' on it?"

"Right this way, miss," she said.

I looked at the bracelet and I looked at the saleswoman and then back at the bracelet. "How much is it?"

"It's about $300," she said. "Would you like to try it on? Or I can show you newer pieces or bracelets from the higher-end white gold collection?"

I stared at the bracelet. It was smaller than I remembered. Lighter. And I found that even in the afternoon glow it lacked the luster it once did. "No, I think I'll pass for now—but I'll be back to look at the gold pieces sometime soon."

And that's when I ran outside and bought stock in Tiffany & Co. (ticker symbol TIF[8]) instead. It felt like a better investment and something I would still care about in a few years—for my portfolio, myself, and that scared little twelve-year-old girl who wasn't so scared anymore. And now, starting with that $600 investment, I can buy more Tiffany bracelets than I can fit on my arm.

So, yeah, it's fine to put some money in Tiffany stock or something else that's meaningful to you and leave it there (I'm not selling mine anytime soon). And if you're going to do it, I prefer that you use an app like Public,[9] which is pretty straightforward.[10] But it's not fine to do this all the time; it's more of a "special occasion" thing (like, you know, if you get a random email from your childhood bully). Remember, you have to pay short-term cap gains taxes (the high, nasty kind) if you sell an investment before a year is up. Our goal here is to build long-term, sustainable wealth, not to channel our inner *The Wolf of Wall Street*. Keep in mind that Leonardo DiCaprio's character in that movie, Jordan Belfort, worked at a firm (and did a ton of shady shit, but that's another story) so he would be considered an "institutional investor" (other big institutions include insurance companies or university endowments). Historically, institutional investors make it out of busts, like the dot-com bubble, because they have access to IPOs on the cheap and have likely already sold what they bought when it first hit the market to someone else or another firm at a profit. You and I, my dear, are called "retail investors" because we don't have the same access and our eyeballs aren't looking at stock charts all day.

Here's the thing, I love following individual companies. I live for it. But I want to be realistic with you and set you up for success. You are not going into a gunfight with a pocketknife on my watch. You can love companies—madly and passionately, even, like I do—but that doesn't mean you need to buy their stock individually. You can cheer your face off for your favorite sports team without putting any of your hard-earned money on the game. You can have an amazing lover that you don't marry. And you can, too, follow companies you are obsessed with without becoming an investor in them. Not going all the way doesn't take away from your admiration. And chances are they are a big enough company that they will already be in one of your index funds, anyway, so you will still benefit from their success, albeit indirectly.

Now, before we move on, I want to clarify what I said earlier about going stock-market shopping when things are on sale ("buy low!") as it relates to individual stocks. This is a good idea when it comes to the overall market. So, if the market tanks, I would double up on the regular dollar-cost averaging you are doing anyway so that you buy more when it's clearly low. However, when it comes to individual stocks, I would be much more careful about this. If a company tanks, yes they could turn it around and you could make a killing with the money you put in when the stock was low. Or, they could be in the shitter for good reason (hi, Borders, Blockbuster, and Toys-R-Us!) in which case your money would be in the shitter too. The lesson here is the same as at the outlet malls: just because it's on sale doesn't mean it's a must-buy.

MISS INDEPENDENT TIP

BULLS AND BEARS, OH, MY!

I'm sure you've heard financial news outlets talking about a "bull market" or a "bear market." Maybe you've heard someone is "bullish" on something or "bearish" on something else. The easiest way to remember which is which in the Wall Street animal kingdom is this: a bull charges ahead, so that's when the market is up or something looks like it's headed in that direction. Bears, on the other hand, hibernate, so when it's a "bear market," it's down and if someone is bearish on something—a stock, the market, even a person—they think it's a sleeper or are otherwise not optimistic about the outcome.

CORPORATE BONDS

A quick word on corporate bonds that I briefly mentioned in Step 7. They are of course technically bonds but they are issued by companies, which is why I put them here. I also put them here because they are more risky. Corporate bonds get issued when a company needs more money for some reason—to expand, to hire more people, to rebuild from a setback. When you buy a corporate bond, you are helping that company do those things in exchange for your money back and a little something extra (interest) for doing so. Corporate bonds typically have much higher returns than government bonds because, again, they're far riskier. If you're thinking about buying corporate bonds, drill down on their rating, which is done by the same credit bureaus that cover government bonds like Standard & Poor's or Moody's. These ratings are much less razzle-dazzle than the Morningstar ones I described earlier in this step.

TIME-RISK MATRIX

The ultimate goal of investing is to take on the lowest risk for the highest return. We will never know the sweet spot for this, but we can plot our time against what we know to be the historic risk profile of different investments. Think back to that "crazy-hot" matrix that went viral a few years ago, poking fun at what level of crazy men will deal with depending on a woman's hotness. I'm not saying I agree with the video, but it was an easy way to think about the exchange that happens between two variables when plotted against each other. (For the record, I much prefer the Hot Emotional Unavailability Matrix video, which is a pretty damn accurate representation of the level of emotional unavailability women will deal with depending on a man's hotness)[11]:

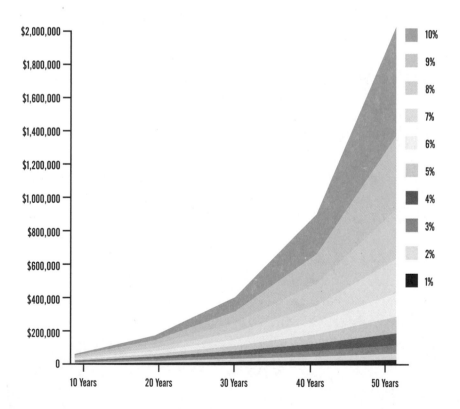

Wall Street and the world of investing is all about taking calculated risk for an expected return. There are core rules that have survived the test of time and proven methods to the madness that you can follow to optimize your chances for the most reward with the least risk. I know it can certainly feel like a wild, chaotic ride at times. In some ways it is. But just like on Mr. Toad's Wild Ride at Disneyland, you don't just hop off in the middle—no matter what. And while there's a chance the ride breaks down for a spell, it has never not started back up again.

BOTTOM LINE

Conventional Wisdom: Target-date funds are the way to go because they do it all for you.

Oh, how I wish anything in the financial world was so simple. Target-date funds can be useful investments as part of your retirement plan or individually as long as you know that there is no guaranteed rate of return, often high fees, and that the strategy is pretty boilerplate.

Conventional Wisdom: I'm doing well because I have super low expense ratio mutual funds.

Well, you may be doing better than if you were not investing at all, but not only do mutual funds typically not beat the market even with all the 5-star ratings in the world; they could also eat into two-thirds of your nest egg with insane fees. Even though the advertised fees seem low, remember that they are marketed that way in the funds' best interest. Aim for 1.5 percent in fees for both your financial advisor and your fund fees combined.

Conventional Wisdom: Buying stock in companies you believe in is a good investment.

Well, that could be. But before you buy stock in any one individual company, see if you are invested in it or could be invested in it via an index fund. If you can't or aren't and you just *must* own it for personal reasons, then keep the investment to a reasonable amount of your net worth—"reasonable" being if you lost all of it, your life and goals would be unaffected.

STEP

THE RISKIEST BUSINESS

A Look Inside the Most Advanced Assets

onsider this step to be the *Vogue* of the investing world. Sure, the photography is fabulous and the outfits are opulent. You imagine yourself wearing them. You know all the designers and their sky-high price tags. But, you aren't the first in line at the Prada store for the new fall collection kaftan. Because . . . who is?!

Short answer: not many people, even the ultra wealthy. The clothes and accessories in *Vogue* are, for the most part, aspirational, not accessible. For most of us, it's not about actually buying the clothes but drawing on them for inspiration, from their silhouettes to their color palettes and how they're styled. Well, the same thing goes for the riskiest investments. Investors know what they are and how they work, and might even draw some inspiration from them for their portfolios, but even the most seasoned investors don't just take them on casually.

In this step, I'll walk you down the dimly lit backroads of Wall Street. We will take a look at more exotic, risky public investments, including commodities, currencies, REITs, derivatives, and cryptocurrency. We will also stroll past more risky private investments, including venture capital, private equity and hedge funds, real estate, and life insurance. The idea here isn't to open your door to every one you meet, but rather to know that these investments are out there as you begin exploring the neighborhood on your own.

RISKY PUBLIC BUSINESS

If any investment offers a high rate of return for a short period of time, it's considered risky. Think about it: someone who wants a 10 percent return must assume there is more risk in their investment than if they'd want 2 percent instead. Risky investments require a combination of experience and risk management (hedging and protecting) especially because there are a lot of HFT professionals who want the biggest return too.

WTF is HFT? It stands for high-frequency trading, which is the term for firms that move huge quantities of investments based on little, technical movements hoping for big returns. That doesn't mean we need all their technology or even that we are trying to compete with them, but it does mean that we need to know they exist and that their edge comes from using technical analysis to predict investment patterns and movements. We are not even going to play in that game. Rather, we will focus our efforts on the opposite analysis game: fundamental analysis—or just looking at the overall economy, the company strength by the numbers that reflect earnings, expenses, assets & liabilities. You know, all the tried-and-true, old-school stuff. This technique focuses on factors that will impact a long-term investment strategy rather than an arbitrage, or exploitation of market blips, for short-term gain.

DERIVATIVES

The derivatives market has gotten a bad rap, understandably so, from the 2008 financial crisis during which banks were selling such complicated versions of investments that they ultimately sank them and the global financial markets too. Traditionally, derivatives are considered to be versions of investments that aren't as simple as buying or selling them in real-time or present-day prices, like call/put options or futures. These investments put you in the speculative investor category instead of the traditional investor category because the bets being taken cost you *more* than your original investment if they fail. It sucks enough to lose all of the money you put into an investment, but imagine if you lose more than that?! That's even suckier.

FUTURES

Futures contracts attempt to have investors benefit (or lose) from what happens to an investment in the future. If the contract goes up, a buyer gets more value while the seller takes a loss. That of course means the opposite is true: if the price goes down, the buyer suffers a loss and the seller gets more value.

Not all brokerages trade futures contracts. The ones that do want to really make sure an investor knows the risk of futures trading. They also may have a minimum net worth or a minimum deposit required just to get in the game. If the value of the contract goes down, you may get a margin call, which means you have to deposit more money in the account to keep it open.

OPTIONS

Options are pretty much what they sound like: the option to buy a stock or commodity at a certain price in the future. If the price turns out to be not what they hoped when the date comes, the investor can basically say "psych, just kidding" and doesn't have to exercise that option.

Most futures contracts give you the option of, well, buying an option. There are two kinds of options: call options and put options. Call options give you the option to buy. Put options give you the option to sell. Futures options are lower-risk than futures contracts themselves, since they come with an out. It is basically putting a deposit on something with the option to buy it at a certain date. Of course, you can choose not to pay the whole thing when the time comes, but you will lose your deposit.

COMMODITIES

My first job in business news was on the floor of the Chicago Mercantile Exchange, or "The Merc." At first, I thought it was some kind of shopping center. I soon found out that it's where commodities were traded—that is, physical items that are publicly traded like coffee, cotton, oil, gold, silver, pork bellies (!!). Yeah, I thought I was getting punk'd when I heard that last one, but nope . . . it's legit.

The most common commodity for mere mortals to get involved with is gold. Gold doesn't offer income or dividends like stocks, but it is considered a "safety" or "safe haven" bet, although the price itself isn't guaranteed to be stable. People think that if paper money goes away, then gold can save the day. I mean, this is a little bit of zombie apocalypse stuff but it's true. The other reason many investors have a little bit of gold in their portfolios, which we will talk about in the next step, is as a protection against inflation.

The rest of the commodities are divided into two categories: hard and soft. Soft commodities are things that are grown like corn, wheat, cattle or meat, sugar, cotton, coffee, and soybeans. Hard commodities are things that are drilled or mined like crude oil, natural gas, aluminum, copper, gold, palladium, platinum, and silver.

Generally, investing in non-gold commodities is tricky because the prices depend on physical supply and demand, which is affected by all sorts of stuff way outside of our control: floods, fires, earthquakes, epidemics and weather patterns. Oh, my. For example, if it's a super cold winter, prices for natural gas go up (because there is a lot of demand as people heat their homes) and if it's unseasonably warm the prices go down (because there is less demand). One of my best friends is a meteorologist and we often geek out (on air and off) about how weather can affect markets more than anything else. Yep. All the MBAs and certifications you can get in business and finance and a freakin' drought happens and takes your portfolio by storm (sorry, I had to).

There are four ways to invest in commodities: through ETFs (yes, there's an ETF for pretty much everything), through options, through futures contracts, or by buying the commodity itself (or a company that produces that commodity). The simplest and also the hardest one is buying the actual commodity, because that means having gold bars or coins or bushels of corn (er, it's mostly just metals but you get the point) lying around your place. That never seemed ideal to me, especially when I was storing my sweaters in the oven for lack of space in my apartment. The next simplest way to go is with a public company that produces a commodity like Rio Tinto Group for minerals or Archer-Daniels-Midland, which processes wheat, corn, cocoa, and other agricultural commodities. Commodity ETFs would have a smattering of those types of companies in them.

The trickiest type of commodity investment is via an option or futures contract. Futures help suppliers and manufacturers lock in prices so that the aforementioned random weather occurrence doesn't totally screw them. So, a farmer might want a futures contract for next year to ensure that no matter what happens, they can get the market price for their crop. In essence they are locking in a price to hedge against uncertainty. On the flip side, let's say a manufacturer makes canned soybeans and they want to make sure that they can count on a certain price for soybeans next year so that if the price goes higher, it doesn't screw up their business. The same thing goes for an airline company that needs to lock in the price of fuel for their operations. Remember: for a long time this kind of trading was regulated to professionals with deep knowledge of the history and how these types of goods tend to move. Unlike with other investments, super small movements in commodities can mean huge swings in the market, which means huge returns or huge losses for any investor—including you.

CURRENCIES

While gold can be a hedge against the dollar, you can also buy into the dollar or other currencies. Currency trading is also known as "forex" trading, which is shorthand for "foreign exchange." Because at the end of the day, currency is literally just paper; it's totally speculative. With commodities, you can look at the actual *thing*—wheat, oil, or those pork bellies that I mentioned earlier—and those are presumably of more value than paper. But with currency, you are speculating on what that paper means, which means that you have to follow geopolitics very closely.

Currency trading is actually the largest, by volume, of all investments out there. Every day, $4 trillion (yes, with a "T") is traded in the currency markets. By comparison, "only" $200 billion is traded on the New York Stock Exchange. The currency markets are also open twenty-four hours per day around the world (closed on weekends) unlike the regular stock market, which is only open Monday through Friday from 9:30 a.m. EST to 4:00 p.m. EST. Like commodities, only recently has currency trading been democratized to allow "retail investors" (in other words, you and me) to partake.

Currencies are traded against each other, like the euro against the US dollar. And while it doesn't really make it easier, there are just eight currencies that are traded most often: US dollar (USD), Japanese yen (JPY), Canadian dollar (CAD), euro (EUR), British pound (GBP), Swiss franc (CHF), New Zealand dollar (NZD), and Australian dollar (AUD). The value of the currencies is determined by basic supply and demand. When there is more need for US dollars—for example, when other countries are importing more of our goods—then the price goes up; and when there are too many US dollars out there in the world, the price goes down.

There's a lot of marketing for forex trading, on Instagram and elsewhere online, that may be legit but makes it sound easier than it is. An average of 75 percent of beginner investors walk away from forex trading empty-handed and feeling scammed. It's not a scam; it's just set up for insiders. If you're interested in learning about and succeeding in the currency world, make sure you really pay attention to interest rates and political tensions around the world.

REITS

Oftentimes when a person is adamant about buying a primary residence but really isn't ready financially or is unsure about the city, I suggest looking at alternative ways to have exposure to what could be big returns in the real estate world without physically taking care of a property. One of the most popular alternatives is getting into a real estate investment trust (REIT). REITs are technically trusts, but publicly traded like stocks. You can buy into a REIT mutual fund, index fund, or ETF. You can also buy individual REITs from bigger real estate companies like Simon Property Group (the folks behind a lot of malls) or Public Storage. You can get into them for as little as $25.

I get it, you know someone who fixed up a house and flipped it or bought a parking lot or commercial real estate and made a killing. Mazel tov! Buying one building or one home is betting that that one particular building or home is going to increase in value. When you're buying real estate that has income associated with it, like a REIT or REIT index fund, you are making money twofold. First, you are getting steady income as you go—REITs can yield pretty fat dividends—and then, if the properties increase in value, you gain on the appreciation when you sell it. Bonus: unlike corporations (like the ones behind stocks), REITs don't pay corporate income tax, so after management costs, the money is distributed pretax to investors.

So, what's the catch? Well, REITs track the overall real estate market and when that's bad, REITs are bad. Back in the real estate bubble of 2007–2008, REIT-related investments fell 20 to 40 percent. Ouch. REITs can also take a beating when interest rates are low, because investors normally look for greater returns elsewhere in the market; when interest rates are high, investors gravitate more toward bonds or other fixed-income investments. REITs are not "bond substitutes" as some think—they are equities and carry that risk—but their movements more closely resemble the bond market. Because they tend to have a lower-than-average correlation with different areas of the market, they make a good hedge in your overall portfolio. And . . . you don't have to mow the lawn or pay someone else to do it for the tenants you don't have!

CRYPTOCURRENCY

You've probably heard someone in your circle rave about their Bitcoin investment at some point since its inception in 2009. I'm totally with you if it sounded too sci-fi to get into it, but even while it's techy and obtuse, it's not super complicated.

Here are some of the basics so you're using the jargon correctly. Bitcoin is the leader of the pack, but it is just one form of cryptocurrency. Others include Ethereum, Litecoin, and Ripple. There are two thousand or so cryptocurrencies, and the ones that are modeled after Bitcoin (a.k.a. wannabes) are referred to as altcoins. Whatever the name for the "coin," it is all digital money—you can't see it or touch it, and there are no actual, physical coins—that is traded on the blockchain. A blockchain is a digital system that is decentralized and free of any government control (so, the opposite of fiat or traditional currency, which is why some consider it another "safe haven" like gold as a hedge against the dollar) and that tracks all the trades that are made in the cryptocurrency world.

Now, all of this is made possible via cryptography (where we get the name "crypto") or code-writing. Cryptography has been around for a long time, perhaps most notably used by militaries to secure confidential messages and instructions via code. This code-writing technology is used in the world of cryptocurrency in three ways: to secure transactions of cryptocurrency, to control the generation of new currency, and to verify the transfer of currency. You buy and sell cryptocurrencies on an exchange like Coinbase, Gemini, or Binance where buying and selling is very similar to stock trading. Some apps that transfer traditional currencies are getting into cryptocurrencies too, like Cash App. Once you own cryptocurrency the best storage method is a wallet—a digital one, of course. Because the world of cryptocurrency isn't regulated like traditional investment trading and is a frequent target for hackers, it's important to protect it with a digital wallet via companies like Exodus, Electrum, Ledger Nano, or Trezor.

CONFESSIONS OF BEING
MISS INDEPENDENT

My Date With A Crypto King

"Thank you for a lovely night," I said, as my date ordered dessert at one of my favorite Mexican restaurants.

"I had an amazing time and I hope we can do it again," he said, as our fun first date started winding down.

"Absolutely! And excuse me for a moment," I said getting up to go to the restroom.

He rose slightly from his chair like the ultimate gentleman, saying, "Of course."

As I walked to the restroom I moved my jaw around. It was cramped from all the laughing and smiling. A sign of a good date, for sure. I stopped at the bar for a second and asked for a sprig of mint (pro tip if you don't have any mints or gum for fresh-tasting/smelling breath). As I approached the bartender, I noticed a couple of guys get up from the seats at the end of the bar and head toward our table. But I didn't think much of it as I scurried to the loo.

I walked back to the table just as those guys were walking back to their perches at the bar. "Are those your friends?" I asked my date, knowing that New York City can be a big small town.

"Oh, well, kind of. I was just giving them something," he said, choosing his words very carefully.

"Um, so you didn't know them before tonight?" I asked, my sketchy detector on high alert. Was it a drug deal? Was he giving them money? What in the hell was going on?!

"I mean, yes, I know them. I was giving them the pin on my jacket that I forgot to take off. The little one with my company logo on it," he said, like it was the most normal thing in the world.

"Your pin? I didn't notice you had one. You gave it to them as a gift?" I asked, now going into full-on reporter mode.

"Listen, there's no easy way to explain this and you're too smart for me to not be completely honest. So, here's the deal: Those guys are my bodyguards. They came over because they noticed that I still had my company pin on, and they didn't want anything identifying me to the people here," he said genuinely, trying to make me think he wasn't totally insane.

"Your bodyguards?! Oh, you're being funny," I said, thinking maybe he was telling another sarcastic joke or provoking me to get back into our verbal gymnastics from earlier . . . back when this date was still fun.

"No, no. It's real. I'm telling you the truth. The crypto world is really insane. The diehard investors come up to me as the CEO of this company and want to take pictures. But that's only at crypto events, not in regular places. I think it's hilarious. I have bodyguards, though, because I have all the passwords to cryptocurrency," he said.

"So, someone could kidnap you to steal the passwords?" I said, trying to make sense of this.

"Yes, someone could in theory come hold me hostage and take millions if not billions worth of our currency and there would be no policing or getting it back."

"But isn't it on the blockchain?" I asked, tapping into my knowledge of cryptocurrency at the time, which was elementary at best.

"It is . . . look at you . . . but that still doesn't protect me from someone taking the passwords and liquidating the company if there was a gun to my head," he said.

I could feel the color drain from my face. "A gun?" I thought, but didn't say out loud.

"But, Nicole, that's not going to happen. I know it sounds like a lot, but it's not all bad. The guys are fun—you'll meet them next time! I know that was kind of a cock block," he said, trying to lighten the mood and get back to our sarcastic sparring.

Just then, the waitress came by to ask how we were doing.

I took a deep breath that was more like a sign.

"The check?" she asked, looking at me.

I nodded, glancing back at the bar.

There are many similarities between investing in cryptocurrencies and traditional investment vehicles as the world continues to grow. You can utilize a broker and you can invest in a fund of cryptocurrency just like you would an index fund. But, while there are plenty of fortunes that have been made with cryptocurrency, it is still the new kid on the block (10 years old as of the writing of this book) and going to go through growing pains. For that reason, I typically advise people not to invest more than 1 percent of their net worth in cryptocurrencies. You can afford to lose 1 percent of your net worth if it goes bust but you can't afford to lose out if that 1 percent becomes more valuable than 100 percent of your net worth.

SHORT SELLING

Any of the risky investments I've talked about you can short sell, or pull a "GameStop" with. Remember that online flash mob of Redditors who came out of nowhere to beat the big financial firms at their own game? That happened when the big dogs "shorted" GameStop thinking that it was going to go down but then a bunch of retail investors (a.k.a. Redditors and regular folks) bought it up, which ultimately fucked them over.

So, what the heck is shorting, anyway? It's not the opposite of "tall," it's the opposite of "long" in the finance world. When you are "long" a stock, it just means you bought it outright and think it's going to go up. And when you do, you try to follow the adage "buy low, sell high." But when you are "short selling" something, you're betting it will go in the popper, so you want to "buy high, sell low." You are also not buying the asset outright, you're borrowing it.

The easiest way to think about it is like borrowing a car. Let's say I borrow yours and as soon as I pull out of your driveway, I post the car on Craigslist and sell it. For easy math, let's say I sell it for $10,000. And then I wait a year, betting the cost of the car will go down once the new model comes out. And let's say after that year, the price does go down to $8,000. Then I buy that to return to you and pocket the $2,000 difference. However, perhaps some celebrity was seen in that car that year and the price skyrockets to $100,000 when I need to give you your car back. In that case, I am out $90,000!

That's essentially what happened with GameStop. Hedge fund guys borrowed the stock thinking it was going to go lower but it shot up astronomically instead. Remember, the rules don't change no matter who invests. A stock can only go down to zero, but can go up without limit. So, when you are long, you can lose 100 percent of the money you invested. But when you short it, the worst-case scenario is so much worse because it can go up without limit. I might even say it's like a game that never stops.

PRIVATE PARTS

Not all investments the wealthiest people make happen out in public. As with most private transactions, private investments have less transparency by their nature. But, what happens behind closed doors is still worth exploring. And private investments are the most literal form of diversification from anything you own in the public markets.

COLLECTIBLES

When I was an anchor on CNBC, I did a series of reports on alternative investments, which included wine, cars, horses, coins, antiques, sneakers, memorabilia, land and art. These investments in actual, physical items have made some investors a fortune, but they've also lost investors a fortune—and a heckuva lotta time to boot. To be the former, you need special expertise in these different areas and oftentimes connections to get your hands on the coveted stuff, like art by important artists that historically goes up in value or first-growth wines from vintners.

PROS

- Less predictable markets can lead to unexpected gains with fewer competitors

- Possibly tax-advantaged or sheltered, carryforward benefits

- Emotional, intellectual, and familial value

CONS

- Lack of transparency can create hidden risks and an information void

- Depending on the type of alternative investment, there can be negative tax consequences

- Complicated inner workings that often ride on connections

Alternative investments are much more of a passion than any other investment. If you have a particular interest in art, let's say, then you probably find identifying, researching, and buying it to be much more enjoyable than any other asset class. Investors who gravitate toward alternative investments are also more likely to be control freaks. After all, it's impossible to control the global markets but it's not impossible to wield a lot of control and power over buying a Van Gogh painting or Elvis's music rights.

It's pretty much the same when you're talking about NFTs or nonfungible tokens, which many consider digital art.[1] The nonfungible part of it means it's unique. So, if I gave you a signed Britney Spears poster and you gave me a Babe Ruth baseball card, we wouldn't have the same thing. But if I gave you a ten-dollar bill and you gave me a ten-dollar bill, we would have the same "fungible" thing. At the time of writing this, NFTs are a brave new world. There's a lot of exploring and a lot of discovering left to do. Heck, I even listed a "Money Rehab" NFT collection.[2] If it sells, then my show team has extra money. If it doesn't, at least we had fun with some digital arts and crafts.

VENTURE CAPITAL

The lure of finding the next unicorn (that is, a private company valued at more than a billion dollars) is real. I would know: I'm an avid and passionate startup investor. I love having a seat at the table to evaluate and help burgeoning technology companies. Being an LP (limited partner) of a venture capital fund can be about just writing a check and peacing out or it can be more involved, almost like a mentor role to the companies, which is the role I prefer.

Most venture capital funds require LPs to be "accredited investors." That is, a person who has at least $200,000 in annual income (or more than $300,000 in joint income with a spouse) and a net worth that's more than $1 million (excluding the value of a home). The minimum amount to invest depends on the fund. Regulators have put these minimum level of wealth rules in place believing that they will be able to understand the risks involved and bear the potential loss associated with these investments better. The biggest risks include: 1) lack of liquidity (in other words, your money is tied up for a longer period of time and the stake is hard to sell); 2) breaking through a startup phase to profitability isn't easy and frankly isn't common; and 3) if profitability of the companies included in the fund doesn't happen, then not only do you not profit but you could lose all your money as well. The biggest reason venture capital firms are unstable is because the companies they invest in—mainly startups—are unstable. The best startup investors go into their investment assuming they are going to lose their money and be pleasantly surprised when they don't.

If that doesn't scare you, there are a bunch of different ways to become an investor. I became an investor in Halogen Ventures because the opportunity came up during a weekly outing with my hiking buddy, who also happens to be the GP (general partner), Jesse Draper. If you don't happen to hike with friends who are starting funds, then there are many fund "matchmaking" sites for accredited investors like FundersClub, Crowdfunder, iSelect, and

EquityZen. There are also sites for nonaccredited investors, too, like Angel-List, SeedInvest, SharesPost, and MicroVentures. Alternatively, you just go and invest in the startup directly without a fund or site if given the opportunity, which would make you an angel investor. Angel or seed investing is done on your own, leading to more risk but also more reward. Access to deals and due diligence on them is why most investors of this nature choose to be limited partners in funds that handle all of that. There are also some publicly traded companies that invest in startups like Hercules Capital (ticker symbol HTGC) and Horizon Technology Finance (ticker symbol HRZN).

The average VC fund manages more than $100 million, which is a pot of money raised by the GP from a limited number of LPs that are individual and institutional investors doled out to different startup companies. Some of the bigger VC funds have a waiting list for investors because of their winning track records. If you love this world and you want to be part of it, try to limit your investment to about 5 percent of your net worth.

FYI

Venture capital funds take a cut of the money investors put in, and they typically charge management fees and carried interest (carry) on a percentage of the profits made on fund investments. This is referred to as the 2-and-20 model, by which VCs charge 2 percent of the fund's total for operational and legal costs and 20 percent carry on any profits the fund makes. Some of the top funds sometimes employ a 3-and-30 model . . . because they can.

Data has shown that the top 2 percent of VCs account for 95 percent of profit generated by all of the more than 1,000 firms out there. The top quartile of VC funds have an average internal rate of return (IRR) of 25 percent with the median of all VC funds at 12 percent. Over the same period of time, the S&P 500 returned about 13 percent. According to the numbers, you're unlikely to do better in a VC fund than you are in the market. But, you'll sure as hell have more fun!

REAL ESTATE INVESTING

I get asked about investment properties more often than many other financial concepts. Apparently the word on the street (Main Street, that is) is that having rental properties is a surefire way to grow wealth. Well, it is *one* way to grow wealth—but it's certainly not a surefire one.

Here's what's historically true: you don't really make money in the house you live in. Let's say you buy a $200,000 house today and in five years you sell it for $300,000. Well, you need somewhere to live so you'll have to buy another $300,000 house that is likely pretty similar to the one you just had. Unless you downsize, it's often a wash.

So, can you make money on owning an investment property? I fully understand wanting to have assets that are concrete (pun intended) versus ones that exist as a bunch of numbers and charts. But before you go into an investment property, plan out how much you'll actually be spending on it versus making off it. Here's a quick cautionary tale from a woman I advised:

> I inherited $15,000 from my grandmother. I thought I would buy a foreclosed house for pennies on the dollar and then rent it out. The home's market value was $100,000 but I got it for $50,000 and put $10,000 down. The monthly mortgage payments were about $500. At the time I had my cousin and her husband move into town so I was able to rent it to them for $700/month. Renting to family wasn't as bad as it sounds. But the backend to owning a property and getting it ready to rent was a royal pain in the ass. While my cousin lived there, I needed to hire a landscaping and maintenance person, so I was probably making $100/month. After they moved out, I felt like I had tried this rental property thing and it wasn't for me with the workload at my job so I sold it. I thought, because I got the house for basically half the price I would at least sell it for $75,000–$85,000. Wrong-o. I sold it for around $55,000. I ended up putting a little bit of money into a light renovation to sell the house and had to comply with the buyer's, um, extensive punch list. At the end of this saga, I estimate that I broke even. I put about $12,000 into the house and got about $12,500–$13,000

out of it, accounting for all the broker's and other fees. In hind-sight, my time and energy were more valuable than the small profit. I wish I would have put that money from granny into a safe investment in the market. I believe I could have at least got the same return or maybe slightly better but I would have saved precious hours of my life.

For every cautionary tale, of course, there is a success story. It's up to you to weigh the risk and reward with not only how you want to make money but also how you want to spend your time. If you are still gung-ho about investing in real estate, then go for it, but do so cautiously and really know what you're getting into. If you are purchasing a foreclosed property like the woman I just mentioned, know that there could be additional mortgages, tax bills and outstanding HOA dues that you would need to pay for and may not be disclosed at the sale. Also, calculate the cost to maintain the property; water heaters and A/C units aren't sexy, but they are expensive. Know your state laws. In many areas it's nearly impossible to evict tenants, even if they don't pay. During the COVID crisis, renters were able to delay paying rent for over a year. It was sweet if you were a renter, but many landlords didn't collect a dime in rent for more than a year.

For me, personally, I would rather spend time with startups than tracking people down to collect rent. But what's right for me is not going to be right for anyone but me. Maybe your passion is real estate, in which case, get smart about it and get after it.[3]

PROTECT YOUR ASSETS

MISS INDEPENDENT TIP

When you're investing in companies or real estate, it's a good idea to open a limited liability company (LLC) to hold those investments. Bill Gates and the Walton family (behind the Walmart fortune) are famously known to have most of their investments in an LLC. Creating this legal entity protects your investments—and therefore your wealth—in case you get sued, while likely offering tax advantages to boot.

It's easy to set one up:

1. Go to the website of your Secretary of State[4] or use a CPA or company like LegalZoom, Nolo, or Rocket Lawyer.

2. Determine how you will use the LLC if it will work for your asset. For example, many home loans will not allow the title to be held by an LLC and you may need to refinance your mortgage to do so.

3. Create a name for your LLC. If it's just for your investments, it can be whatever you want as long as it's not already registered in the state. Bill Gates's LLC is Cascade Investments LLC, while the Waltons' is more obvious: Walton Enterprises LLC.

4. You'll need to file Articles of Organization and pay a small fee (average is $100).

5. Get an Employer Identification Number (EIN), which is basically like a social security number for your entity.

6. Set up a bank account and transfer money into that account to fund your investments.

Successful real estate investing in hopes of creating a steady passive income stream takes time. Breaking even doesn't happen overnight and making a profit certainly doesn't either. But it can happen and when it does, it can significantly increase your cash flow. The best part of real estate investing is that you can't lose all of it like you can in a fund or in the market. You'll still have that house or building even if the current value isn't what you dreamed it would be.

LIFE INSURANCE

Life insurance is viewed way differently from other kinds of insurance, like car or home insurance. Those insurance products are pretty much there to protect you in case of an emergency or disaster. Life insurance is a different beast that people often view as an investment.

There are two types of life insurance: term and whole. Term life insurance has a lower annual premium but a higher payout for your beneficiaries in case of your death. For example, a $1 million policy could cost $500/year. If you die after twenty years, your heirs will get a million bucks for you paying just $10,000. The thing is: beneficiaries rarely claim these benefits. And you don't get any of them because you're, well, dead. Whole life insurance has higher premiums but has cash value that goes up at a fixed rate. This is the type that people view as an investment vehicle because you can borrow from it whenever you want and it grows tax-deferred (like a 401k, where you don't pay tax as it grows, but when you take it out) and it gives you dividend checks in retirement.

Critics of whole term life insurance as an investment say that the guaranteed rates of return aren't much more awesome, if at all, than what you would get from the stock market. Proponents say that the stock market doesn't offer a guaranteed rate of return, and it's another way wealthy people who max out their other retirement vehicles can go to have their money grow tax-deferred or minimize estate taxes. If you buy into that, then I would also take a look at what the media has often called the "rich (wo)man's Roth," or private placement life insurance (PPLI), which is designed to shield your nest egg from income taxes even upon your death. Removing taxes can, of course, help you reach your wealth goals faster. And, ultimately, just like I talked about in Step 8 with annuities, the integrity of the product comes down to the actual insurance company behind it.

I want to leave you with a story about salt.[5] Yes, salt. It used to be the world's most valuable asset. More valuable than gold; more valuable than diamonds. Wars were fought over salt.[6] But then, it became the most ubiquitous commodity in the world. It's laden on the floors of Red Lobster and strewn down the sweaty happy trails of college coeds taking body shots. It's relatively meaningless on a macro level today. That would be unimaginable for the people who literally killed for it back in the day. But if it can happen to salt—once the most coveted, *en vogue* asset of them all—then it can happen to any other commodity. In investing as in life: nothing is forever.

BOTTOM LINE

Conventional Wisdom: Investing in gold is a scam you see on late-night commercials.

There's a difference between owning actual gold coins or bars and owning the metal as a traded commodity or part of a commodity-based fund. Owning some gold without having to physically lock it up has historically been a safe haven trade and a hedge against inflation.

Conventional Wisdom: My smart friends are making a killing in Bitcoin, I must get in!

You are, of course, free to get into Bitcoin or any other investment your Miss Independent heart desires. Bitcoin is just one of the many cryptocurrencies you can buy. The whole crypto world is only a decade old so if you do get in, don't invest more than 1 percent of your net worth.

Conventional Wisdom: Investing in startups is just a Silicon Valley thing.

Well, there is certainly a lot of startup investing that happens in Silicon Valley, on Silicon Beach (Los Angeles), or down Silicon Alley (New York City). But, there are many websites for accredited investors and others for non-accredited investors that let you become a startup investor wherever you are.

STEP

12

KEEP IT TOGETHER

How to Build and Protect Your Portfolio

Throughout this book, I've taught you how to set yourself up to grow wealth and enjoy the many freedoms that come along with it. Following this plan—and actually taking the actions outlined in the steps, not just reading them—will get you to your Miss Independent goals. I have no doubt about that. But, I don't just want you to get rich. I want you to *stay* rich, for life. I don't just want you to get it all, but to keep it all. And, yes, by now *I'm* invested in your long-term success, too—so, do mama proud.

I wish I could tell you that building wealth had a start line and a finish line. It doesn't. It's a practice. And like any practice, when you slack off, you can feel it. Good financial skills and habits are hard to build, but by setting up an automatic system for yourself and getting into a groove with managing your investments, it will become harder for you to slack even if you wanted to—and those habits are more likely to stick.

Why do you think even the most wealthy people continue to work super hard? Some of the wealthiest people I know work like they are poor because they legitimately enjoy the game, and they want to win it. The financial system itself is a game, but you don't need innate skill to come out on top. By now, you have the tools and know the rules; you are set up to soar. In this final step, I'm going to help you take a helicopter view (maybe your own!) of your whole financial landscape. And from there, I'll show you how to reach new heights by not only increasing, but protecting, its value.

NEW YOU, NEW WORTH

Yas, girl, it's a new you. The old you, along with millions of other Americans, used to live your financial life like this: earn, spend, get taxed, save, get taxed. The new you has rethought your order of operations and adopted the Miss Independent mindset: earn, get taxed, save, get taxed, spend, invest, reinvest.

Most people stroll the financial streets that their parents laid down before them, or take the paths that groupthink leads them down: work hard, pay half of your hard-earned money in taxes, and save what's left at a shitty interest rate that's also taxed. Clearly, that has not worked out for them (or likely you) because you picked up this book. Here is the less conventional but richer mindset to cultivate: work on your financial intelligence (FQ) and prioritize fleshing out the asset column of your beautiful new balance sheet.

NEW NET WORTH

Calculating your net worth can feel empowering, especially when you are on top of your game. As a refresher, your net worth is simply calculated by subtracting your liabilities (mortgage, student loans, car loans, credit card debt, and so on) from the assets that you have accumulated so far (and I hope that, after working through Steps 1 through 11, you've added a few more to the mix!). This calculation shows that you can be a millionaire without making a million dollars in income. In fact, most "millionaires" don't make anywhere close to a million dollars in income or have a million dollars just sitting in their bank accounts. Instead, their million(s) comes from a variety of assets, all adding up to one strong and stable portfolio. They have structured the money they do have in a way that makes their money make more money for them. To make sure that your net worth remains on track—that is, trending upward—it's a good idea to calculate it once a year. Don't obsess over it, just set a calendar reminder (I may need a calendar invite intervention but I had to get one more in).

The reason I keep bringing Uncle Sam into our conversations is because oftentimes people's net worth can get thrown out of whack because they are taxed up the wazoo when they go to sell or liquidate their assets. That is why tax strategy must be a forethought and not an afterthought to your investment strategy. The average American works four to five months per year just to pay off taxes. Once you've factored in vacation, that's almost half of your working months every single year! It doesn't need to be that way. Because we have a progressive tax system in the United States (the more you earn, the more you pay), it may seem like high-class problems to pay more taxes. But wealth taxes, like estate tax and gift tax, can eat into that.

CHARITY

There is tremendous grace in volunteering your most valuable asset (time) even if you don't have money to give. But, when you *do* have money, that grace gets gusto with the impact you are able to have. As Margaret Thatcher famously said, "No one would have remembered the Good Samaritan if (s)he'd only had good intentions. (S)he had money as well."[1]

Donating to charity is awesome for three reasons: 1) It helps people. 2) Helping people has been shown to make you, yourself, happier. 3) It gives you more tax benefits. If we double-click on the third benefit—that is, for your taxes—here are six things you should keep in mind:

1. Donate to a qualifying charity or organization. It must be tax-exempt as defined by 501(c)(3) of the IRS code.[2]
2. Before you donate, ask how much of your contribution will be deductible.
3. Document your contributions, saving the receipt from the organization and the bank statement or credit card statement it came from. If it came directly out of your pay, save the corresponding pay stubs.
4. If the donation is for more than $250, get a letter of acknowledgment from the organization stating the amount, whether or not you got something in exchange for it (hopefully not).

5. If you donate more than $500 in noncash, "in-kind" items—like clothes, food, even your car—you have to fill out an 8283 form. If it's more than $5,000, get an appraisal.

6. Don't forget that volunteering counts! Not for your time, but for all the expenses around the time you spent volunteering, like gas or public transportation.

I'm sure I don't need to convince you that giving is an important part of living, but in case you need some more woo-woo, I truly believe in the law of attraction when it comes to money. The more you put out in the world, the more that comes back to you. What you put out, you attract.

We all know stingy people who have a lot of money and generous people who don't have a lot of money. Being generous has more to do with your state of mind than the state of your bank account. Rich *and* generous is what we're striving for.

CREATING YOUR PORTFOLIO

I've alluded to this principle in pretty much every step in this book, but I am going to say it again now so it sticks: diversify, diversify, diversify. Diversification is having exposure to different kinds of investments rather than putting all of your eggs in one proverbial asset basket. The point of doing this is that if one of those eggs cracks, you can still make a yummy omelet. You get the point. There are so many variables and things that can happen within specific companies, industries and in the world that can screw up your assets. Creating a diversified portfolio helps protect you not *if*, but *when* that happens.

ASSET ALLOCATION

It's widely known in the investment world that you need to spread out your assets. The biggest question is: How? Short answer: The more variety the better, and that means having a variety of asset types (everything in the last six steps is fair game including stocks, bonds, cash, real estate, commodities, and so on) and a variety of risk (just like the last six steps broke out assets in increasing order of risk).

The longer answer is tied to this question: How much goes where at this point in your life? As your life changes, so will your asset allocation. So, while it seems like a big, weighty decision, remember that it's not permanent.

The traditional rules are that you should gradually move from more aggressive (more risky) to more conservative (less risky) as you get older. I already told you about a classic way to determine that mix, remember? Your age is the percentage of bonds or fixed income you should have with the rest of your investment dollars going to equities or stocks. So, if you're thirty-five, it would look like this:

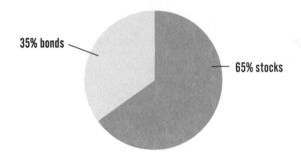

A simple conservative portfolio might look like this:

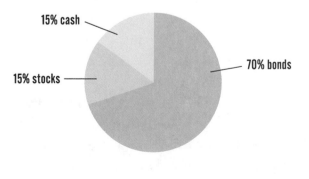

A simple moderate portfolio might look like this:

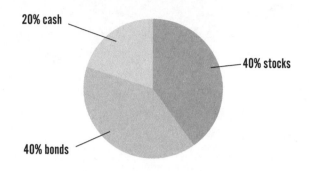

A simple aggressive portfolio might look like this:

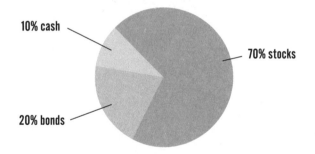

RAY DALIO'S ALL-WEATHER PORTFOLIO

Another portfolio, which is much more specific and has gained a lot of popularity is the "all-weather portfolio." This model was first introduced by Ray Dalio, the hedge fund manager behind Bridgewater Associates, the world's largest hedge fund, who is widely considered one of the most successful investors of our time. When Ray talks, investors listen. Here's what Ray's all-weather portfolio looks like:

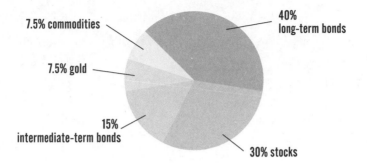

According to Ray, there are four things that affect the value of assets:

1. Inflation
2. Deflation
3. Rising economic growth
4. Falling economic growth

Based on those factors, Ray says that we can expect four "seasons" of the economy:

1. Higher than expected inflation (rising prices)
2. Lower than expected inflation or deflation
3. Higher than expected growth
4. Lower than expected growth

His portfolio has actually "weathered" all of those seasons over time. When historically back-tested, this portfolio made money 85 percent of the time. It also would have lost "just" 20 percent during the Great Depression, while the S&P 500 lost 65 percent. In some of the other big market drops (1973 and 2002), Ray's construction actually made money while the market suffered. Historically, this particular portfolio has made it through bull markets, bear markets, recessions, and everything in between. If you want to try an all-weather portfolio for yourself, don't be overwhelmed; you can do it using different ETFs that cover each of those asset classes, setting it up with your brokerage or working with your financial advisor.

BUFFETT PORTFOLIO

Another portfolio I like is the one that Warren Buffett reportedly wrote as instructions for his wife and their trust for when he dies: "Put 10 percent . . . in short-term government bonds and 90 percent in a very low-cost S&P 500 index fund. (I suggest Vanguard's.) I believe the trust's long-term results from this policy will be superior to those attained by most investors—whether pension funds, institutions, or individuals—who employ high-fee managers."

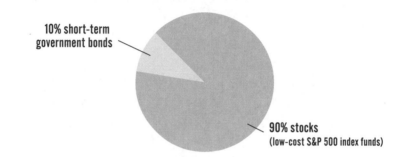

10% short-term
government bonds

90% stocks
(low-cost S&P 500 index funds)

Again, Dalio's and Buffett's portfolios are rough outlines. You can color inside or outside the lines depending on your particular assets, and ultimately the lines are drawn to your individual needs, time frames, and goals. It also comes down to your own preference and tolerance for risk.

Ultimately, I want you to get a good night's sleep, so if you're scared now, honor that feeling. Forget about me, forget about Ray, forget about Warren. Don't go skydiving if you're actually peeing in your pants; the people around you will thank you. There may come a day when you're just plain scared, not peeing-in-your-pants scared, and you zip into your flight suit and jump out of the damn plane—but if that's not today, that's okay.

Remember that certainty was the number one thing on Maslow's hierarchy of needs, which I mentioned back in Step 2. Don't discount that instinct. However, also on the hierarchy of needs is uncertainty and variety, so don't discount those, either. Yes, portfolio building is a delicious paradox.

REBALANCING

When I said that an allocation is not forever, I meant that you will ideally be rebalancing your portfolio regularly. Rebalancing a portfolio is simply modifying the allocation of your assets as the investments, the market, and your life change.

Let's revisit the all-weather portfolio as an example. Here's how you would rebalance that particular portfolio setup:

1. Look at how much your portfolio has changed since you last checked it. Which investments got bigger and need trimming? Which got smaller and need a little boost?

2. Invest more or sell to get the balance back to your initial allocation setup (30 percent stocks, 40 percent long-term bonds, 15 percent intermediate-term bonds, 7.5 percent gold, 7.5 percent commodities). So, let's say your stocks grew (yay!); you'll have to either invest more in other assets so that the stocks get back to the 30 percent target or sell some stock and funnel more money into the other categories to balance them out.

The idea of rebalancing is similar to maintaining a shrub. If you want to keep it a certain height forever, then you'll need to trim the excess as it grows to get it back to that height. Or, you can grow the other plants around it so that it remains *proportionally* the same size in relation. You can set up a rebalancing schedule monthly, quarterly or annually. Generally, if your assets have grown or shrank more than 5 percent from the target, you will want to prune a bit. I personally like a good thorough check-in with my asset allocation at the end of the year, with minor tweaks along the way. (Dare I suggest you set a calendar reminder for this?)

TAKE INTEREST

While you are doing your regular rebalancing, it's a good idea to go online shopping for the latest rates on your interest-bearing accounts, like your money market accounts and other cash-equivalent accounts. In order for banks to remain competitive, interest rates change all the time. If there is a markedly better rate somewhere else, switch. Yes, loyalty at a bank is important for long-term relationships, but having more money makes the bank care about you more. Go where you can get *that*.

PROTECT YOURSELF

You have worked so hard throughout these twelve steps to not only get your financial life together but grow your wealth. I hope you are proud of yourself. I sure am! Now, you'd better not let anyone get their paws on those hard-earned assets.

WIFE YOURSELF

Whenever a woman—whether she's a client, friend, or reader—says that she is worried that her future spouse is going to ask her to sign a prenup, I scream: "Awesome!" She is usually pretty confused at first, but I explain that she should reclaim this conversation. Reframe the narrative. He is not making you do anything. A prenup is a great thing, and if he doesn't suggest it, *you* should. You value yourself, you value your worth, and you want to protect it. That's awesome, if you ask me. Women these days are getting married later on average, which means we have more to our names, thus more of our own assets that we need to protect.

Another reason you should want a prenup, aside from protecting your assets and intellectual property, is because you don't just share assets in a relationship, but also debt. And, honey, we don't want any of that.

I hear the argument that prenups are not romantic; after all, isn't marriage forever? I am the ultimate romantic. There is nothing hopeless about being a romantic. But there's also nothing romantic about being hopeless. I have a few friends who have ceremoniously burned the prenup paperwork after they got married as a symbol of that romance. The agreement is still valid, of course, but if you are among the 50 percent of couples who stay married, you'll never need to use it anyway. However, if you're on the other side, and your marriage ends in divorce, a prenup gives you a say in how your assets are divided, instead of leaving that up to the laws of your state. This is especially helpful if you have kids.

INSURE YOURSELF

You likely already have basic insurance like car insurance, homeowners/renters insurance, and health insurance. (I prefer to use a reputable insurance broker for my policies, but you can DIY this with online insurance companies—reputable ones, of course!) As you grow your wealth, there are some other insurance options to consider:

- **Umbrella insurance:** This picks up where home and car insurance leave off, and can be used to cover injuries, property damage, certain lawsuits, and personal liability situations. For example, I have a $2 million umbrella policy that extends my coverage to that amount. This is an additional charge of about $500 a year on top of what I'm already paying.

- **Professional liability coverage:** The most common example is medical malpractice insurance, which covers doctors if they are sued for allegedly making a mistake. Any field can have this. Some of the most vulnerable professions to lawsuits, including doctors, are architects, lawyers, real estate agents, engineers, and IT consultants.

- **Business liability coverage:** Depending on your business, there are different options that can protect you. For example, business owner policies are popular with small and midsize companies because they roll property, liability, and other kinds of coverage all up into one. If you serve on a board, even as an unpaid member of a nonprofit, you may want to look into directors and officers insurance, which protects you from a personal lawsuit.

FYI If you have a body part that is so vital to your business that, if something happened to it, you wouldn't be able to earn a living—you can insure it. A surgeon might insure her hands while an athlete might insure her legs. I have my voice and face insured. Celebrities take this very seriously. Heidi Klum's legs are insured for $2 million (each!). America Ferrera's smile is insured for $10 million. Miley Cyrus's tongue is insured for $1 million. And Dolly Parton's "girls" (her famous 40DD breasts) are insured for close to $4 million.

TRUST YOURSELF

I get it: dying or becoming incapacitated is probably not your favorite thing to think about, let alone talk about. That's why financial advisors refer to this type of planning by its euphemism: "estate planning." But, protecting your family from huge taxes or fees in case something happens to you, or you die (remember, we are all just walking each other home anyway) is a conversation you can't afford *not* to have.

Super rich folks set up systems well before they are actually needed so that their loved ones avoid estate tax, gift tax, and probate, which is a long and expensive process of allowing the courts to go through and divvy up your assets (not to mention make them public, which is not ideal). But let me be clear: estate planning is not just for the super rich. I know the word *trust* conjures all sorts of *Gossip Girl* trust fund kid imagery, but that's just one extreme example. Those of us with more modest means—who are on our way to becoming super rich—can do right by our money and our families by planning ahead too.

If you don't have a will already, you should set that up. And you should do so this second if you have kids or are planning to have them soon. (If you are looking for advice on what to put in said will, refer back to the examples I present in *Rich Bitch*.) Once you have your will taken care of, you should set up one or more of the following trusts:

- Testamentary trust: This is basically a will and details where you want your assets to go when you die.

- Asset protection trust: This protects you from future attempts by creditors to take your assets.

- Living trust: Unlike a will, a living trust can protect you and your family while you're still alive.

    Revocable living trust: can be changed or revoked at any time while you're alive.

    Irrevocable living trust: can't be changed but could protect assets more and work better for, say, surgeons who are susceptible to being sued for alleged malpractice.

    Grantor Retained Annuity Trust, or GRAT: is a way to gift family members a lot of money by minimizing taxes. Tax is paid when you set it up and then the family member takes it out tax free. It's also the favorite vehicle of a lot of startup founders to minimize their tax liability before they make it big.

    Intentionally Defective Irrevocable Trusts or IDIT (also referred to as Intentionally Defective Grantor Trust or IDGT): sounds fishy but it's structured with a purposeful flaw to gift family members money—or often a family business—with protection from estate tax, creditors or their spouses getting their paws on the money should they divorce.

There are many different kinds of trusts for your particular needs and family structure that can be set up pretty inexpensively online at places like

LegalZoom or Trust & Will for less than $300. You don't need to be a trust fund baby to have a trust fund, baby.

POOR BITCH MOVE	SUPER RICH MOVE
Not getting a prenup	Suggesting a prenup
Having only basic insurance	Insuring your business/assets thoroughly
Only having a will	Having a will and setting up a trust

THE ULTIMATE ASSET

I hope you realize by now that this book was never really about money. Nope. It was about freedom. *Your* freedom.

There have been many studies showing that three main things—experiences, prosocial spending (fancy psych speak for "hanging out with people"), and time—lead to happiness. And while money may not be able to buy you happiness directly, it *can* afford you the means to have more experiences, give more to others, and outsource tasks you don't want to do so that you have more of your most valuable asset: time. Money can buy you the help, tools, and resources you need to more freely invest in yourself and your loved ones. It gets you one step closer to the things that *do* bring you happiness.

I've had some dark days, personally and financially, as I'm sure you have. We all have. I've been poor in circumstance and in spirit. I vowed that I'm not going back there. No, I'm not saying I won't have dark times ahead, because I will. But, I won't ever go back to scarcity, not literally and not mentally.

We can only control one thing in life: ourselves. And as part of that, we control our minds. I can promise you that I will never espouse anything but a mindset of abundance and wealth again, no matter what darkness or crap comes my way. I will never beg for crumbs, actual ones or emotional ones. How others treat me, how the world treats me is not up to me—but how I respond to it is.

So, while I can't buy peace, I can buy therapy. And while I can't buy brilliance, I can buy classes. I can't buy health, but I can buy great health care. And even though I can't buy culture, friendship, time, sleep, or an appetite, I can buy a first-class ticket for me and my best girlfriend to go to Paris, stay at a great hotel with a fluffy bed, and eat croissants every day while my assistant holds down the fort back home.

I hope that you join me (figuratively, that is—but come with me to Paris if you want!). Moreover I really, truly hope that you live a rich, full life in all ways. I hope that you take the stressor of money out of your life so that you can fill it with whatever else you want: trips, adventures, babysitters, dog sitters, great food, the best doctors, a house, a car, a kid, another degree, or anything else you can dream up. I hope you give generously to the causes you love. I hope you fund research that makes the world a better place. I hope you make career decisions that set your soul on fire. I hope you get crazy, weird, and wild every once in a while. And I hope you chill in your jammies all day once in a while. I hope you live a Miss Independent life however *you* define it.

I can't promise you a problem-free life, because that doesn't exist. I can only give you the tools so that you can troubleshoot when chaos happens, as it inevitably will. It's up to you to use them. I can teach you how to make money, but you're the one who has to get fulfillment from it.

The only way I know how to tell a story is to tell it honestly. So, there you have it: my story so far. I've told you a lot about my own problems and personal quest for fulfillment to hopefully inspire you and make you laugh with me or even at me. As long as you're smiling when you think about money, I promised you from the jump that I would take one for the team. Above all else, I want you to remember that you're not the only one who doesn't have a perfect life. That's the ultimate secret: none of us do, even (perhaps especially) those who look like they do. The sooner you own that, and the faster you are unapologetically, brutally honest about it, the closer you will be to the life you want.

So, what's *your* story, Miss Independent?

BOTTOM LINE

Conventional Wisdom: Earn, spend, get taxed, save, get taxed.

Earn, get taxed, save, get taxed, spend, invest, reinvest.

Conventional Wisdom: I'll never sign a prenup, it's not romantic!

I know this is the thing women tend to say, but don't be that woman. Take back the narrative, reclaim your power. You should be the one to suggest a prenup to protect all of the amazing assets you've accumulated thus far. After all, loving yourself is pretty fucking romantic.

Conventional Wisdom: Money can't buy happiness.

You can't go to a store and buy happiness, no. It's not sold online, either. But, you can buy resources, tools, and help to get you one step closer to the most studied components of happiness: experiences, helping others, and time. Money buys you the freedom to pursue happiness—and what's more powerful than that?

ACKNOWLEDGMENTS

Miss Independents are independent not because they act on their own but because they have the strong support of others to help them thrive individually and as part of a team or community. Without these people, I wouldn't be the Miss Independent I am today.

To Steve Troha, my superstar book agent, thank you for always being the proudest dude in every *Rich Bitch, Boss Bitch, Becoming Super Woman* and *Miss Independent* room. We've not only raised the bar but we've set the bar. We've come a long way, Steve Book, and we're far from done.

To Sara Kendrick and the amazing HarperCollins Leadership team, thank you for believing in me and my mission of financial literacy. I may not go about it in the most conventional way but together, we can educate women to become their best, most independent selves. That might not be world peace, but it's definitely changing the world and that's not nothing (please forgive this double negative).

To Jami Kandel and Hilary Hansen, my badass PR team, thank you for helping me see my crazy ideas through to spread my message about money to a mainstream audience. You've helped me appear in places I may not belong but showing up with financial talk in a sneak attack way has made a difference in women's lives over and over again.

To Jared Greenwald and team ICM, my agents extraordinaire. Thank you for helping me elevate my reach in all the ways I wanted and many I didn't know I did.

To my Washington Speakers Bureau team, thank you for accepting me as what seems like the only non–former president. I am in awe and honored every time you email me. Working with you makes me remember that imposter syndrome never really goes away.

To my Money Rehab and iHeart dream team, Morgan Lavoie, Catherine Law, Mike Coscarelli, Cristina Everett, Michelle Lanz, Mangesh Hattikudur, and Will Pearson, thank you for believing that I could carry my own daily show. I am grateful for your listening to the sound of my own voice more than I wish upon anyone. And to our show mascot, my own little Doggie Coin, Penny. Thank you for making life so much more entertaining.

To Jason Feifer, my *Hush Money* cohost and work husband. Thank you for saying "yes" to my rosé-induced idea of having a he-said-she-said money show. Thank you for always naturally disagreeing with me even though you're wrong.

To all my favorite Miss Independents, Sarah Zurell, Shachar Scott, Stephanie Abrams, Lavinia Errico, Chloe Coscarelli, Leanne Hilgart, Tracy DiNunzio, Paula Sutter, Randi Zuckerberg, Taryn Southern, Sari Eitches, Helene Pyne, Krista Williams, Susan Hendricks, Baya Voce, Jennifer Miller, Kristy Reed, Tiffany Jackman, Sabrina Andersen, Lena Hall, Hitha Herzog, Susie Spanos, Deanna Siller, Rhona Banaquid, Meredith Rollins, Rebecca Minkoff, Aliza Licht, Grace Jin, Elizabeth Stephen, Caroline Stephen, Soni Rice, thank you for inspiring me.

To Ellen Lapin London Crane, my physical twin and soul sister, thank you for always being my most trusted confidant. I could not have birthed one, much less four, without you. Over the years, you've taught me to sweat it out when in doubt and ask, "What Would Ellen Do?" That answer is always the right one.

To Joe Sanberg, my partner and cocreator, thank you for building and dreaming with me. You are my safest place and greatest adventure. You haven't completed me or saved me, but my life is even better than I ever could have imagined for having you by my side.

And to myself, who is proud to call herself Miss Independent but who knows that doesn't mean you have to go at everything alone. Thank you for graciously depending on others while standing strongly on your own. You've exceeded all of the hopes and dreams that eighteen-year-old Nicole had for you.

DICTIONARY

Accredited Investor: under Securities and Exchange Commission rules, someone who is eligible to participate in certain risky investments because they have a net worth of at least $1 million or an income of $200,000 ($300,000 for married couples).

ACH Transfer: Automated Clearing House, a type of direct transfer of money to or from your bank account. It's often used to pay bills.

Adjustable-Rate Mortgage: a mortgage with an interest rate that varies with the market rate of interest.

Affiliate Income: payments made from companies to people who recommend their product, especially on social media. Where are my social media influencers?

Age-Weighted: a defined contribution pension plan that makes larger contributions to older workers, who also tend to make more money.

Altcoin: any cryptocurrency that isn't bitcoin. There are thousands of these on the market.

Angel Investor: an individual investor who provides startup capital to a new business.

Annuity: a contract that pays a specified amount of money each year.

APR (Annual Percentage Rate): an interest rate that includes added costs and fees for borrowing money.

APY (Annual Percentage Yield): the rate of interest earned on savings when compound interest is taken into consideration. It's a more accurate calculation of your return than APR.

Arbitrage: literally a risk-free profit, this involves making a profit by buying an asset at a low price and then selling it almost immediately at a higher price.

Asset Allocation: a method of diversification that looks to balance risk and return by spreading investments into different categories, like stocks and bonds.

Assets Under Management: the total value of the funds that an investment firm manages for clients.

Automatic Bank Account Transfer: an arrangement with a bank that moves money from one account to another without any additional work.

Balance Sheet: a basic financial statement that shows what you own and what you owe.

Bankruptcy: a legal process to handle situations in which a person or business has more debts than can be repaid.

Basis Point: one-hundredth of a percent, commonly used to quote interest rates and rates of return in the financial markets. 1.00 percent is equal to 100 basis points. If the rate goes to 1.01 percent, then it has increased by one basis point.

Bitcoin: a digital currency, also called a cryptocurrency, created in 2008 by someone using the name Satoshi Nakamoto. Each transaction is tracked in a digital key known as a blockchain.

Blockchain: a digital key that tracks transactions in a cryptocurrency.

Blog Income: revenue earned from advertising or sponsored posts on your personal blog.

Bond ETF: an exchange traded fund (like a mutual fund) that invests in bonds.

Bond Index Fund: a mutual fund that invests in bonds and that tries to track the performance of a bond market index.

Break-Even Point: the point where revenue equals expenses, so profit (and losses) equal zero.

Broker: the person or firm that acts with the buyer and the seller to get a trade done.

Brokered CD: a certificate of deposit that is issued by a bank but sold through a brokerage firm.

Burn Rate: how much cash you use up in each period without considering new money coming in.

Business Owner Policies: insurance policies that are designed to protect the owner of a business against liabilities and losses.

Call/Put Options: an option is a type of derivative that gives you the right, but not the obligation, to buy or sell an asset at a predetermined price on a predetermined date. A call option gives you the right to buy, and a put option gives you the right to sell.

Capital Gains: the increased value between the price you paid to buy an asset, like stock or a house, and the price you received when you sold it.

Capitalization: the total value of a company in the stock market, found by multiplying the number of shares by the price per share.

Carried Interest: also known as carry, this is the share of profit that the general partners in a private investment partnership receive. It is designed to be an incentive, and it is taxed at capital gains rates rather than as interest.

Cash Management Bill: a short-term fixed-income security sold by the Treasury Department to raise money when there's a temporary shortfall. The terms range from a few days to three months.

Certificate of Deposit (CD): a type of savings account that pays higher interest than a regular savings account as long as the money is not withdrawn for a specified period of time.

Commodity: basic materials and crops. Examples include corn, soybean, silver, and oil.

Compound Annual Growth Rate (CAGR): this is the mean annual growth rate, including the effects of compound interest, for an investment.

Compound Interest: interest paid on interest that was paid earlier. This is good if you are saving money, bad if you owe money.

Consumer Price Index (CPI): a calculation by the US Department of Labor of the change in overall price levels based on the change in prices for a fixed set of goods. Researchers go to stores all over the country once a month to see what things cost, then turn it into an index and report it.

Coupon Payment: the fixed payment that a bond issuer makes to bond holders to cover the interest on the loan. In the old days, these were actual coupons. When they came due, people would get all dressed up and go to the bank to deposit them. Now, it's an electronic payment.

Cross-Testing: a way to evaluate whether a pension plan discriminates in favor of the highest paid employees by looking at projected benefits at retirement time.

Currency: money, honey! Usually, currency refers to money from other countries.

Day Trader: a person who buys and sells shares many times during the day, hoping to make profits from small movements in prices.

Debt-to-Income Ratio: the amount of money you must pay on your debts each month divided by your monthly gross income.

Defined Benefit Plan: a retirement plan that pays workers a specified amount at retirement, often based on the amount of earnings at retirement.

Deflation: a steady decrease in price rates over time. This seems like a good thing, but it's not, because people are afraid to invest, and businesses are afraid to hire.

Delta: the difference between two things. Think of a river splitting into a delta. In business, it often refers to a price change, so the delta between one dollar and three dollars is two dollars.

Depression: a recession that lasts for years. The Great Depression refers to the 1930s, which was a period of high unemployment and serious economic problems.

Derivative: a contract that is based on the underlying value of another security. Examples include options and futures.

Dip: a temporary decline in prices.

Directors and Officers Insurance: insurance that protects the officers and board of directors of a company or a nonprofit organization against liabilities.

Discount Brokerage: a brokerage firm that has low or no fees for trading. It also provides few other services.

Diversification: what your granny called "not putting all your eggs in one basket," this is the process of mixing your investments so that you do not have too much exposure to any one.

Dividend Income: money that you may receive from stocks you own if the companies choose to share a portion of profits with shareholders in the form of cash.

Dividends: payments out of profits that some companies make to their shareholders.

Dodd-Frank Wall Street Reform and Consumer Protection Act: a 2010 law that overhauled financial regulation following the 2008 financial crisis.

Dollar-Cost Averaging: sometimes called a Constant Dollar Plan, this is a way to buy shares of stocks or mutual funds by dedicating a specific dollar amount each period. It helps average out the effects of ups and downs.

Dot-Com Bubble: a big increase in prices in the shares of the first internet companies in the late 1990s. It popped in 2000 when people realized that only some of them were real businesses.

Dow Jones Industrial Average: a market index of thirty of the largest public companies in the United States, maintained by Dow Jones & Company.

Downside: what can go wrong.

Duration: a measure of how much a bond's price will change if interest rates change. In general, the larger the duration, the more the price will change.

EAR (Effective Annual Rate): the cost of borrowing that includes all costs and fees as well as compound interest.

Earned Income: money you make from your job.

Emotional Intelligence (EQ): a measure of how much you are aware of, able to control, and express your emotions. If you have a high EQ, you do a great job of handling relationships with other people.

Employer Identification Number (EIN): an Internal Revenue Service number that tracks a business for tax purposes. It is like a Social Security number.

Equity: another word for ownership. It is also a synonym for stock, which is ownership in a company.

Escrow: money, securities, or other property that are held in trust until a transaction is finalized.

Exchange-Traded Fund (ETF): like a mutual fund, an exchange-traded fund allows a large group of people to buy into a common investment. ETF shares can be bought and sold during the trading day, which gives them more flexibility.

FDIC: The Federal Deposit Insurance Corporation, a government agency that regulates banks and insures deposits in the event of failure. I was really happy that they existed in the 2008 financial crisis.

Fed Funds Rate: the interest rate that the Federal Reserve Bank pays to banks that put money on deposit overnight.

Federal Reserve: the central bank of the United States. Also known as the Fed, the Federal Reserve regulates banks, researches the economy, and sets interest rates.

Fiduciary: a person who holds assets in care of their owner with a legal responsibility to act in the best interests of that asset owner.

Financial Advisor: a person in a professional position to give financial advice.

FINRA: Financial Institutions Regulatory Authority, the organization that regulates brokers and stock exchanges.

Fintech: financial technology, an emerging field that looks at ways that technology can make it easier for people to manage money.

Fixed Annuity: a contract that gives someone a fixed payment every year for a specified number of years or for the rest of their life. The return on the investment is based on an interest rate. These are often used for retirement income.

Fixed Income: a type of security that pays a fixed rate of return, usually a bond.

Fixed Index Annuity (FIA): a contract that pays someone a fixed payment every year for a specified number of years. The return on the investment is based on the return of a stock-market index.

Flight to Safety: moving assets from riskier investments to safer ones in a time of economic crisis.

Forex: foreign exchange. Forex traders buy and sell different currencies all around the world.

Front-End Ratio: also known as the Mortgage-to-Income Ratio, it is your monthly mortgage payment divided by your monthly gross income.

Full-Service Brokerage: a brokerage that charges customers fees but also provides a great deal of financial advice.

Fundamental Analysis: a system of finding the value of an investment by looking at the value of its business and its expectations for growth.

Futures: this is a type of derivative that gives you the obligation to buy or sell an asset at a predetermined price on a predetermined date. Basically, it's a contract that lets you lock in the price of an asset now for delivery in the future.

General Partner: the person or firm that organizes a private investment partnership. The General Partner chooses the investments, taking most of the risk but also taking much of the return.

Glide Path: the way that the asset mix of a portfolio changes over time, especially as you get ready to retire.

Global Fund: a mutual fund that invests in stocks of countries all over the world, including the United States.

Great Recession: a period of global economic decline, from 2007 to 2009, because of the failure of several financial institutions around the world.

Gross: value before associated costs are removed.

Hedge: insurance against something bad that might happen to your investments. You can literally buy insurance as a hedge—homeowner's insurance is a form of hedging—or you can set up your portfolio so that there is protection against things going wrong.

Hedge Fund: an investment fund that is managed to get the maximum return for a given level of risk. These are usually limited to high-net-worth individuals and institutional investors.

High Yield: a return on an investment that is greater than average, often because the risk of the investment is greater than average.

High-Frequency Trading: computerized trading by hedge funds and big institutions that allows them to make many trades in a very small amount of time: literally, less time than it takes for you to blink.

Income Tax: a fee charged by the government based on the amount of income you report.

Index: a measurement of market return. It is made up of a list of typical items (stocks, for a stock market index; common consumer goods, for a price index) and then looks at how they change in price over time.

Index Fund: a mutual fund that is invested in all the stocks in a market index so that its performance will match it.

Individual Retirement Account (IRA): a defined-contribution retirement plan that allows workers who are not covered by an employer plan to make contributions before taxes.

Initial Public Offering (IPO): the process of a private company making its stock available to the public market.

Intellectual Intelligence (IQ): your ability to learn, reason, plan, and solve problems.

Interest Income: interest that you earn on your savings accounts or from any loans you make.

Interest Rate Risk: the risk to bond prices from a change in interest rates. When rates go up, bond prices go down.

Interest: the cost of money, expressed as a percentage. It's what you earn on money you save—and pay on money you borrow.

Interest-Only Mortgage: a mortgage where you only have to pay back the interest every month. If you have an interest-only mortgage, you should have a plan for paying back the principal, or you can get really stuck.

Internal Rate of Return (IRR): mathematically, this is the rate of return that makes the present value of future cash flows equal to the price of the investment. This calculation is often used to measure the performance of private investment partnerships.

International Fund: a mutual fund that invests in stocks of companies headquartered outside of the United States.

Investment Advisor Representative (IAR): a person who works for a brokerage firm or a registered investment advisor who gives investment advice. IARs must be licensed by FINRA, and the advice they give depends on the licenses that they hold.

Investment Horizon: the length of time you plan to hang on to your investments before selling.

IRA (Individual Retirement Account): a defined-contribution retirement plan that allows workers who are not covered by an employer plan to make contributions before taxes.

Jumbo CD: a certificate of deposit that requires a significantly higher deposit than a standard CD. It usually pays a significantly higher rate of interest, too.

Large-Cap: short for large capitalization, these are the public companies with the largest valuations, like Microsoft, Facebook, and Apple.

Large-Cap Growth Fund: a mutual fund that invests in large public companies that are also growing faster than the economy in general.

Large-Cap Value Fund: a mutual fund that invests in large public companies with relatively low-priced shares. These are often industrial companies or utilities.

Leading Indicator: an economic statistic that gives a hint about where the market is going. Examples include new unemployment claims and manufacturing orders.

Licensing Income: earnings from allowing your copyrighted or patented material to be used by someone else.

Lifecycle Fund: a mutual fund that is designed to follow the risk and return needs over a person's life. Generally, it will have riskier investments in its earlier years and then move to income-generating investments when its shareholders near retirement age.

Lifestyle Creep: when we start to think of luxuries as necessities. Once you were happy when you could afford your bus pass, and now you really need a new BMW to get to work. Or do you?

Limited Liability Company (LLC): a US corporate structure that allows shareholders to pass through the income to their personal taxes while giving them the liability protections of a corporation. These are the common structure of private investment partnerships.

Limited Partner: an investor in a private investment partnership who has less risk but also receives less return. The limited partners put in cash but do not make investment decisions.

Liquid/No-Penalty CD: a certificate of deposit that allows for withdrawals before the maturity date with no penalty.

Liquidate: sell. Turn it all into liquid cash!

Liquidity Event: this is the time when you get money out of an investment and turn it into cash. It could be your choice, or it could be someone else's choice—for example if a company gets sold.

Living Trust: a trust established between two living persons, such as a parent and a child. If you're fancy, you can call this an Inter Vivos Trust.

Long-Term Capital Gain: the profit earned on the sale of an asset that was held for more than one year. These are taxed at a lower rate than short-term capital gains.

Macro: this is the big picture, the major events, the zoom-out perspective of the world.

Margin Call: if your account is at risk of big losses, your broker will ask you to deposit cash or securities. If you can't, your position will be sold out from underneath you.

Market Risk: also known as systematic risk, it's the risk you take for being in the market. If there's a crisis that affects everything, it is going to affect you.

Market-Linked CD: a certificate of deposit whose yield is tied to the return of a stock market index.

Maturity Date: the date that a certificate of deposit can be closed without paying an interest penalty.

MBA: Master of Business Administration degree, awarded to those who study a program of finance, accounting, marketing, and management.

Media Income: money from appearances on TV, radio, podcasts, etc., or from contributing to print outlets or blogs.

Medium-Cap Fund: a mutual fund that invests in the stock of medium-sized public companies, often companies just smaller than those in the S&P 500 index.

Micro: the zoom-in perspective on the world referring to small, everyday routines and ordinary events.

Money Market Fund: a type of savings account that pays a higher rate of interest than a traditional savings account. If they are offered by banks, they have federal insurance. Money market funds sold by brokers do not have federal insurance but often pay higher rates of interest.

Money Market Savings Account (MMA): a bank account that pays higher interest rates than a regular savings account. It usually requires a high opening account balance.

Money Purchase Plan: a program that allows people to buy into an annuity that will give them payments in retirement.

Multilevel Marketing Income: earnings from selling goods or services on behalf of someone else. In an MLM system, participants receive commissions on their sales as well as the sales of any new sellers they recruit.

Mutual Fund: a type of pooled investment. Many people put their money into the fund, which is then managed by investment professionals. A load fund charges new investors an upfront fee; a no-load fund has no upfront fee.

NASDAQ: one of the major stock exchanges in the United States. The letters stand for National Association of Securities Dealers Automated Quotation System, and it is pronounced Naz-Dack.

National Credit Union Administration: a federal government agency that regulates credit unions and insures deposits in the event of failure.

Negative-Amortization Loan: a loan where the payment doesn't cover all of the interest. The extra interest gets added back to the principal. Ouch!

Net: value found after removing all associated costs.

New Comparability: a type of retirement plan that allows businesses to make larger contributions to older and highly compensated employees and smaller contributions to younger and less well-paid employees.

Option: an option is a type of derivative that gives you the right, but not the obligation, to buy or sell an asset at a predetermined price on a predetermined date. A call option gives you the right to buy, and a put option gives you the right to sell.

Overleveraged: having too much debt.

Overweight: putting a larger-than-average share of your portfolio into a specific asset.

Paper: short for commercial paper. These are super short-term loans, sometimes as short as overnight. The short term means that paper has very little risk. Companies use paper to make sure they have the cash they need for large payments. Also, what this is printed on.

Par Value: the face value of a bond, usually $1,000.

Paycheck Protection Program (PPP) Loan: loans made to businesses during the COVID-19 pandemic that would be forgiven if the borrowers maintained their headcount.

Payroll Savings Plan: a program offered by some employers that allows employees to make savings contributions straight from their paychecks.

Pension: an employee benefit that gives you an income in retirement.

PIIGS: bonds from Portugal, Italy, Ireland, Greece, and Spain, countries that ran into serious trouble during the financial crisis.

PITI: principal, interest, taxes, and insurance, all of which may be rolled into your monthly mortgage payment.

Points: this is a payment you can make when you sign your mortgage that will reduce your interest rate. Each point is 1 percent of the amount borrowed.

Portfolio: all your investments and financial assets.

Price-to-Earnings (PE) Ratio: a way to measure the value of a public company by looking at the share price divided by a year's earnings.

Price-to-Rent Ratio: also known as the Rental Price Ratio, this is the cost of a house divided by the annual cost to rent a similar property.

Principal: the base amount of a loan or a savings account.

Pro Rata: proportional.

Profit and Loss Statement: an analysis that looks at how much money is earned and how much of it is spent on different expenses.

Profit Income: this is how I define money you earn from your side hustle, to separate it from other types of money that you receive.

Publicly Traded Company: a company that has stock listed on a public stock exchange, where anyone can buy and sell shares. Public companies must also disclose their financial information, and there's often really juicy stuff in those filings.

Rate of Return: the increase in value of an investment over a period, including any income from dividends or interest, divided by the value at the beginning of the period. In other words, the profit on an investment expressed as a percentage.

Real Estate Comps: a comparison of the values of properties of a similar size, quality, and location.

Real Estate Investment Trust (REIT): think of this as a mutual fund for real estate. Investors put their money into a fund that buys apartments, office buildings and other income properties.

Rebalancing: the process of adjusting your portfolio so that it gets back to its target asset allocation or follows its glide path.

Recession: a slowdown in the economy. It is usually marked by two quarters of declining Gross Domestic Product numbers.

Refinance: taking out a new mortgage with more favorable terms and using it to repay your current mortgage.

Registered Investment Advisor (RIA): someone who gives investment advice who is also registered with the Securities and Exchange Commission, which regulates a RIA's work but does not endorse or approve it.

Rental Income: money paid for the use of your property. For many people, this comes from apartment tenants or Airbnb guests.

Resale Income: money that you receive from selling the things you are no longer using, whether at a garage sale, online, or through a fancy auction house.

Residual Income: commissions or other payments for work that has already been completed, especially performance in a movie or television show.

Retail Investor: a brokerage firm client who is an individual, as opposed to a big pension or endowment.

Return on Investment (ROI): the increase in value of an investment over a time, including any income from dividends or interest, divided by the value at the beginning of the time period.

Risk: the likelihood of things going wrong. This is an assessment that looks at probabilities as well as flaws in the project.

Roth 401(k): a defined-contribution retirement plan offered by employers that allows workers to make contributions that are taxed when made but not when withdrawn. It also allows employers to contribute money out of profits.

Royalty Income: payments that come from sales of intellectual property, such as books or music.

Rule of 55: an IRS rule that lets people take money from their 401(k) or 403(b) accounts without paying a penalty tax if they leave their jobs during or after the year that they turn fifty-five.

Rule of 72: a way of estimating how long it will take for an investment to double. Divide 72 by the annual rate of return (as a whole number, not a percentage), and you'll get the approximate number of years it will take to double your money.

S&P 500: a market index of 500 public companies designed to represent the US stock market, maintained by Standard & Poor's.

Savings Account: a basic bank product that gives you a very low return, but is federally guaranteed and often can be opened with a small deposit.

Savings Bond: a US government bond that is marketed to individuals for savings.

Savings Club: a type of bank account that can be used to save up for something specific. Many people use these for their holiday budget.

Secondary Market: trading of assets after they have been issued.

Securities and Exchange Commission (SEC): the US government agency that oversees the financial markets and ensures that investments have adequate disclosure so that people can make decisions about whether to go ahead.

Series EE: the basic type of savings bond, sold at half its face value. A $50 Series EE bond costs $25 and will be worth $50 on its maturity date.

Series I: a savings bond with an interest rate that varies with the rate of inflation.

Short-Term Capital Gain: the profit earned on the sale of an asset that was held for one year or less.

Short-Term Capital Loss: a loss realized on the sale of an asset that was held for one year or less.

Simple Interest: the interest calculated on the principal amount.

Small-Cap Fund: a mutual fund that invests in the stock of smaller public companies, some of which may be speculative.

Social Savings Club: a group of people who get together and make regular contributions into a pool that then gives the money back to members on a set schedule. These can be great, or they can be sources of heartbreak.

Speaking Income: payments for giving speeches at events.

Stock: ownership of a corporation, often divided into shares that can be bought and sold.

Sunk Cost: money you'll never get back, so ignore it when evaluating choices.

Supply and Demand: the basic force in economics that sets prices. Prices are at equilibrium if there is enough supply for everyone who wants to buy something, and no more.

Tax Deductible: an expense that can be used to reduce taxable income when calculating income taxes.

Technical Analysis: a system of finding the value of an investment by looking at supply and demand changes in the price charts.

Term: the length of a time until a bond matures.

Time Value of Money: a basic concept in finance that says that the money you have now is worth more than the same amount in the future, if only because you cannot spend it. You can get more money in the future by investing, if you are willing to give up the use of the money for a while.

Treasury Inflation-Protected Securities (TIPS): a type of bond issued by the federal government with a fixed interest rate and principal that varies with inflation. This way, you are ensured of your return regardless of what happens to price levels.

Unhedged: a portfolio or a financial asset with no protection against things going wrong.

Value Company: a public company that trades at a low share price relative to its earnings or assets.

Variable Annuity: an annuity contract that invests in a range of securities, so the amount of its annual payment will go up and down with their return.

Vesting Schedule: the percentage of a retirement benefit that someone is entitled to each year until they have 100 percent access. A typical vesting schedule gives someone 20 percent access their first year on the job, 40 percent access in year two, 60 percent access in year three, 80 percent access in year four, and finally full vesting—100 percent access—in year five.

Yield Curve: a graph that shows interest rates for different time periods for bonds of the same quality. It can be used as an economic indicator.

Yield: the percentage return found by dividing income from interest or dividends by the principal amount.

401(k): a defined-contribution retirement plan offered by employers that allows workers to make contributions before taxes. It also allows employers to contribute money out of profits.

403(b): a retirement account for nonprofit employees that allows them to set aside money before taxes.

1031 Exchange: this is a way to avoid paying capital gains taxes on real estate investment properties. You must sell one investment property and use the proceeds to buy another one.

2008 Financial Crisis: a deep recession caused by the failure of large financial institutions in the United States and in other countries, in most cases because they were overextended on real estate loans.

NOTES

INTRODUCTION

1.	If you don't know what a word means as we go along, don't worry. I've put together a handy dictionary (see page 227) just as I did in my previous books. I know the language of finance can be the most overwhelming part of your journey to greater wealth, so I wrote the definitions in such a way that you don't need a dictionary to understand them, and in the same tone I would use if I were relaying the information over cocktails.

2.	Of course, I have the alphabet soup of financial certifications, including AIF (Accredited Investment Fiduciary) and have been through the CFP (Certified Financial Planner) program.

STEP 1

1.	At the end of each step, as in all my books, I will challenge conventional wisdom to help you realize that nothing is gospel—especially not in the financial world. And, yes, maybe conventional wisdom actually works for your situation. Mazel tov. I just ask you to stop and question if it works for *you*. Don't forget that just because something has always been done a certain way doesn't mean that's the way it always needs to be done.

2.	The statistics are staggering and scary: Surveys have found that 85 percent of women who leave an abusive relationship eventually return. According to the National Coalition Against Domestic Violence, many of those women who return do so because they lack the financial independence to live on their own; all too often, their abuser holds complete control over the family finances, leaving them with few options after they leave. If you or someone you love is the victim of domestic violence, contact the National Domestic Violence Hotline at www.thehotline.org/ or 1-800-799-SAFE.

3.	"U.S. Bank Survey Says Women Are Leaving Money and Influence on the Table," U.S. Bank, March 5, 2020, https://www.usbank.com/newsroom/stories /survey-says-women-are-leaving-money-and-influence-on-the-table.html.

4. I am 1,000 percent supportive of whatever gender, pronoun, or association you have and whomever you fall in love with. But for the sake of the readability of this book and explaining the many (often gendered) money clichés out there, I am going to write heteronormatively. By all means, the information in here is for everyone.

5. In case you're interested, *Hush Money* is a podcast I cohost on iHeartRadio with Jason Feifer, the editor-in-chief of *Entrepreneur Magazine*, about the hush-hush money conversations no one likes to have, but we do.

6. "Household Work Shared a Little More Evenly," Sverige Radio, August 31, 2011, https://sverigesradio.se/artikel/4673288.

7. Drew Weisholtz, "Women Do 2 More Hours of Housework Daily Than Men, Study Says," *Today*, January 22, 2020, https://www.today.com/news/women-do-2-more-hours-housework-daily-men-study-says-t172272.

8. Cher, in a 1996 interview with Jane Pauley, https://www.youtube.com/watch?v=dZsL5R_CR-k.

9. Check out *The Rich Bitch Guide to Love and Money*, free to download at my website, nicolelapin.com.

10. Janna Herron, "Millennials Still Lean on Parents for Money but Want Financial Independence, Survey Says," *USA Today*, April 18, 2019, https://www.usatoday.com/story/money/2019/04/18/millennial-money-why-young-adults-still-need-support-parents/3500346002/?mod=article_inline; Richard Fry, "It's Becoming More Common for Young Adults to Live at Home—and for Longer Stretches," Pew Research, May 5, 2017, https://www.pewresearch.org/fact-tank/2017/05/05/its-becoming-more-common-for-young-adults-to-live-at-home-and-for-longer-stretches/?mod=article_inline.

11. Ideally you're coming into this book with no debt and savings, but if you're not there yet, I'm not kicking you out. *Miss Independent* is meant to be aspirational, in the same way that not everyone who reads *Vogue* is buying couture gowns. It's still fun to dream about the day when you can.

12. Maria Vultaggio, "Most Americans Lack Savings," Statista, December 18, 2019, https://www.statista.com/chart/20323/americans-lack-savings/.

13. Jack VanDerhei, "Retirement Savings Shortfalls: Evidence from EBRI's 2019 Retirement Security Projection Model®," EBRI, March 7, 2019, https://www.ebri.org/retirement/publications/issue-briefs/content/retirement-savings-shortfalls-evidence-from-ebri-s-2019-retirement-security-projection-model.

14. Amanda Dixon, "Survey: 21% of Working Americans Aren't Saving Anything at All," Bankrate, March 14, 2019, https://www.bankrate.com/banking/savings/financial-security-march-2019/.

15. Within the scope of this book, I will focus on the many ways in which Wall Street has alienated would-be investors—especially women—with needless jargon and barriers to entry. But make no mistake: there are myriad larger, systemic ways in which the financial world has excluded many groups since its inception, especially people of color and people with disabilities. To learn more and for additional resources, visit the National Urban League (nul.org) and the National Disability Institute (nationaldisabilityinstitute.org).

16. Andrea Romano, "Millennials Are Going on the Same Vacations Because They're Too Tired to Research," *Travel & Leisure*, March 13, 2019, https://www.travelandleisure.com/travel-tips/travel-trends/millennials-scroll-fatigue-tired-of-researching-vacations.

17. Kathryn Kattalia, "On Average, Women Spend 399 Hours Shopping a Year, Survey Finds," *Daily News*, March 4, 2011, https://www.nydailynews.com/life-style/average-women-spend-399-hours-shopping-year-survey-finds-article-1.116819.

18. "This Is How Much Americans Spend to Host Parties," *New York Post*, November 5, 2019, https://nypost.com/2019/11/05/this-is-how-much-americans-spend-to-host-parties/.

19. Marie Ennis-O'Connor, "How Much Time Do People Spend on Social Media in 2019?" infographic, Medium, August 8, 2019, https://medium.com/@JBBC/how-much-time-do-people-spend-on-social-media-in-2019-infographic-cc02c63bede8.

20. Matthew Needham, "How Much Time Do Successful Investors Spend Each Day Following Trends and Charts and Other Stock Related Information?" Quora, July 31, 2016, https://www.quora.com/How-much-time-do-successful-investors-spend-each-day-following-trends-and-charts-and-other-stock-related-information.

21. Ben Carlson, "How Much Time Should You Spend on Your Finances?" A Wealth of Common Sense, October 24, 2019, https://awealthofcommonsense.com/2019/10/how-much-time-should-you-spend-on-your-finances/.

22. "How Much Time Does the Average American Spend on Personal Finance?" The Ascent, A Motley Fool Service, October 11, 2019, https://www.fool.com/the-ascent/research/average-american-time-personal-finance/; Ben Carlson, "How Much Time Should You Spend on Your Finances?"

STEP 2

1. Being Rich Enough also assumes you don't have credit card debt (or other high-interest debt) to pay off. It's really hard to budget for even the basics if

you have debt following you around. So, if you do, head back to *Rich Bitch* and make a plan to "prioritize to pulverize" your debt once and for all.

2. Jim Wang, "Average Income in America: What Salary in the United States Puts You in the Top 50%, Top 10%, and Top 1%? (Updated for 2021)," Best Wallet Hacks, updated January 27, 2021, https://wallethacks.com/average -median-income-in-america/.

3. Sterling Price, "Average Household Budget," Value Penguin, updated April 26, 2021, https://www.valuepenguin.com/average-household-budget.

4. This is assuming a 10 percent stock return, 5.2 percent bond return, and 3 percent inflation rate. After the first year, you withdraw 4 percent of your retirement savings, but each year after you would withdraw the initial 4 percent, adjusted for inflation. In order for this to actually work in retirement, you first need twenty-five times your yearly retiree "salary" in the bank as the lump sum.

5. Alexandria Bova, "The Minimum Salary You Need to Be Happy in the Biggest Cities," Yahoo!Finance, November 8, 2019, https://finance.yahoo.com/news /minimum-salary-happy-biggest-cities-100000022.html.

6. "Saltwater Fishing Boats for Sale," Boat Trader, https://www.boattrader.com /boats/type-power/class-power-saltfish/.

7. "Saltwater Fishing Boats for Sale," Boat Trader.

8. "Louis Vuitton Bag Price List Reference Guide," Spotted Fashion, updated December 2020, https://www.spottedfashion.com/louis-vuitton-bag -price-list-reference-guide/.

9. Search on Tradesy, https://www.tradesy.com/i/louis-vuitton-keepall -37022-60-duffel-brown-monogram-canvas-weekendtravel-bag/27367863/.

10. Brian Resnick, A Psychologist Explains the Limits of Human Compassion," *Vox*, September 5, 2017, https://www.vox.com/explainers/2017/7 /19/15925506/psychic-numbing-paul-slovic-apathy.

11. "Millions, Billions and Other Large Numbers," Antidote, February 1, 2018, https://www.druide.com/en/reports/millions-billions-and-other -large-numbers

STEP 3

1. There are some great and legit MLMs out there, including Avon, Mary Kay, and Tupperware. But there are also some major scams. Before getting involved in one, check out the Better Business Bureau and Federal Trade Commission to learn more about the company's track record and ensure there haven't been any complaints filed against it.

2. If you want to futz around with your specific calculations for compound interest, head over to nicolelapin.com/tools.

3. *Caveat emptor* is Latin for "buyer beware." This phrase is often used in finance to talk about how, at the end of the day, the buyer is the only person responsible for the quality of the goods before purchase.

4. The way taxes are calculated is progressive, so not all of the $1 million is taxed at 37 percent. As of 2020, the first $9,876 is taxed at 10 percent (the lowest rate), then from $9,876 to $40,125 is taxed at 12 percent, and so on up to the highest rate (37 percent), which affects the income above $518,401. That's how you calculate your Effective Tax Rate (as opposed to just your tax bracket, which is your Marginal Tax Rate).

5. Federal Income Tax Calculator, https://smartasset.com/taxes/income-taxes#i4NtpcOrGo.

6. We all have a boss, even if we work for ourselves. Whoever pays our bills are our bosses and that can be in the form of clients or investors if you own your own business.

STEP 4

1. Find your own balance sheet printout at nicolelapin.com/balancesheet.

2. Anna Zakrzewski, Kedra Newsom Reeves, Michael Kahlich, Maximilian Klein, Andrea Real Mattar, and Stephan Knobel, "Managing the Next Decade of Women's Wealth," BCG, April 9, 2020, https://www.bcg.com/publications/2020/managing-next-decade-women-wealth.

3. Lois P. Frankel, *Nice Girls Don't Get Rich: 75 Avoidable Mistakes Women Make with Money* (Grand Central Publishing, 2005).

4. Now that we're shifting gears to building assets, it's even more important to start with a clean slate in terms of debt. So, if you still have a debt monkey on your back, revisit *Rich Bitch* to come up with your plan to "prioritize to pulverize"—and then meet me back here.

5. Jim Rasmussen, "Billionaire Talks Strategy With Students: Columbia University Group Hears From Famous Alumnus Berkshire Hathaway," *Omaha World-Herald*, January 2, 1994.

6. About $13 trillion (yes, with a "T") is managed in different kinds of mutual funds.

STEP 5

1. Obviously you don't live forever but if a financial plan is set up correctly, it can be passed on in your family even after you pass.

2. By the way, it wasn't always like this. Only in the 1940s did people start paying the government out of their paychecks before even seeing the money. That's because you and I couldn't be trusted to budget enough money to pay up when the tax bill came due in April. So, Uncle Sam set up a national automatic "pay me first" system—and so can you.

3. If you want to see the power of a little increase in the amount you put into savings over time, check out "The 1 percent More Savings Calculator" from the *New York Times*. I was going to make my own, but they nailed it already, and I'm so glad they did.

4. The concepts of "fixed" and "growth" mindsets originated from researcher Carol Dweck. In a "fixed" mindset people believe their talents and intelligence are fixed and can't improve. In a "growth" mindset, people believe they can learn and, well, grow to achieve success. While Dweck's research is in psychology, this terminology is often used in business settings.

5. Go to findanadvisor.napfa.org.

6. I know I'm stating the obvious, but it bears repeating: nothing in life, including on Wall Street, is 100 percent safe. The "safe assets" I refer to are thus not 100 percent safe, either. They still carry some risk, but less so (sometimes significantly) than the assets under "risk assets."

STEP 6

1. I don't work with any online, app-based, or traditional banks. I'm simply giving you some options to see what resonates for you and fits your needs and desires best. Of course, there's no way to list them all, so this is merely a sampling to get you going.

2. An abbreviation for one of my favorite Latin phrases *"quod erat demonstrandum,"* literally meaning "what was to be shown."

3. Megan Leonhardt, "American's Spend Over $1,000 a Year on Lotto Tickets," CNBC, December 12, 2019, https://www.cnbc.com/2019/12/12/americans-spend-over-1000-dollars-a-year-on-lotto-tickets.html.

STEP 7

1. Mosey on over to Treasury.gov for daily yield reports. Don't be scared. I would be stoked to look over at a girlfriend's phone and see her looking at the yield curve rather than being an Instagram private investigator.

2. The curve is said to be steepening when long-term bonds outperform short-term ones, because it indicates more growth ahead. If short-term bonds are

rising slightly higher than long-term ones, then the curve is considered to be "flattening." If it's flattening fast, it will be "inverted."

3. This sounds a little cutesy, but it is based on a theory by Dr. Harry Markowitz, awarded the Nobel Prize in Economic Sciences in 1990.

4. Interest is not taxed, but capital gains are still taxed. Those would be triggered only if you sold the bond for more than you paid for it.

5. For example, a Ginnie Mae bond, a mortgage bond backed by the government, is $25,000 total, but you can buy into that bond fund for just $1,000.

6. On most stock market and investing reports, including the ticker you see on financial news outlets, red = negative and green (or sometimes black) = positive.

7. Reputable banks include our Canadian friends too. Zero Canadian banks failed during the Great Recession.

8. Sometimes foreign bonds are issued in dollars and those are referred to as Yankee Bonds. (Don't take offense, Mets fans.)

9. Not to be confused with a hedge fund, which is a totally different thing.

STEP 8

1. Tennessee Williams, *Cat on a Hot Tin Roof* (New Directions Publishing), p. 55.

2. The average life expectancy in the United States is eighty-one for women and seventy-six for men. Of course, the odds of living longer than that increase once you get to sixty-five, so that's why I cited this statistic; it's more accurate when having a discussion around retirement.

3. People are also able to pass their Social Security benefits to their spouse now. Plus, Social Security is also paying for other government programs. You don't need a doctorate in economics to know that that's just not sustainable and will likely run out before millennials reach retirement age.

4. The ages listed here are as of 2020.

5. Try my retirement calculator at nicolelapin.com/tools.

6. The 4 percent rule gets a lot of flak because it's seen as very conservative and likely to make you the richest lady in the graveyard. I get it: we can't take it with us, so let's use it to make our lives and the lives of those around us better while we can. I would be remiss if I didn't mention these rules of thumb. But retirement is one of the biggest financial decisions you will make, so customized is always better than off the rack.

7. Not including any pensions or home value.

8. "Ram Dass Quotes," https://www.ramdass.org/ram-dass-quotes/.

9. Although obsolete, you may have a Keough (pronounced kee-yo) plan hanging around; more commonly known as H.R. 10 plans these days. These are a cross between a solo 401(k) and a SEP IRA for self-employed folks. They allow for far higher contributions than any other plan and make the most sense for doctors or lawyers in private practice.

10. 403(b)s only invest in annuities and mutual funds while 401(k)s can have any investment in them.

11. Make sure you know how many years it takes for your match to be fully vested, which means yours.

12. Contribution limits for all retirement vehicles change often, but I'm listing them here as of 2020.

13. If you lost your job before age fifty-five, you would have to wait until 59.5 to take money out without penalty. This special rule also works for 403(b)s and kicks in early at age fifty for public safety workers like fire fighters, air traffic controllers, and police officers.

14. No one likes taxes, but if there is an option to pay them now, so you'll never have to pay them again, as with a Roth option for 401(k)s or IRAs, take that option. Or, better yet, have one of these in your portfolio in addition to the tax deferred options.

15. There is a nice fee tracker tool at www.AmericasBest401k.com.

16. My company, as an S-corporation, has this as do many sole proprietorships.

17. There's a penalty for early withdrawals from traditional IRAs and 401(k)s except in cases of death or disability. If that happens, God forbid, the penalty and tax ramifications are going to be low on the list of your concerns, anyway. You can also withdraw from a traditional IRA if you're paying for yourself or your kids to go to college or to help pay for your first home (up to $10,000). There is one more wonky way to get around penalty withdrawals, and that's with the 72(t) IRS rule, which lets you take out money based on life expectancy, but check with a tax professional for that one.

18. If you're married, the best thing to do is to list your spouse as the beneficiary on your retirement plan, allowing them to do a spousal rollover if you die. If you have kids, and both you and your spouse die, then they would become the beneficiaries.

19. To be super clear, this doesn't mean opening up multiples of each type of account. Don't run around to different banks trying to get a bunch of different Roth IRAs. Just make sure you have one Roth option and one tax-deferred option in the mix.

20. If you are getting Social Security money, then try to delay the payments as long as you can—ideally until you're between sixty-seven and seventy, even though you can start taking money out at sixty-three. Every year you delay allows your benefits to continue to grow.

21. The Secure Act passed by Congress at the end of 2019 allowed for more access to annuities in retirement accounts.

22. To read more about the ratings of different mutual funds out there, check out Morningstar.com. The ratings are pretty basic: "gold," "silver," and "bronze." It also has a star rating system like Amazon reviews. Whenever possible, cross-check any mutual fund you have on Morningstar. (Note that you have to pay a subscription fee to access some of the more advanced features.) You can also check out the Mutual Fund Education Alliance at mfea.com.

23. You can always investigate your own company by looking up the company's 10-K, which is what every publicly traded company has to file with the Securities and Exchange Commission (SEC). You can also listen to the company's quarterly earnings calls to Wall Street analysts or find the transcripts on business news websites like seekingalpha.com. These will give you a less biased view into how the company is actually doing.

24. This is not a big secret. I talk about it very openly in my last book, *Becoming Super Woman*.

25. Karlyn Borysenko, "Burnout Is Now an Officially Diagnosable Condition: Here's What You Need to Know About It," *Forbes*, May 29, 2019, https://www .forbes.com/sites/karlynborysenko/2019/05/29/burnout-is-now-an -officially-diagnosable-condition-heres-what-you-need-to-know-about -it/?sh=203c05cf2b99.

STEP 9

1. The largest study ever done on home prices by Robert Shiller (of the Case-Shiller housing index) found that home prices have been flat for a century (!!) when adjusted for inflation. One of the reasons people assume you can make a killing from buying a home is that they don't account for inflation (or expenses you'll never get back like repairs or closing costs) when looking at the sold price.

2. After you buy a house, take a good look in the mirror: that's your landlord. Termites? All you. Busted pipe? All you. Boo.

3. Beyoncé's dad is the cutest and very outspoken about why he prefers to rent instead of buy. Watch one of his videos online where he riffs about it. Please adopt me, Mr. Knowles.

4. To calculate true profit, make sure you are accounting for expenses and other money put into the house or home buying process that you don't get back (ahem . . . closing costs) plus adjust for inflation.

5. Kiyosaki basically says that if you rent out your house at a profit (meaning that you have money left over after all expenses are paid), then that is an asset, as are businesses that you own but don't work at or manage—even as small as a vending machine. That strategy would give you enough cash flow to live off and make your primary home a place to live, not an asset to make money from.

6. This is another reason more rich people rent than you might think. They often live in more expensive cities like New York, London, or San Francisco where renting makes way more financial sense than buying.

7. Also potentially property insurance, mortgage insurance (if less than 20 percent of the value of the property was deposited), home inspections, real estate agent commission, loan origin payments and/or renovations.

8. A lot of successful property investors will tell you to rent your home but own your rental properties.

9. If you want to see depressing graphs of how much you end up paying the longer you take to pay off your mortgage, look for Home Loan Amortization charts. A standard graph shows that you pay off as much principal on your house with a thirty-year mortgage in the last ten years as you did in the first twenty!

10. By now you shouldn't have shitty credit, but if you do (like below 600), you are considered high-risk for lenders and you'll get screwed with interest. If you fall into this category, that's another reason to look hard at renting while using that down payment money in the market, which doesn't need your credit score. Plus, you can spend the time you're *not* spending mowing your own lawn on rehabbing your credit score!

11. Start by going to annualcreditreport.com.

12. Always say yes to an increase as long as you can stay at the same spending level, because that increases your utilization score (how much credit you have available as it relates to how much of it you actually use).

13. These are small but help diversify the types of credit you have, which accounts for 15 percent of your score.

14. If you put less down, you're ultimately paying more. For example, if you buy a $200,000 home with 5 percent down instead of 20 percent, you'll pay about $35,000 more in interest at the end of a thirty-year loan. Obviously, you'll also be paying more to cover the principal as well. Also, the less you put down, the more risk you have of going underwater (owing more than the house is actually worth).

15. Visit the National Council of State Housing Finance Agencies at ncsha.org to start.

16. There shouldn't be, but triple check that there are no penalties for paying your mortgage off sooner.

17. Fun fact: the word *mortgage* is derived from Latin and means "death pledge." Yikes.

18. This is a concept investors refer to as "using other people's money." But just because you can take "free money" (which is not actually free money, but money you borrow at lower rates) doesn't mean you should.

STEP 10

1. The average annual expense ratio for passively managed funds (like index funds) in 2018 was 0.15 percent, compared with actively managed funds (like mutual funds) in which the average expense ratio was 0.67 percent.

2. No, that's not a typo—there are 505 companies in the S&P 500. It's like there are fourteen schools in the Big 10 Conference. Weird, but true. It hurts my label-making, put-it-in-a-bento-box, organizational spirit.

3. They don't only track indexes. The fund can also have different kinds of assets like gold, real estate, renewable energy and so on.

4. This shouldn't really matter to you. It's unlikely that you're going to need to liquidate money super fast in the middle of the trading day and it can't wait a day or two. The fact that ETFs can be bought and sold during active market hours is mostly beneficial to professional day traders.

5. "Books" in the finance world aren't like my books. They refer to what they own. The phrase "talking your own book" refers to portfolio managers talking up their own holdings. When I had guests on my finance shows, we would put disclosures up on the screen showing what they owned so the viewer could determine if the advice they were giving was unbiased. Spoiler alert: oftentimes it wasn't.

6. These five companies are known by the acronym "FAANG." (Even after Google became Alphabet, the name stuck with investors, who use it a lot.)

7. In which case you should pick up some more advanced books than this one!

8. When you are reporting on business news, you have to disclose your investments, which I did, so as not to try to influence the stock in any way.

9. There is a social networking component to Public and I am active on there with my real-time investing thoughts, if you're interested in joining me.

10. You can also buy stocks through whatever brokerage you chose for your other investments.

11. Posted by Girl Behavior on YouTube (https://www.youtube.com/watch ?v=YDqoqeOXolA). I highly recommend watching it if you need a break from investments for four minutes.

STEP 11

1. Every time an NFT is sold on the blockchain, the original creator gets what is basically a royalty.

2. The lexicon I told you I was teaching you about finance for the beginning is constantly changing and evolving. An NFT, for example, is a relatively new addition to financial terminology. I learned about it recently along with everyone else. But that's another reason to have your baseline understanding down pat so that you can continue to build upon it as financial innovations happen.

3. Also, please make sure early in the process that whatever investment property you are looking at allows rentals or Airbnbs, lest you get stuck with owning a place with no tenants to fill it. I, um, heard that from a friend.

4. This doesn't have to be your own state. Wyoming and Delaware offer more advantages and protections for LLC owners, making them popular choices for new filings.

5. I've always been fascinated by the history of salt, so when my friend Jesse was telling me about her fund, Halogen—which comes from the Greek words "halo" (salt) and "gen" (formation) to mean "salt former" and refers to the six salt-forming elements on the periodic table—I had a feeling it was a good fit.

6. The words "salary" (value) and "soldier" (war) have their origins in "salt."

STEP 12

1. Margaret Thatcher, television interview, 1986, https://www.youtube.com /watch?v=QDF6blmU3co.

2. You can check this on the IRS website under "Tax Exempt Organization Search."

INDEX

ABOUT THE AUTHOR

*A*merica's go-to money expert, **Nicole Lapin** is the only finance expert you don't need a dictionary to understand. She got her start in the business world at age eighteen, reporting from the floor of the Chicago Mercantile Exchange for First Business Network. Nicole went on to become the youngest anchor ever at CNN and then to claim the same title at CNBC, where she anchored the only global finance show on the network, *Worldwide Exchange*, while contributing financial reports to MSNBC and *Today*. She has served as a business anchor for *Bloomberg TV* and a special money correspondent for *Entertainment Tonight*. Nicole is currently the host of the nationally syndicated business reality competition show *Hatched* and contributes regular financial reports to *Good Morning America* and *The Dr. Oz Show*, among others.

Nicole cohosts a podcast on iHeartRadio with the editor-in-chief of *Entrepreneur* magazine, Jason Feifer, called *Hush Money*, which tackles taboo money topics. Her daily show *Money Rehab with Nicole Lapin*, also with iHeartRadio, consistently ranks at the top of Apple's business charts.

Nicole's first two books, *Rich Bitch*, an instant *New York Times* bestseller, and *Boss Bitch*, became hits with female audiences looking to take charge of their money and careers. She has disrupted the traditionally male-dominated, boring finance space by offering actionable advice with her signature sassy and accessible style. Her third book, *Becoming Super Woman*, which teaches women to go from burnout to balance in a simple twelve-step plan, is now out, along with its companion, *The Super Woman Journal*.

Nicole launched a series of online masterclasses—The Money School, The Boss School, and The Balance School—that expand on the lessons in her first three books. She was named Money Expert of The Year for the second year in a row and is the first female winner. Nicole was also the first-ever monthly finance columnist at Hearst Magazines. Nicole has earned the Accredited Investment Fiduciary (AIF®) certification. She graduated valedictorian of her class at Northwestern University's Medill School of Journalism.

ALSO BY NICOLE LAPIN
(AND AVAILABLE FOR PURCHASE WITH THE QR CODE BELOW)